To Pete Coors! Thanks!

FORWARD

Colonel "Bud" Day;

This book covers many topics and subjects. The talks that have been transcribed are great ones. The moral teachings revealed are outstanding. I have known Guy for many, many years. He is a hero in my book. He walked the walk.

I strongly recommend and endorse this book and know that any who read it will be greatly touched and affected in a positive way. I particularly strongly recommend it be read by young men in the military, especially in the Air Force.

Words never die and these words will last and be doing much good long after I and Guy are long gone. Guy has given and will be leaving behind a great gift to his countrymen and women and I am very proud that my name will be used to help others read and keep this book on their bookshelf for years to come.

In the spirit of our great country,

Sincerely,
Colonel George E. "Bud" Day, U.S.A.F.
Medal of Honor

A fighter in World War II, the Korean War and the War in Vietnam, Colonel George E. "Bud" Day is the most decorated Air Force officer in history, and the most decorated living military officer in America.

D1533412

i

TABLE OF CONTENTS

"The Hun"
F-100D Super Sabres in Vietnam
35th TFW, 352nd TFS "Yellow Jackets"

© Mark Karvon

INTRODUCTION

The title of this book reflects that it is a book about being locked up with God. This happened to me during the Vietnam War. I was an American prisoner of war - P.O.W. I spent over five years in a prison, and there I was with God and only God besides a few cellmates.

This is mainly a book of the speeches I have given over the last decade or so that reflect my experience as a war prisoner. I have integrated the stories and experience of this period of my life with the faith and experience of my life since.

The talks have been transcribed and placed together here. I have refined and polished them. Some are shorter than others because of the various time constraints. I have selected what I felt were my best. They have been sorted by category as the table of contents reflects.

However, I placed the first in its own category and titled it *My General Talk*. This is the one I most commonly give. It gives a good general overview of my experiences in the Vietnam War and my total dependence on and trust in the Maker.

The second category titled *Faith* all relate to deep spiritual truths that I have grown to love and respect because of my initial experiences as a POW. To get through five years in a prison camp under horrible conditions was a real journey of faith. I returned to this country an entirely different man. I had grown in my faith. I had learned how to trust God, to love Him and to forgive others. These talks reflect what being locked up with God for five years did to me.

The third category titled *Family and Manhood* reflect what has occurred to me and what I hold out as ideal in regard to being a man and a father and husband of a family. I have been through much in my lifetime. I have had and raised a large family. I am now old and have had time to reflect what is important and what means the most. I have also made many mistakes in my life and only by the grace of God have made it to this point and still have a family. This category is given to help young men get off to a good start.

The best way to learn is by experience. That is, the experience of others who have been through it and made all the mistakes one can possibly make. This is the case with me. I am offering these three speeches to all young men so that they can profit by my life of having to learn the hard way. If young men can read these, they won't have to fall and struggle as I have had to do. They can fly high and have a very productive life being a man and, if called, also a father and husband of a family.

The final category of talks titled *War and Patriotism* include those that give more detailed stories of my combat and POW experiences in South and North Vietnam. This war is history and most don't even remember it, but reflecting on a war and hearing what a person has experienced who lived through one can help anyone to grow in love of country.

The reader, if he or she is a soldier, can also learn much in case they are ever called to be in a war. Being in the military is a vocation all by itself. It is a vocation of love because a soldier is ready to lay down his or her life for another both in the combat zone or wherever they are called to serve their country. A soldier must be ready to not only die for others but also suffer as I did and many others did in an enemy prisoner of war compound.

This category also includes a talk about leadership. This will help any young man or woman know what it takes to be a great leader.

There is also a speech about Lance Sijan and one that was given at an Air Force Base to honor two other Medal of Honor winners, Bud Day and Leo Thorsness. Reflecting about the life of real heroes always does a soldier good, for all soldiers are called to be heroes in their vocation of love.

I hope and pray that this book helps our country be great and remain great for ages to come. I will soon die as all do, but words never die. My hope is that these words will go on helping my American brothers and sisters keep America great.

May God bless you and our country forever. Amen.

GUY IN NORTH VIETNAMESE PRISON CAMP, OBTAINED BY DOD

ACKNOWLEDGEMENTS

For many years after returning from prison camp in North Vietnam, I found that relating the lessons learned there were a help to a number of veterans and fellow workers in business in dealing with the stresses of marriage and the work environment. I believe those lessons have made me a much better husband, father, employee and manager. This fact was not appreciated by me, but my wife, Sandy, and my brother, Peter, finally convinced me that it really was the case.

It is impossible to convey the incredible love, loyalty and support that Sandy has given me throughout our marriage of almost fifty years, but without it I would have simply failed in every way. Most recently, her support for the endless travel and work necessary to give the numerous talks each year over the past ten years has been perfect. Her encouragement enabled me to continue in so many instances when I was satisfied to just give it up. And her judgment and positive suggestions have been outstanding. She has spent endless hours listening to the countless variations of addresses for different groups. I learned early on that her criticisms and suggestions were always accurate and her "that was good" was the defining standard for an excellent talk.

About four years ago, my youngest brother, Peter, suggested that a book might be in order. He had helped me tremendously through the years tailoring my experiences to fit talks given to many diverse audiences. And Peter also came up with the idea to simply include the speeches that had resulted in the best feedback from the audience as to their helpfulness. That's why I have called it a book of my "best" talks.

When I speak of good leadership, it is because I witnessed it, not in my actions, but in those of my commanders and fellow POWs. The greatest leaders I have ever seen were Air Force Majors James Landers and Herbert Neatherly (later Colonels) of the "*TONTO*" Forward Air Controllers with the 173rd Airborne Brigade at Dak To, Vietnam; General Leo Schweitzer, USA, Commander of the 173rd Airborne Brigade; Colonel George "Bud" Day, our superb *MISTY* Fast FAC combat unit founder and Commander, Colonels Bill Douglass and P. J. White, *MISTY* Commanders; Lt. Lance Sijan, Medal of Honor recipient and North Vietnam cellmate; Major Robert Craner (later Colonel), my commander and cellmate in North Vietnam; Colonel Robert Risner and

Colonel John P. Flynn (both later generals), 4th Allied POW Wing Commanders in North Vietnam.

Teamwork was taught to me in the numerous military and civilian organizations I have been associated with, but there has been no better teacher than that exhibited by the POWs and POW Leadership in the rugged and apparently hopeless conditions of the North Vietnam Prison Camps.

Courage was taught to me by the "*MIKE*" Forces of the US Army's Special Forces; the LRRPs and Airborne Troopers of the *173rd Airborne Brigade*, especially Captain (later colonel) John Moon; the South Vietnamese Airborne Infantry; the *Tonto* and *Misty* Forward Air Controllers, especially Arthur (Buddy) Roberts, Brian Culbertson, Charlie Neel, Jim Mack, Jim Fiorelli, Bob Craner; all *MISTY*s and I mean **ALL** *MISTY*s; Lance Sijan, Richard Tangeman, the Combat SAR (Search and Rescue) Forces that rescued me after my first shoot down; and the POWs of North Vietnam. When I say I was surrounded by heroes, it is perfectly true.

Forgiveness was taught to me by the greatest forgiveness I have ever seen, that of Lance Sijan for his captors as he was beaten to death.

Loyalty was taught to me by my wife, Sandy, and my brothers, Terry and Peter.

The wonderful truths of the Catholic Faith, which saved my life in North Vietnam, were taught to me by the dedicated and joyful Nuns in the elementary school of St. Anne's in Fairlawn, N.J., in the early 1950s, especially Sr. Thomas Ann in eighth grade. In recent years, my brother, Peter, has steered me to one outstanding spiritual book after another, and these now include some he has written himself.

The living Catholic Faith of the marriage vocation was taught to me by my mother and father, who lived a life of selfless love for their six children until the day they died.

I believe the courage and peace for daily battle in war and in peacetime since was given to me by God as a result of attendance at daily Mass in the tents of Dak To, Vietnam, said by the wonderful Catholic Military Chaplains assigned to the 173rd Airborne Brigade, and by the priests throughout the United States since my return.

The editing of the talks for this book has been a marathon because I use a lot of gestures in my talks and so the recorded words alone could not adequately describe the experiences. The primary editors in chronological order were my wife, Sandy, then Lou and Mary Jo Rubino, my great friends in Minster, Ohio. Ms. Becky Koverman and her good friends of the Holy Redeemer Book Club of New Bremen, Ohio, patiently reviewed the first draft and suggested many wonderful changes and revisions. They were followed by my daughter, Amber, my very best editor, then our other children Dawn, David and Sheri, Ginger, Ryan and Rachael, Tyler and Carolina, Matt and Misty, and Jacqueline. My brother, Terry, contributed a great deal of material and insight for major portions of key chapters. My wonderful young friends Nathan and Jacob Tangeman, graciously performed a detailed careful edit. And an outstanding edit and superb encouragement was given by my perfectly loyal and great friend, Colonel Charlie Neel, the Pilot in Command of the mission of my first shoot down who, when we were badly on fire, turned disaster into rescue by his courageous and sure piloting.

And, of course, the person in a category all alone and uniquely responsible for this book, most importantly the inspiration, outline and/or edit of all my talks, the unswerving encouragement of its completion, as well as the definitive and final arrangement and edit, is my brother, Peter.

The Title of this book is used by kind permission of the Diocese of Springfield, Massachusetts (diospringfield.org). Peggy Weber, a lovely lady who writes for the Diocesan Newspaper, *The Catholic Mirror*, wrote an article with that title about a talk I gave to a Diocesan Men's Conference in Springfield. The numerous drawings of the POW experience throughout the book were used with the kind permission of Captain John M. "Mike" McGrath, USN (ret) and the *Naval Institute Press*, which published his outstanding book, *Prisoner of War*. The numerous photos of the Special Forces camps in South Vietnam and many others taken from his aircraft were used with the kind permission of Colonel Dana Kelly, USAF. The Painting of the two F-100s on the *Table of Contents* page was used with the kind permission of Colonel Mark Karvon, USAF. The Painting of the two F-100s returning to base after mission complete in Chapter XIII was used with the kind permission of Roger "Willy" Williamson, USAF.

So I take credit for nothing good in my life or in this book, but rather every problem with them, because the simple truth is that every good that ever happened to me was the result of blessings by God or others, and the only problems were or are due to my own clear mistakes.

This page blank.

MY GENERAL TALK

TALK NARRATIVE: The following talk has been given in part or in whole many times all over the country and even in Europe and Japan. This talk is as the title reflects, my general talk, and will give the reader a good overview of what happened to me during the Vietnam War or at least some of the main events. The talk also includes some text on what happened in the POW camp. The reader should read this talk before reading any of the other talks in the remainder of the book in order to help grasp the big picture and have the back-ground to understand the circumstances and occurrences men-tioned in the other talks that follow this one.

Introduction

Captain Guy Gruters served as a fighter pilot and Forward Air Controller during the Vietnam War and flew more than 400 combat missions. In December 1967 he was shot down and spent the next five years and three months as a prisoner of war in communist prison of war (POW) camps, including the notorious Hanoi Hilton.

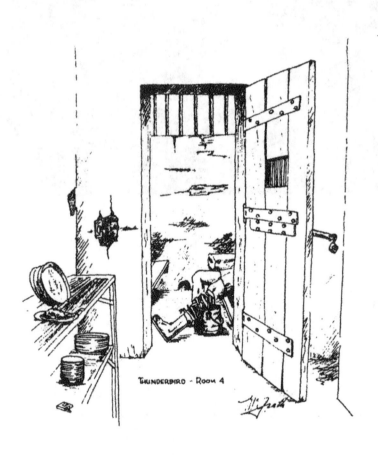

TYPICAL CELL IN THE HANOI HILTON. USED WITH PERMISSION FROM *Prisoner of War*, BY CAPTAIN JOHN M. (MIKE) McGRATH, USN (RET), NAVAL INSTITUTE PRESS

Captain Gruters was awarded more than 30 combat medals, including two Silver Stars for gallantry in action, two Distinguished Flying Crosses for heroism, two Bronze Stars for valor, two Purple Hearts for wounds due to hostile action, and over twenty Air Medals. Captain Gruters has spoken around the country and overseas sharing his unique message, a joyful, positive one, full of faith and hope. He and his wife, Sandy, have been married over forty years and have seven children.

Here now is Captain Guy Gruters.

PRAY FOR PEACE

I would like to thank everyone for coming. I'm here to bear witness to God's presence in a communist POW camp and the love that is found in war. Speaking for all veterans, I ask you to please remember everyone who has served, especially those who have lost their lives or their health. I ask you to please pray for peace in the world. Nobody wants peace more than veterans of war.

CONDITIONS IN PRISON CAMP

I was shot down by the North Vietnamese during an airstrike. I was captured after ejecting from my F-100.

All of us who were captured were imprisoned for the remainder of the war. We suffered terribly. We were beaten. We were put in stocks and manacles in solitary confinement. We were tortured, some of us for months, some of the senior officers for four years or more. We were denied medical attention and starved. We were not allowed to correspond with our families for the first few years that we were up there. We were hot in summer and cold in winter. I have never been hot or cold like that before or since. We spent hours daily just trying to communicate, which was strictly forbidden. There was a rule of silence. We were tortured badly when they caught us communicating.

We never knew whether we would ever get out. That was the toughest thing to take mentally because it looked like we would spend our whole lives as captives. There was no pressure whatsoever on North Vietnam, especially after the U.S. stopped the bombing of the North in 1968. The U.S. didn't go after the source of the trouble, which was North Vietnam, who was allowed to raid South Vietnam at will from its secure bases in North Vietnam, Laos, and Cambodia, which we could not eliminate due to the US State Department's "Rules of Engagement." These facts are well-documented in books and stories, but they're not the real story.

NORTH AMERICAN F-100 SUPER SABRE FIGHTER AIRCRAFT FLOWN BY MISTYS

MORE THAN SURVIVAL

The real story is that we didn't just survive up there. Surviving at all costs is when people are willing to do anything just to get through. "I'm going to live, I don't care if I have to betray my country. I will give them what they want. I don't care. I'm going to get out of here. I'm going to be helpful to them, and do what they say." Instead, we fought them every step of the way as a well-disciplined military unit. We established contact through the walls, using what was called the tap code. We would tap out one letter at a time through the walls. We kept the American Fighting Man's Code of Conduct, which directed that the senior ranking officer be in charge of every cell, of every cell-block, of every prison camp. We remained a fighting team. We continued the fight in hopeless conditions so we could return with honor.

AS EVERYONE WHO IS NOT LIMBER AND IN GOOD CONDITION KNOWS, IT CAN BE QUITE PAINFUL JUST TRYING TO TOUCH THE TOES. FORCING A MAN TO BEND, AS SHOWN HERE, CAN CAUSE EXTREME PAIN IN HIS BACK, AS WELL AS A FEELING THAT THE LIGAMENTS IN THE BACK OF HIS LEGS ARE BEING RIPPED RIGHT OUT OF HIS BODY. STRESS POSITIONS SUCH AS THESE WERE FAVORITE TORTURE METHODS OF THE NORTH VIETNAMESE BECAUSE OF THE EXCRUCIATING PAIN THAT CAN BE EXACTED. AND JUST AS IMPORTANT, NO TELLTALE SCARS WILL REMAIN (UNLESS THE TORTURERS MADE MISTAKES — AS THEY OFTEN DID). USED WITH PERMISSION FROM *Prisoner of War*, BY MIKE MCGRATH, NAVAL INSTITUTE PRESS, PAGE **88**

I think we beat the communists even though we were under their power physically in prison camp. They beat and tortured us constantly without reprisal. But I think we did very well. I believe it was due to God's grace because of our Christianity and sincere prayer. Our leadership was God-fearing. The first communication each prisoner received told us about the church service each Sunday at mid-day in each individual cell. We would all say the Our Father, the 23rd Psalm, and the Pledge of Allegiance. Even though we were generally kept solo or with one other man in each cell, we knew that at twelve noon on Sunday we were saying our prayers in union with every other POW in North Vietnam. Of course, we also prayed extensively as individuals. I believe this and the prayers of our families and the American people gave us the grace to fight as well as we did.

MISTY FORWARD AIR CONTROLLERS

In South Vietnam, I served with the US Army's 173rd Airborne Brigade as a Forward Air Controller or FAC (See Chapter 13 for detail). I subsequently transferred to an Air Force unit called *MISTY*, called the Fast FACs, because we traveled at fighter speeds (400 to 550 miles per hour) instead of light plane speeds (80 to 100 miles per hour). *MISTY* was the call-sign for an all-volunteer, top-secret unit of 14 fighter pilots who flew over North Vietnam. We would fly low-level scouting missions in North Vietnam to find targets. Most of the strike fighter flights carrying bombs came in at 16,000 feet. But we would be from altitudes down on the treetops up to about two or three thousand feet looking for targets and so had excellent visibility. We found targets of opportunity such as hidden convoys which were impossible to see from higher altitudes. After we'd find a target, we would have first priority on all fighter strikes into North Vietnam, of which there were between fifty and one hundred each day. We would call the top brass in the control ship orbiting over Laos and they would divert the fighters to us for attacking the targets we found. We would dive and mark the targets with smoke rockets. The smoke rockets had exploding warheads with white phosphorous which would appear as puffs of white smoke on the ground.

**O-1 WITH "WILLY PETE" (WHITE PHOSPHOROUS) MARKING ROCKETS ON WING
THE SAME ROCKETS WERE USED BY THE *MISTY* FAST FAC F-100 AIRCRAFT**

Then the strike fighters would come in and destroy the enemy positions clearly pointed out by the smoke rocket.

Each mission, we rendezvoused with and refueled twice from a KC-135 Tanker Aircraft airborne over Laos.

This refueling let our missions be four and a half to five and a half hours long, of which three to three and a half hours were under heavy fire from the ground. We had among the highest loss rates of any unit in North Vietnam. One of the proudest and most satisfying accomplishments of my life is that I was a member of the *MISTY*s. The stories of a number of those fighter pilots, including one of mine, are documented in the book, *MISTYs*, by Major General Don Shepperd, USAF (Ret). Please see my website, guygruters.net, for a link to this book and others on the *MISTY*s.

SPECIAL FORCES BEHIND THE LINES

Due to the enemy's excellent camouflage of many targets in North Vietnam, two-man special forces teams were assigned the mission of finding them. We had approximately thirty such teams on the ground behind the lines. They were inserted, supplied, and extracted by air. They would scout through the jungle to find military targets for our strikes, looking for ammo dumps, supply dumps, armored vehicle and truck parks, etc.

EXCELLENT TARGET

On one date, at two o'clock in the morning, we received a call from one of these teams. They gave us the coordinates of a big ammo dump in North Vietnam. We were off before dawn to strike this target. Captain Charlie Neel was the aircraft commander and I was in the back seat of a two-seat F-100F Fighter. As we came into North Vietnam, we were on the deck turning and twisting back and forth to evade the heavy cannon fire. There were 150,000 to 180,000 active anti-aircraft gun sites in North Vietnam, according to our intelligence services. We made our way to the coordinates that had been given to us, but the sun was just barely up. At first we couldn't see anything under the trees. We came back around through the mountains and made another approach from a different heading, and we still could not pick it up. We made about ten passes over that target. The ground fire became heavier each time. That is why we never wanted to go back over the same target, but it was essential in this case to confirm its location before calling in the strike fighters.

The Special Forces ground teams risked their lives constantly, but especially when they contacted us on the radio. As soon as they transmitted coordinates as they did to us that morning, the enemy would triangulate on their radio emissions and know their position. The enemy would deploy patrols including dog teams to surround and destroy them. So when the Special Forces took the risk to give us a target, we always wanted to make sure to hit it.

Finally, when the sun was high enough to reflect off the equipment hidden below the jungle canopy, we managed to see the various equipment, fuel and ammo dumps side by side with endless rows of tanks and trucks, about a quarter of a mile by a half mile or so. This was in early November of 1967, and the target was a forward staging base for the *Tet* offensive of early 1968. Of course, we didn't know about the *Tet* offensive at that time, but it was clearly the best target we had ever seen. We called for a scramble of Gunfighter Flight from Da Nang. Gunfighter was a flight of four F-4 fighter aircraft that were held on five minute runway alert 24/7. This meant pilots were always with their planes so they could take off within five minutes for an emergency strike.

RENDEZVOUS WITH GUNFIGHTER FLIGHT

The four fighters in "Gunfighter" Flight flew north.

F-4 PHANTOM FOUR-SHIP; "LEAD", "TWO", "THREE", "FOUR"

The control ship over Laos also started diverting other fighter flights to a map location called "feet wet off Dong Hoi," which meant holding in a flight pattern over the water until *MISTY* picked you up and brought you to the target. Meanwhile, we flew over to Laos to refuel from an airborne KC-135 tanker in the air and crossed into North Vietnam on the way back to rendezvous with the fighters. That only took about ten or fifteen minutes. On the flight back across North Vietnam, we went over the target on the deck to check it out again, then crossed the coast eastbound and picked up Gunfighter Flight, which was orbiting at 16,000 feet. We climbed up to 5,000 feet, had them in sight, and asked them to follow us in to the target. In each of these *MISTY* F-100s we had two pilots, one flying in the front seat, and the other man on the maps in the back who would control the fighters. It was a single seat fighter normally, but we used the two-seat version called the F-100F. We were all qualified F-100 pilots. After being checked out, the practice was to switch seats every other mission.

HIT OVER DONG HOI

We led the fighters back into North Vietnam. Passing over the city of Dong Hoi we were turning and twisting at about 5,000 feet. The muzzle flashes of the gunfire on the ground looked like the stars in the sky. There were literally thousands of guns of all calibers firing at us.

RADAR CONTROLLED ANTI-AIRCRAFT CANNON

One of the 37mm shells hit our F100F aircraft in the rear fuselage. Charlie asked, "Guy, what was that?" I said, "Well, Charlie, it could be the air-handler recycling." But almost immediately, it felt as if a giant grabbed the plane and shook it. A fighter plane is just a pilot sitting on an engine, surrounded by ammo and fuel on and in the wings and fuselage. So when something happened to the engine, which was a powerful jet engine equivalent to 16,000 horsepower, bad things happened to the pilot. When that airflow was disrupted in the compressor blades of the engine and they stalled out, the entire aircraft shook violently. We had on strong seat belts and harnesses, g-suits, oxygen masks, etc., and it still shook us around as if we were rag dolls.

CAPTAIN, LATER COLONEL, CHARLIE NEEL, USAF

Another second went by and the fighter shook us again. Meanwhile the two big emergency fire and overheat lights on the dashboard illuminated and when I looked in the rear view mirror, the whole tail section was on fire. Out of the corner of my eye, I saw the warning light panel down low on the right side of the cockpit. The lights told us we were losing many systems. The main electrical was out - showing red light, auxiliary electrical was about to be lost - caution light – and systems like hydraulic and fuel were also showing trouble. These were critical systems. This cross-check took just a second or two. I looked back up to the mirror and now the entire mirror was filled with fire. That's how fast the fire spread. The mirror was a rear-view mirror for air-to-air combat, so it was a large, curved, wrap-around type. This meant the entire aircraft was on fire.

A BALL OF FIRE

At this time, the F-4 lead, "Gunfighter" lead, started yelling, "MISTY, get out. You're a ball of fire. You're a ball of fire. Get out, *MISTY*.' He could only see flames. The cockpit section was not engulfed yet, but he couldn't see that from his location in the air. Charlie, meanwhile, had wrestled back control, put our fighter into a hard six-G turn back to the ocean, and kicked the engine into afterburner, so that we could get back to the coast as quickly as possible. So I said, 'Negative, we are going to try for the coast.' Nobody wanted to be captured, because no one who was captured was heard from again. That would the end of us, as far as we knew. Any pilots found dead had been horribly mutilated. We were supposed to eject from a fighter when it caught fire because they have a consistent tendency to explode, but we had an inclination in *MISTY* to ride it to the water or the mountains rather than eject, as long as the plane would fly. We believed it was our best chance for survival.

RUN FOR THE COAST

Charlie started a gradual climb out as we turned for the water. Gunfighter became upset on the radio because he was concerned we would blow up any second. He even more strongly advised that we get out. 'Get out, get out at all costs. Climb out of the cockpit if the [ejection] seat is jammed, but do something." And again I told him, "Negative, we are going to ride for the coast." Then we listened to their advice for the next few minutes without responding. Meanwhile, another couple four-ships of fighters had arrived in the area. We flew eastbound back over the city.

I remember looking outside and thinking, "If we go down here, there is no way out," and, "Well, you wanted to be a good soldier. This is part of it. Can you take it?" I was talking to myself about the disastrous situation we were in. It was really very similar to the feeling just before going into the boxing ring or playing football, but much worse. It was a quiet, internal fight against fear and for self–control.

Badly on fire, we managed to make the coast in about three minutes, although it seemed half my life.

As we approached the coastline, Charlie said, "Okay, Guy, we will go just after we hit the beach." When we passed it, he said. "Go." I lifted the handles up and the canopy blew off. I squeezed the handles and the ejection seat blew me out over the tail. Charlie immediately squeezed his handles and he went flying over the tail. I had a good chute, but the seat did not separate well and hit my right wrist as it came by, shattering the bone and severing the main tendon to the thumb. We had climbed to 8000 feet by the time we ejected. I started drifting down. We were about a mile offshore and were sitting ducks in the air. The gunners from the shore were shooting at us with machine guns and cannon. Miraculously, they didn't hit Charlie or me on the way down.

Charlie was hit in the head by the seat as he ejected. It split his helmet in half. He was knocked out and hanging limp in his chute. I was greatly concerned and tried to slip my chute over to him. I had been through airborne training with the Army and knew how to slip a chute. Initially, I was 200 yards from him and closed to about 100 yards, but I couldn't get to him in time. I couldn't use my right hand. So I couldn't slip very well. He had to be reached so his eighty-five pound survival kit, which was strapped to his bottom and acted as a seat cushion, could be deployed. Otherwise, he would hit the water unconscious with eighty-five pounds of dead weight strapped to him and gone down like a rock. I could not reach him in time.

FIGHTERS STOP THE GUNFIRE

However, he regained consciousness just above the water and immediately deployed his heavy seat pack. This also automatically inflated and deployed his survival raft.

I hit the water with a deployed, inflated raft. I pulled the raft in with the lanyard it was on and climbed in. The water was erupting around us from the shore gunners' cannon fire. I tried to paddle away from the shore, but noticed the heavy bleeding from my right hand caused a cloud of blood in the ocean. I was concerned that the blood would draw sharks, so I stopped paddling and started to kick. But due to my injuries I was unable to un-strap my flight boots and so kicking was ineffective. I thought, "Well, nothing much I can do here to increase the distance from the shore."

I took the survival radio out and started controlling the fighter strikes against the shore guns, because I could see the gun positions. The fighters started walking their bombs, rockets and strafe down the shore. The shore gunners switched their fire from us to the fighters attacking them, which was a great relief. I helped to direct the fire on those guns for some time. I think Charlie and I are among the few Forward Air Controllers to ever help direct fighter strikes from a one-man survival raft.

A short time later a Navy P-2 Neptune patrol bomber came on station. I guided him to my location. As he flew overhead at fifty feet above the water, he dropped a white phosphorus smoke marker to help the rescue crews locate us. As soon as he did, the gunners on shore had a perfect aim point again. All hell broke loose where I was with various sized explosions from the coastal artillery. The Navy pilot saw the problem and put his plane's wingtip on the ocean in a hard tight turn and dropped out 10 to 15 other smoke markers, which immediately disbursed the fire from the shore, since they didn't know which marker was the correct one.

SHORE BOATS

Unknown to us, about a dozen motor boats with ten to twelve enemy soldiers in each had departed from shore to retrieve us or kill us. They started from a location a half mile or so north of us.

Charlie was an outstanding fighter pilot, a "fighter pilot's fighter pilot." Charlie methodically examined his survival kit, seeing what he could use to better mark our position for rescue and found twenty pen-gun flares. He started shooting off the flares to mark our location for the fighters and rescue forces.

The boats starting out from shore to get us passed me, because they were coming from a position on the shore to the north of us. They were closer to Charlie's position than to mine. One of the fighter pilots saw the enemy boats nearing Charlie's position as indicated by his flares and rolled into a steep dive on them. He put his fire control switches on "arm all, fire all." This would fire all 120 rockets off his wings when he squeezed the trigger. He didn't have time to alert us because he was right on the boats and the boats were just about to get Charlie.

FIGHTER PILOT SAVES US

He was traveling 650 knots at about a 60 to 70 degree dive angle. He pressed dangerously low to make sure he didn't miss.

What was in this man's mind as he risked his life by this action? Only one thought, "My brothers need help. They are in trouble. They are going to be captured and could be murdered in a few minutes." Certainly he knew that his plane was receiving heavy fire from the shoreline batteries and that he was pressing much too low. Was this man concerned for his life? No, he was focused on the act of helping his brothers in trouble. He had no problem with his own possible death. This is the love

15

found in war. This is the greatest love a person can show. It was the love of giving up your life for another. It was a daily occurrence in a soldier's life. My brothers in those planes and choppers showed great love as they risked their lives for us. I thank God for each of them and for their actions that day.

Charlie watched the fighter come down the slot and calculated there was no way he was going to be able to pull out of his dive in time. Charlie later told me he thought in his mind, "You're dead, buddy - too low, too late." The fighter pilot fired all rockets and started his pullout. He badly overstressed the fighter on the pullout, pegging the G-meter at near 13 g's, and still kicked up a rooster tail on the ocean with his exhaust, but made it. All he cared about was protecting us and he did not mind dying to do it. The rockets were fired so close to the water they did not have time to spin-arm. The 2.75 inch diameter exploding warhead rockets have to go 1500 feet to arm themselves before they explode. So he was within 1500 feet of the ocean when he started his pull.

Charlie was on the outside edge of the rocket pattern. A rocket hit right next to his raft, but didn't explode. But most of the rockets hit the boats. Even though they did not explode, they sank about half the boats. He was right on target. As a result, there were enemy soldiers in the water screaming in terror, obviously asking for help. The other soldiers, instead of helping their buddies, turned and ran for shore. We heard the horrible screams of men dying over the next five to fifteen minutes. Never saw anything like that in the U.S. military. I served with the Navy, Army, Marines and Air Force in heavy actions. I never saw anything like that. I couldn't believe it. They left their buddies to drown.

JOLLY GREENS "THAT OTHERS MAY LIVE"
After about 45 minutes in the water, two "Jolly Green Giant" air-sea rescue choppers arrived.

I thought the fire was too heavy for them to come in close to shore where we were, but both did. One flew to each of us. It was now about nine o'clock in the morning in full sunlight. One chopper hovered over me, a perfect target for the shore gunners. The two air-sea para-rescuemen, the men responsible for helping pilots into the chopper, were trying to lift me up and get me in. I couldn't help much as I had no strength left. I was completely waterlogged and they couldn't lift me up. We were taking heavy fire. I told them, "You have to go, you can't stay here." They made a call to the pilot but instead of leaving, the pilot set the chopper down in the water like a boat. One of these men jumped over my head into the ocean. Now he was worse off than I was.

The next thing I knew, he came up from under me. He had swim fins on and pushed me up hard. The other man grabbed me and pulled me over the edge of the chopper's deck. We lifted the swimmer in. The pilot took off. Fighter pilots called the Combat Search and Rescue Crews (SAR Crews) the "bravest men in the world." That was the truth then and I am confident it still is today.

"JOLLY GREEN GIANT" AIR-SEA RESCUE CHOPPER (HH-3C)

We flew to the Marine base at Dong Ha for refueling. Charlie and I went to the hospital for evaluation. Charlie was released, I had surgery to fix my hand and wrist, spent two weeks in the hospital, and another five weeks with a cast on.

While in the hospital, I heard that Charlie had gone back to flying with *MISTY*. About a week later he was capping (protecting) a downed pilot just north of the DMZ (Demilitarized Zone) in an open field when a considerable force of NVA infantry tried to approach the pilot from a tree line at the edge of the field. Charlie's repeated strafing runs at low altitude kept them from the downed pilot. He pressed low time after time to save this man despite heavy ground fire. He didn't consider the risk he took. He was the best. Charlie was scheduled for an assignment to England with an *RAF* (Royal Air Force) Lightning squadron after his tour with *MISTY* was over, a wonderful tour for a fighter pilot. As an aside, later on in prison camp, where happy thoughts were rare, it was a personal comfort to me that he had received this assignment.

I rejoined the *MISTYs* after about a month and a half.

SHOT DOWN AGAIN

On my second mission after returning, I was shot down again. We were the only plane in North Vietnam because of the weather conditions. We were under the clouds, with a low ceiling of 1500 feet. Strike fighter flights with bombs did not fly in such conditions, but *MISTY* did. We shot up a number of convoys with our cannon fire.

There was an anti-aircraft gun location of thirty-six guns, six six-gun batteries, which were extremely accurate, and had almost shot us down a number of times. We were trying to fix their position for an attack the next morning. But they got us first. We were hit hard with a heavy explosion by a 57mm cannon shell just behind the rear cockpit, knocking out both main and alternate hydraulic pumps instantaneously. This meant all flight controls ceased working immediately. We had no control of the aircraft. The plane immediately flipped over on its back, diving right into the ground. We both managed to eject upside down. Fortunately, the chutes opened before we hit the ground. A squad of North Vietnamese soldiers finally captured me after chasing me for about forty-five minutes.

PRISON NUTRITION

I would like to tell you a little bit about the prison camps in North Vietnam. The food was different than any we had ever experienced in the United States. Only bread and water were provided for those first years. The bread consisted of little loaves of white flour bread, which were full of rat excrement. Every cubic centimeter had a piece of rat excrement in it. As a result, there were all kinds of worms and weevils in this bread, some of which were quite large. We would bite into the bread, and the worms would bite us. Then we would bite and kill the worms and eat them. But I appreciated the insect life in the bread, because that was the only nutrients we were getting. The water was the same. They boiled it but it was full of hundreds of little worms that we could just barely see, about a sixteenth of an inch long or so. We would drink a large number of these worms every time we had water.

PRISON SANITATION

We had a bucket for our bathroom in the cell. I was in with another man for two and a half years. And in the winter, that bucket would not be large enough for our waste. We were permitted to wash out our cell one time in five years. So we had raw sewage in our cell all the time. We were brought to a cistern once a week to wash ourselves. We only had two liters of water a day for drinking and none extra for washing.

THIS IS THE HANOI HONEY BUCKET, OR HO CHI MINH'S FOOD BANK, AS SOME MEN CALLED IT. EACH CELL HAD AN OLD RUSTY SLOP PAIL FOR TOILET FACILITIES. THE TOP EDGE WAS USUALLY SHARP AND RUSTY, SO MOST MEN WOULD USE THEIR RUBBER TIRE SLIPPERS FOR A SEAT. THE OCCUPANTS WERE ALLOWED TO EMPTY THEIR BUCKETS ONCE A DAY, USUALLY IN THE MORNING...LIVING WITH THE RESULTING STENCH IN CRAMPED QUARTERS WITH ONE OR TWO OTHER MEN, ALL OF WHOM CONSTANTLY HAD EITHER DIARRHEA OR DYSENTERY, REQUIRED A GREAT DEAL OF PATIENCE. USED WITH PERMISSION FROM *Prisoner of War* BY MIKE MCGRATH.

THIS WAS ONE OF THE WASHROOMS IN LITTLE VEGAS (SECTION OF HANOI HILTON). MEN WERE PUT IN ALTERNATE WASHROOMS SO THEY COULD NOT COMMUNICATE. WE WERE GIVEN ONLY A MINIMUM AMOUNT OF TIME TO WASH, AND USUALLY THERE WAS NOT ENOUGH WATER. THE GARBAGE WAS KEPT IN THE WASHROOMS AND THE PIGS AND CHICKENS HAD FREE RUN OF THE GARBAGE. IF A MAN WAS TOO SICK OR WEAK FROM BROKEN BONES, AS I WAS, HE SIMPLY DID NOT GET TO WASH HIS BODY OR HIS CLOTHES UNTIL HE WAS STRONG ENOUGH TO MAKE IT TO THE WASHROOM UNDER HIS OWN POWER. SOME MEN WERE PLACED IN IRONS AND LEFT TO LIVE IN THESE OPEN WASHROOMS AS A FORM OF PUNISHMENT. THEY HAD NEITHER MOSQUITO NETS NOR PROTECTION FROM THE ELEMENTS. USED WITH PERMISSION FROM *PRISONER OF WAR*, BY MIKE MCGRATH.

There were interrogations going on all the time, one, two or more times a week. We were beaten and kicked around as we were brought to them. You have heard of being kicked around or slapped around. I never knew what that meant until prison camp. The guards didn't speak any English. They weren't allowed to speak Vietnamese. They never wanted us to learn any Vietnamese, and we never heard any Vietnamese. I think they were afraid of us convincing a guard on the inside to help us escape.

KICK TO THE BROKEN ARM. THE GUARDS AND TORTURERS LOVED TO KICK AND BEAT THE WOUNDED ON THEIR WOUNDS. THIS IS HOW THEY BEAT AND KICKED LANCE SIJAN TO DEATH. USED WITH PERMISSION FROM *PRISONER OF WAR*, BY MIKE McGRATH.

Imagine that you were walking along and the guard wanted you to go left, then he would kick you with his right foot real hard in that direction. And then later on, he kicked you the other way for a right turn. We were given directions with slaps similarly. The prison camp experience was a good antidote for my pride. It brought me very close to God because it was such a humiliating experience in every way. We couldn't fight physically. We had to fight spiritually with our prayer and mentally with our mind.

KILLED MY FRIEND

They beat and tortured one of my good friends to death. He died suffering terribly. I developed hatred for these guards and the officers that were running that camp. It resulted in strong suicidal thoughts. I almost killed myself as a result of the hatred.

POWER OF PRAYER

I finally got down on my knees and asked the Lord to please help me because I could see that I was dying from it. God gave me the grace through consistent prayer over months to overcome the hatred and to overcome despair. But I never would have understood despair if I hadn't experienced it like that. My thoughts were that, "Our situation looks hopeless. We are going to die up here. I can never get back to my wife and children. It's just so terrible and there is no way of getting word out." It was easy to despair. It was easy to just quit eating to commit suicide. We had a number of men do that. I turned to God and he got me through the experience by giving me the grace to effectively do what the Church calls "live the moment."

LIVE IN THE PRESENT

My cellmate, Maj. Bob Craner, was seven years older than I and much wiser. He said, "Guy, We have to stop living in the past or the future." The trouble with prison camp is that the reality was so bad that our minds rejected where we were. It was similar to having a child dying of cancer or some other horrible tragedy in life. It was easy to think about how great life was before capture, or how great it would be in the future. But our minds tried to run away from the present. The Catholic Church teaches that you don't ever run away from the present, as it would be cowardice and lack of faith in God. We must handle the troubles of the present, trust God and his mercy for the past, and trust God and his providence for the future. Our job is always to handle the situation that God gives us in the present moment. The cellmate I was with, by the grace of God, figured out how to handle the despair we were developing.

We were constantly thinking about returning to our families and the States. Then one day Bob said, "Guy, we have to stop thinking about the States. Let's only allow ourselves to think about our families for fifteen minutes a day. And the rest of the time, we will do the best we can here." I said, "OK, lets try it." So we controlled our thoughts. We would not allow ourselves to think about the States or our families or the future or anything else. This prison camp was our life. This was going to be our existence for the rest of our lives. That would have to be it. We were going to do what we could right there. This attitude turned around the despair. We came up with mental and physical activities to do. We would tap through the walls to our fellow POW's and helped establish an organization to fight the enemy together.

THE PRESENCE OF GOD

I remember thinking after three or four months there, because it was such a horror story, "I wonder if God is in this communist prison camp?" I wasn't praying to God, I was just asking the question of myself. I thought he wouldn't come to North Vietnam. It was too evil, too rotten, too filthy, just horrible. I believed he was probably at the border waiting for us to come back! I think this illustrates my lack of faith.

MASS DURING COMBAT

During the ten months prior to my second shoot down, I would go to Mass and Confession was given everyday. We had great priests serving as military chaplains. My code was the Ten Commandments. If I broke one of them, I would confess it and try my best to not break it again. Because of that, I had great peace. In the fighting, I was a good soldier because of it. I didn't worry because I knew I was trying to do the right thing. When I asked the question in my mind, "I wonder if God is up here?" I meant it. I thought at the time that God was just taking care of the big things. I had gone to Catholic schools, but obviously I never fully believed in the power the nuns told me He had. But after my sincere question in prison camp, within a few months He greatly increased my faith and revealed to me He was controlling every detail of life. He brought a fellow POW to me that taught me the mysteries of the Rosary. I prayed the Rosary over and over again, day after day. It gave me tremendous peace and joy. To this day, I have never had the peace and joy deep in my heart that I had in prison camp from those prayers. It was unbelievable how he took care of me, supported me through some tortures, and saved me from others. He comforted me. I understood the saying, "God is a real help in time of trouble." I will tell one quick story to explain what it was like.

THE GOVERNMENT IS GOD?

I went in for an interrogation. There was a different line of questioning pursued by the interrogators each time. The communist line for this one was, "Tell these air pirates that they are lucky to be alive, that the government gives them everything. What a great communist government we have to give you food." The interrogator started with that. I said, "Listen, I appreciate that the government is distributing the food, but the food is from God. God made the seeds, the sun, the rain and the soil. Which seed did your government make? God is the one that provides the food. Your government can't make food. It just distributes the food. The food is from God. I thank God for the food. I thank your government for being God's instrument."

This interrogator went ballistic. "There is no God! The government is god! The government is the one that gives you the food! The government gives you everything!" So I start raising my voice and he does too. The session deteriorated quickly.

After a little while, I was saying things to him like, "Listen, when you die and you are going to die, you are going to be on that side of the table and Jesus Christ is going to be on the other side! There is going to be no Politburo at the table! He is going to go through every thought, word, and deed that you did! And he is going to judge you on them! There is no way of getting around it! It is going to happen to you! And your acts of killing and hurting my friends here are going to be on that table! So you better stop it! You better be sorry for it because you are going to die and you are going to meet Jesus Christ!"

YOU WILL HAVE NOTHING

He had five thugs grab me. He was screaming at me as I left the interrogation. " I will show you! You will have nothing! Nothing, do you hear me, you will have nothing, nothing!" He was screaming as loud as he could. The five guards didn't understand the English he was yelling at me. They took me out and brought me to a hot room there. It was August, about 11 o'clock in the morning. I had to climb into the hot box through a hatch. While I was climbing in, one of the guards reached down and picked up a piece of cardboard, stiff, about the size of a magazine. He made a fanning motion with it and gave me the cardboard. This kind act from a guard was the first and only time this happened to me in five years.

I took the piece of cardboard and climbed in the hot box. They closed the hatch. There were no windows. I was on my knees. I was not even using the "fan." I was on my knees thanking God, literally crying with joy that he hadn't completely disowned me because of my pathetic attempt at evangelization.

When I first understood the infinite power of God, I thought "I'm going to tell everybody that God is really there. He is all powerful. The whole world is going to believe me, because of course they are going to listen to me. And that will be the end of the trouble in the world – because there will be no more atheism anywhere." That is how naive and prideful I was. But based on the reaction of the interrogator, I realized, "I'm really not getting through to this man very well." So I was in the hot room crying with joy and saying, "Thank you, Lord, thank you, Mary. Thank you for staying with me." Because the only thing I had was God. Our families couldn't help. The country couldn't help. Our buddies couldn't help. Nobody could help. We were on our own and all we had was God. It was truly God alone.

About that time, I heard the sound of thunder in the distance. Within twenty minutes, there was a big thunderstorm right over the camp, dumping about two inches of rain and cooling that hot room down. It was no longer torture. They took me out of it and put me on my knees in ropes, but that was nothing like the hot box.

THERE IS NO COINCIDENCE

People can say, 'Oh, that was just coincidence that it happened like that." But I know it wasn't coincidence. God let me understand that it wasn't. He was with me like that all the time. He gave me tremendous confidence in his care no matter what happened to me. He really was my shepherd. He has absolutely infinite power and I know that to this day. There is no coincidence or fate whatsoever. Nothing wrong happens unless He allows it to bring greater good, like the crucifixion. He has total infinite, perfect power, and it is perfectly used. This life is just a school of love. We have free will, but He uses consequences of our acts and anything that happens to teach us lessons to make us better, to lead us to be more loving children, to lead us to Heaven.

I AM VERY THANKFUL FOR PRISON CAMP

This prison camp experience resulted in great joy and blessings. I'm so happy I had it, because it brought me very close to God while I was still in my twenties. I knew that I would only be up there as long as He wanted, which happened to be five years, but that's fine. It could have been a lifetime and I would have had no regrets, because of the grace of faith.

THE SON TAY RAIDERS

We had very brave men of the Special Operations units try to get some of us out of prison. Did you ever hear of the Son Tay raid into North Vietnam in November of 1970? They went in with helicopters and descended on a POW camp. At the time, POWs were at five or six or seven different little camps all over North Vietnam. The raiders attacked one of those camps where 50 of our men had been, but they had been moved shortly before. The raiders killed all the guards. It was a successful raid to that point, but it was considered unsuccessful in the United States because they didn't get any POW's out. But to us it was the greatest raid of all time, because it forced the North Vietnamese to consolidate all the camps into one. Instead of one and two man cells, they moved us all into large 45-man dungeons in Hanoi at the Hanoi Hilton.

ON 20 NOVEMBER, 1970, A SPECIALLY TRAINED U.S. ARMY UNIT MADE A DARING AT-TEMPT TO RESCUE SOME OF THE POWS FROM SON TAY, 23 MILES EAST OF HANOI, BY HELI-COPTER. ALTHOUGH THE PRISON CAMP WAS FOUND EMPTY, THE PRISONER'S MORALE WAS BUOYED WHEN THE NEWS REACHED THEM.

AFTER THE SON TAY RESCUE EFFORT, THE "V" PANICKED AND BROUGHT MOST OF THE POWS FROM THE OUTLYING CAMPS INTO THE EASILY DEFENDABLE PRISON HOA LO (HANOI HILTON), IN DOWNTOWN HANOI.

WE WERE CROWDED INTO LARGE 60' BY 24' ROOMS. THERE WERE 56 MEN IN MY ROOM. WE QUICKLY ESTABLISHED COMMUNICATION LINKS WITH SOME OF OUR SENIOR OFFI-CERS WHO HAD BEEN ISOLATED FROM US FOR YEARS. OUR NEW CAMP NAME WAS CAMP UNITY. I MADE THE ACCOMPANYING DRAWING OF ROOM 4 FROM A PENCIL SKETCH I MADE IN PRISON, JUST BEFORE I WAS RELEASED. USED WITH PERMISSION FROM PRISONER OF WAR, BY MIKE MCGRATH.

THIS IS THE TOILET FACILITY OF ROOM 4 IN CAMP UNITY. THIS DRAWING IS MADE FROM A PENCIL SKETCH I MADE ON THE MORNING I LEFT HANOI FOR THE PHILIPPINES. IT SHOWS THE FRENCH BUILT TOILETS WHICH INCLUDED TWO PEDESTALS TO STAND UPON. IT WAS A TREMENDOUS IMPROVEMENT OVER THE HONEY BUCKETS. USED WITH PERMISSION FROM *PRISONER OF WAR*, BY MIKE MCGRATH.

SIX OF SEVEN KILLED

There had been about 2400 aircrew shot down by that time and not rescued. Out of those 2400 men, about 1 in 7 were alive. That was the 308 of us. After the raid, they put us in seven dungeons of approximately 35 to 50 men each.

They put us all together so they could defend us against another special forces' raid. It was wonderful. Now we had many men in a cell. We started classes on the concrete floor. We scavenged pieces of brick to use for chalk. We had three math classes and Russian, Spanish, French and German language classes from various men. There

27

was no comparison of what it had been like being alone or with one other man to the diversity of men and activities in those dungeons.

RISNER WAS IN COMMAND

Colonel Risner was the man in charge over all of our POWs in North Vietnam. We had communication directly with Risner through the walls in these dungeons. Risner was a great Christian. By this time, everyone believed we had survived this experience only with God's help. Risner said, "Okay, now we will have a Church service on Sunday at 12 noon, with everyone joining in. We will have a two hour service thanking God for everything." Risner gave us ten songs to sing that almost everyone knew like the *Star Spangled Banner, Battle Hymn of the Republic, Amazing Grace,* and so on.

CHURCH SERVICE

On Sunday at 12 noon, in this communist prison camp with its strict rule of silence, 308 men belted out the *Star Spangled Banner.* The guards came in with machine guns. They put the leaders up against the wall and took them out and to the torture rooms. They put them in leg and wrist irons on concrete slabs. This gets old in an hour. After ten or twelve hours it is very painful. The leaders were in irons for a long time.

The next men taking command stood up and said, "Gentlemen, they interrupted our Church Service." We started again, singing the *Star Spangled Banner.* They came in again and took these commanders to more torture rooms. The next men stood up and said, "Gentlemen, they interrupted our Church Service." We started again.

We knew in every cell and in every cell block and in every camp exactly who was in command, and who was the next in command down the line. The communists never broke that. That is the *Code of Conduct* and it works. We took orders from whoever was date-of-rank in charge in every cell, in every cellblock, in every camp.

They finally ran out of torture rooms. The North Vietnamese could not stop the Church Service and we completed the program.

A man from Ohio, Ed Meckenbier, was in our cell. They called him in on Monday. With ear on the ground, you can hear people talking in rooms 50 feet away. I was the assigned monitor listening in on the interrogation. This is a first hand account of that conversation. They said to Meckenbier, "We are going to stop this Church service at all costs. If we have to torture and kill you all, we are going to do it. You can't have it. There is a rule of silence. We don't want anything to do with God here." And Meckenbier said in a dead-calm voice, "You can do that. You can do whatever you want, but as long as one man is alive, we are having that service." They believed it and were not willing to kill all of us. From then on, we had that Church Service and they never tried to stop it again.

We had that service for the last year and a half. I wanted to explain that, because it wasn't just me that had the religious conversion experience. All of us knew we had been brought through prison camp by God alone. Everyone knew it and nobody was going to desert God.

U.S. IS BLESSED WITH CHRISTIANITY

What happened to us was very simple. We fought in the war like millions of other Americans. We are very fortunate to have always had many men and women who were willing to fight for our country. In World War II, we had sixteen million men in arms. In the Korean War, it was six million. And in the Vietnam War, it was nine million. We have always had very brave men who fight extremely well, and it has been a great blessing for our nation. I believe this is due to our Christianity. In my opinion, Christians have always made the best soldiers in the world. There is a tremendous confidence and peace in a Christian soldier that is not present in soldiers of other religions. They don't have it. We have it. I hope we never lose it. I believe the country will lose our freedom if we lose our Christianity.

The other beautiful thing about those dungeons was that we had the ability to have Church Services on holidays. We had a service at Christmas, Easter, the Fourth of July and Thanksgiving.

We would always have Larry Barbay (later Colonel after return) from Louisiana sing his favorite song for us about his son. He had five children. For the seven years that he was up there, he never received a letter from his wife. He loved his wife and five children so much, but didn't receive any letters. I believe the reason was that Larry looked like an extremely tough man. Actually, Larry was an extremely tough man. John Wayne looks like a tough guy, but Larry was more ruggedly handsome than John Wayne. I believe the communists were afraid of him.

So the North Vietnamese would never give him a letter from his wife even though she wrote faithfully all those years. We all felt sorry for Larry because we believed his wife had left him. But she hadn't. They are together to this day and have a beautiful family.

LARRY HAD A HEART OF GOLD

We always asked Larry to sing his favorite song at each holiday. There were all those rough, tough fighter pilots and there wouldn't be a dry eye in the dungeon during that song. Every one of us believed that we were going to die up there. That's what it looked like. If you had told us we were going to get out in five or ten years, we would have been ecstatic. Again, the toughest thing to take was that it looked like we were going to live the rest of our lives up there without seeing our families again. There was no pressure on the Communists to release us.

We all had families. Most men had more children than I did, but even I had two at the time. Larry would sing his song and we would all consider ourselves the missing father of the song. I will sing it to you now. Put yourself back in time as one of those men in prison camp in 1971 in North Vietnam, who believed they would never go home;

I asked a little boy to call his daddy.
He said he couldn't and sighed.

And when I asked him what was wrong,
Here's what the boy replied.

My daddy is only a picture,
in a frame that hangs on the wall.

Each day I talk to my daddy,
but he never talks at all.

I tell him all of my secrets,
And all of my little plans,

And from the way he looks at me,
I know he understands.

The angels took daddy to heaven,
when I was just going on three.

But I bet they never told him,
how sad and lonely we'd be.

I try to cheer up my mommy,
when the tears roll down her face.

My daddy is only a picture,
but I'm trying to take his place.

Thank you very much for your attention.

This page blank

2

THE SAVING VALUE OF THE CROSS

TALK NARRATIVE: There is a group of pious Catholic Families in Plainfield, New Jersey and in other parts of the United States called the "People of Hope." They meet on a regular basis for Saturday morning breakfasts and have a speaker talk on topics of interest. I was asked to relate the effects of the POW experience on my faith and how God may use suffering to greatly improve our faith.

Thank you for such a warm welcome. As all of you know, I have been asked to talk about my experience in prison camp. I was a fighter pilot shot down behind enemy lines and subsequently a prisoner of war in North Vietnam. Although we attacked only military targets, the bombs we dropped sometimes killed not only soldiers, but also civilians. This was an unintended consequence, but our captors didn't understand and were angry.

Unlike many air crewmen floating down in a parachute, I was not killed immediately because I was captured by disciplined soldiers. The soldiers were apparently under strict orders to keep us alive because we were of value to their government as a bargaining chip in the peace talks. The North Vietnamese civilians were not so constrained.

I would like to discuss "The Saving value of the Cross," that is, the spirit of sacrifice and self-denial. During the approaching Lenten season, the Church emphasizes the importance of imitating Christ and how we all should voluntarily make sacrifices to grow closer to God. This is good because it exercises and strengthens our free will. Then, when it is tough to make the right decision, we are strong enough to do it.

I was in my early twenties when I volunteered to go to Vietnam. I was very healthy and strong, both physically and emotionally. I had been through four years of school at the Air Force Academy. It included significant physical training and mental discipline. I was on Judo and Boxing teams there, and took parachute training with the US Army. I also attended Purdue University where I earned a masters degree, then completed pilot training and fighter gunnery school. Afterwards, I volunteered for Vietnam.

It was a different world back then. Our country was fearful of communism and rightfully so. We were engaged in a war in Vietnam to stop communism from spreading and taking over the whole world. Communism had already grown like a horrible cancer to include Russia, China, all of the Eastern European nations, North Korea, and North Vietnam. Now South Vietnam was being invaded.

It had to be stopped. This is what the leaders of our country thought. I agreed and as a soldier was happy to be able to contribute to this struggle.

I was a professional soldier and a fighter pilot flying a very fast and powerful airplane when I was shot down. The education and training I had as an Air Force officer resulted in skill and competence but also resulted in a lot of pride. When I was captured, tortured, and had to witness a fellow soldier being tortured to death, I became furiously angry. I developed a great hatred for the enemy. I hated them so much that I dreamed of torturing and killing them daily.

I had been in prison camp for only a few months, when it became apparent that I was in trouble from a spiritual standpoint. Having so much hatred for the guards and the interrogators who tortured us resulted in strongly desiring to obtain revenge. But there was nothing I could do. I was kept in a locked cell under their total physical control. I was continuously deeply humiliated. But since my pride was so great, instead of growing in humility, I rebelled and grew in hatred.

I found myself constantly trying to determine ways to obtain revenge. I concluded that the best way was to stop eating. They could not force me to eat. This would teach them, I thought.

By the grace of God, I woke up to my mistake in time. I became aware of my sin. I was going to commit suicide by willfully starving to death. I knew from my Catholic upbringing that this was wrong, that to commit suicide was wrong under any circumstance. This realization brought me out of the rut I had fallen into.

I fell down on my knees and prayed to God to save me and he did. I told God I was sorry for this sin, and instead of hating my enemies I began praying for them. This turnaround was very difficult for me. It did not happen overnight, but it did occur.

I can now reflect back on what happened to me in prison camp.

I was prideful because of my accomplishments before Vietnam. Then I was shot down and captured, kicked and slapped around by the guards, put in irons, treated like an animal, tortured, and forced to witness the death by torture of friends without any recourse. These were great crosses of suffering and humiliation. I thought the situation was terrible. But these crosses saved me from my great sins of pride and hatred that otherwise might have resulted in my eternal death.

For five years the crosses continued. However, after turning to God in prayer, I had the right attitude. I had accepted the spirit of sacrifice and self-denial. I had found God in prison camp. Truly I had been saved because of the crosses I had to carry.

But this was not all that happened in prison camp. I was just barely kept alive. I was given only water to drink and it was limited to between one and two quarts a day. The water was not clean and pure, but full of worms. I was given only bread to eat and it was full of rat excrement and worms. We had no bathroom in our cell. We used a bucket that was emptied daily, but it also overflowed daily and filled the cell with raw sewage. The heat was unbearable in the summer. The cold was unbearable in the winter.

My flesh was crushed by the conditions. But I had God, and my spirit became strong because of the constant self-denial.

Our Church teaches the value of fasting during lent because of the war between our flesh or "self" and our spirit. It teaches the value of mortification or death to "self." We are all human beings. We have a nature that craves to be cared for and spoiled. It is a fallen nature, a corrupt nature, a defective nature. It is a tendency to sin, a force within us that nourishes selfishness, which is opposite to what our spirit craves, that is, love of God and neighbor.

Christ states clearly in the gospel that we must deny our "selves." We must pick up our cross to follow him. Lent is the season of the year to renew our commitment. If we do not do such, then our human nature will win over the wonderful spiritual nature we received at Baptism.

We must all realize that because of the curse of original sin we have to deal with this selfishness. The only person who was not born with original sin was Mary. She was immaculately conceived. Every other human being has a tendency toward selfishness, which must be overcome. This is the war all Christians have to fight. It is why St. Paul said near the end of his life, "I have fought the good fight. I have finished the race." We all must overcome the "self" in us by accepting the cross of self-denial.

If we spoil a child while raising him or her, the child will grow to be very selfish and not loving. Similarly, if we spend our lives in the pursuit of fortune, pleasure or fame, we too will become very selfish and self-centered and not loving.

Lent is meant to help us refocus on this important truth, that we must overcome our "self" to be one with God.

This was made very clear to me in prison camp after my conversion. I lived in conditions in which my flesh suffered and my spirit thrived. It states very clearly in Holy Scripture that we unite with God in spirit. But if we focus on pleasing ourselves we will be separated from God. The goal then of all Christians is to be made over in Christ, to be united with Him, our spirit to be one with His.

In prison camp I felt very close to God. I prayed and fasted constantly. I did not participate in worldly activities and had no wealth. My "self" was very small. I was close to God. My spirit was united to His. That is why I can stand up in front of you and say that having to go through the prison experience was the best thing that ever happened to me in this life. I experienced the saving value of the cross, the cross that crushed the "self" in me.

Oh! How I long for those close times with God that I experienced in prison camp. But I do not experience them now, for I spend my life caring for my "self." I eat well. I drink what pleases my taste buds. I stay warm in the winter and cool in the summer. I spend hours and hours watching the news and filling my mind with useless and unnecessary thoughts.

I know the enemy now. I know him well. He is the "self" in me and his tactics are to distract me from spending my life focused on God. He does not want me praying and reading spiritual books. Anything but such as that. Anything he can do to distract me or divert my attention, he does.

I have learned from reading about the saints that the greatest fight that a Christian must wage is against the "self" within his or her own mind. Some authors call one's mind the "Citadel of Self." It is the headquarters for our selfishness. Our mind is the battleground. We must fight the good fight, for it is in our minds that we unite with God in spirit when we pray. If our mind is full of useless and unnecessary thoughts, it is difficult to pray and be one with God. Instead, we spend hours distracted by life's activities and demands.

In prison camp I spent hours contemplating nature. I used to watch the ants and the spiders fight. I saw God's hand in all of nature and praised Him. I prayed and filled my mind with good thoughts, which drew me closer to God. He showed me His Love.

When I returned from prison camp, I was a different person than when I left for Vietnam. I spoke of forgiveness and love. I had been changed. I had been renewed. I had been saved by the cross.

I long for the closeness I had with Him in prison camp. There, I experienced God firsthand. I am seeking a better spiritual life now. My children have all grown up. I am retired from my work life. I still have the world and my "self" that tempt me. My "self" is so at home in the world and with my flesh. I must combat this enemy now as I did in prison camp. I must fight the good fight against this force in me, the tendency to avoid sacrifice and self-denial and to do my will instead of God's Will.

The Saints I read about knew this. They denied their "selves" heroically, so that they formed good habits, called virtues. To practice virtue is how we overcome our "selves." Thus, I know I must strive to learn about the virtues so that I can practice them and imitate Christ.

I know the path to take. It is to welcome suffering and sacrifice in my life. It is to embrace the saving cross of Christ to facilitate union with God.

Even though I am weak, I only have so much time to fight the good fight and win the race. No longer do I have the prison camp environment to help me do such. I am on my own as is everyone else.

Please pray that I get serious and with God's grace get rid of my "self." Please pray for me that some day it will be Christ that lives in me and not my "self."

I'll do the same for all of you. God bless you.

"It may be the will of Heaven that America shall suffer calamities still more wasting and distresses yet more dreadful. If this is to be the case, it will have this good effect, at least: it will inspire us with many virtues, which we have not, and correct many errors, follies, and vices, which threaten to disturb, dishonor, and destroy us. The furnace of affliction produces refinement, in states as well as individuals. And the new governments we are assuming, in every part, will require a purification from our vices, and an augmentation of our virtues or there will be no blessings... But I must submit all my hopes and fears to an overruling Providence; in which, unfashionable as the faith may be, I firmly believe."

John Adams, July 3, 1776

Your Cross

"The everlasting God has, in His wisdom, foreseen from eternity the cross that He now presents to you as a gift from His innocent Heart. This cross He now sends you He has considered with His all-knowing eyes, understood with His Divine mind, tested with His wise justice, warmed with loving arms and weighed with His own hands to see that it be not one inch too large and not one ounce too heavy for you. He has blessed it with His Holy Name, anointed it with His grace, perfumed it with His consolation, taken one last glance at you and your courage, and then sent it to you from Heaven, a special greeting from God to you, an alms of the all-merciful Love of God."

St. Francis de Sales, Doctor of the Church (one of 32 in 2000 years), author of *Introduction to the Devout Life.*

As St. Therese lay painfully dying during her last days;

"I have asked God to send me a beautiful dream to console me when you are gone," said a novice.

"Ah, that is a thing I shall never do - ask for consolation! ...since you wish to be like me, you well know what I say:

Oh! Fear not, Lord, that I shall waken Thee:
I await in peace th' eternal shore...

"It is so sweet to serve the good God in the dark night of trial; we have this life only in which to live by faith."

The Little Way: Counsels and Reminiscences, St. Therese of Lisieux, Thomas Taylor.

This page is blank

3

THE VALUE OF SUFFERING

TALK NARRATIVE: For many years, Ms. Joan Kiser has been instrumental to the wonderful care provided for the patients of the Center for Neurological Development in Burkettsville, Ohio. Joan asked for a speech addressing suffering for a retreat attended by the patients of many area facilities similar to Burkettsville's. This retreat for the disabled was held at a Retreat Center in North-west Ohio in 2006. Father Louie Schmidt, a wonderfully gentle and holy priest, a great friend of mine and of all who know him from the St. Charles Seminary at Carthagena, Ohio, also attended.

I have been asked today to talk about suffering. As I look at you all, I see you know all about suffering, but perhaps I can help you to understand a little better why suffering is allowed by God.

First, I would like to tell you about the greatest suffering I went through in my life. Then you may agree I can speak with some authority on the subject.

When I was in my twenties, I was a soldier. I volunteered to fight as a fighter pilot in the Vietnam War. I volunteered for duty and signed up for a second tour. Flying a fighter plane, I volunteered for a top-secret unit where I flew over North Vietnam as a scout at low altitudes to find enemy targets and call in other fighter-bombers to take them out. It was a dangerous job. I was shot down twice. The second time I was captured by the North Vietnamese Communists. I was a prisoner of war for five years and three months. During those years the real suffering of my life occurred.

I was treated harshly by the people that caught me. The soldiers almost beat me to death shortly after I was captured. Then I had to walk slowly while my hands were bound behind my back with ropes and my feet were hobbled with ropes through three villages as the population was encouraged to beat me with clubs and kicks. The North Vietnamese soldiers finally stopped them, locked me up in a cage, and put my hands and feet in irons.

In the village I was kept in, I suffered my first humiliation when I had to go to the bathroom. There were no toilets there. I had to go in the open field over a hole in the ground and about 300 people, men, women, and children stood there and watched me each time I went.

I also suffered greatly witnessing the suffering of others. I tried to help a fellow pilot that had been shot down about a month earlier. He was severely wounded, a mass of infected lacerations, and starvation had reduced him to skin and bones. The guards would beat him unmercifully in his cell only six feet away from mine. He would not talk, for if he did then the enemy would use the information to kill other American soldiers. All POWs had to withhold information and refuse to be used for propaganda purposes. Many POWs were killed in prison camp, tortured to death like this man was. It broke my heart to see and hear the Communists beating him to death over the next month.

We suffered greatly interiorly and mentally, realizing we couldn't help the wounded and that our captors could do the same to us at any time.

I suffered repeated humiliations as a Prisoner of War. Not knowing any English, the guards led us around like dogs, kicked us or hit us with rifle butts to turn us right or left or go faster or just for the heck of it. There was absolutely no privacy to handle bodily functions while using a bucket in our cell, or during the weekly wash we were allowed.

I was a young man full of pride and wanted to get back at them. I tried to aggravate them in many little ways. For example, I would smile brightly at them. This caused me a number of beatings and one time I was slammed across the mouth with a two by four. Then I had a mouth full of loose teeth for a long while.

When I was transferred to the main prison camp, I was tortured with ropes and irons forcing wrists and ankles in odd positions, and my elbows were tied touching each other behind my back. They had many kinds of torture to make you talk and they would push you to near death. There was no relief. Eventually I told them false information and after awhile they would let me out of the torture rooms to return to a concrete cell.

There were no lights and no air circulation. I slept on a board. Our bathroom was a bucket. They fed us bread and water. The bread was full of rat droppings and living worms or weevils. The water was loaded with little dead worms. That is all I ate and drank for years on end. There were bugs everywhere. One time I counted 16 mosquitoes on my little toe alone when I was contorted into a position on my knees during torture, just a few seconds after being put down. That's how fast the mosquitos covered us. Any exposed skin was black with them. Any movement of our bodies at all resulted in a loud buzzing sound from a cloud of many hundreds being displaced. There were spiders as big as the cross section of a lampshade. Their bodies were as big as my fist. There were rats everywhere, which would run across the room all night long. Because of the filth, the POWs had a number of internal parasites. I pulled (twelve) foot-long worms out of the mouth of my commanding officer after three years up there. Even twenty-five years after my return to the States, a doctor found major infestations of eleven parasites in my body, including two liver flukes and a lung fluke. These came very close to killing me and would have if she had not found them.

If we were caught communicating to each other through the walls, we would be tortured. In the winter, they would strip us down, and we would have to kneel for days. They would come every hour, dump cold water over us and beat us with large bamboo clubs. In the winter, we shivered for long periods from the cold (entire days or weeks, shivering without relief). In the summer, we almost died from the heat, for the cells had tin roofs and just a small vent for air. We used to lie down on the filthy concrete floor to breathe air from the cracks at the bottom of the door.

I suffered from feelings of hopelessness. My country had apparently abandoned me. The steps to win the war were not being taken. The bombing, the only pressure we had on North Vietnam, was stopped in 1968 and we were told we would never go home. Many died not only from the torture but also from lack of confidence in the country that they were fighting for. I suffered because I was away from my family, my wife and two children, as well as my own parents and brothers and sisters. After two and one-half years, I did finally receive a letter, which was permitted to be only six lines long.

I would pray and ask God, "Why did I have to suffer? Why did strong young men, the best the country had, have to be treated like this, tortured, or starved to death? Was there a God; did He love us?" Well, some men were not sure and they were probably the ones who died of hopelessness.

Then I almost died of starvation. My pride resulted in terrible anger and I started to hate the guards. I was going to get back at them. It seemed the only way I could was by not eating. Then I realized that I was being led by the bad guys to commit suicide. This is why I turned to God. I prayed very hard and asked for forgiveness. I forgave everyone who was hurting me. I started to pray for the conversion of the communists. It took me over six months to really mean these prayers. But this confession gave me a new life. I was at peace with the terrible conditions. I knew God was with me and loved me. He came back to me because I stopped hating others. I have never had greater joy and peace in my life than I had in prison camp over the next years.

Why did God allow all this? Well, first of all I could see that all the suffering I went through had brought me back to God. My focus before prison camp had been on completing my goals and doing my job to the best of my ability. I had not thought about God except in Church and did not ask Him for help or give Him any credit for the success I had. I had been far away from Him in that I was full of pride. For I was young and a fighter pilot. I graduated from the Air Force Academy with honors. I earned a master's degree from Purdue University in Astronautical Engineering, and did well in pilot training, fighter training and in combat. These accomplishments blinded me. All the suffering purified me of a lot of this pride, by humiliating me and bringing me to my knees. It separated me from the world that kept me so busy that I never had much time to pray and think about God. Now I sat in a prison cell without the world. Now I could get close to God.

So the suffering was a blessing and grace from God, for if I had not gone through it I would not be close to him as I have been ever since that day. I make sure to pray hard in the morning, go to church each day, and try to pray throughout the day.

I turned to God in the prison camp. He let me see he was with me and he loved me. Even after I was sure of this, I still had to live in a prison camp. But I stopped rebelling against the pain and suffering. God gave me the strength to endure the torture and horrible conditions. He really was my shepherd. He got me through. I did not die there. Six out of seven men did.

After I returned to America I had time to reflect about the suffering I had gone through. I still suffer physically. When they tested me at the Veteran's hospital, the board of doctors declared me to be 260 percent disabled. My back was damaged by the ejections. I have severe arthritis in my wrists, ankles, knees and elbows from the rope tortures. My hearing is shot from the explosion of the engine on my first shoot down. I have a heart condition from the poor diet. So my suffering did not completely end when I came home.

But one reason God allowed all of this may have been because of my vocation. I was a soldier. I was willing to give up my life to save others. This is the greatest love anyone can have. A soldier or a policeman or a fireman is a very good Christian in this regard. I fought in the war to save other's lives and that is why I suffered and still do. Tens of thousands died and tens of thousands suffered and suffer now more than I did or do now. God allows suffering because He allows us to share in the saving of souls, which may be ours or others. This is a key truth. This life will always be one of suffering because of the sins committed on earth. But only a Christian can understand and suffer with joy, for he or she knows that it is by the cross that souls are saved. We all have been given life, but this life is very short. There is a life after this one.

Jesus gave a perfect example. Jesus died on the cross after the greatest suffering that ever was or ever will be, then rose from the dead to show all that there will be life after death. We all have bodies, but we also all have a soul, a spirit. This is who each of us really is, and which will live on after our body dies. The body is not who we are, but rather just a container for our spirit on earth. Our spirit is who we really are.

God sees us and knows us as the character we have, not as the body we have. We will be judged on our character, not our body. Our body is relatively unimportant and will die and decay. Even if someone's body is still and unable to move, when you talk to the person, they are unique, they have personality and wonderful character. The soul is immortal and made to be with God in perfect peace, joy and love forever.

I like to think of it this way. When my car gets old, I take it to a car dealer. I park that car and get out of it. I pay for the new car, get in it and drive away.

Well, that is what happens to each one of us on our final day of this life. We will park this old body and rise to Heaven above. If we take the effort to repent and pray hard now, there will be no more suffering, no more pain, and no more humiliation in Heaven. This is our Christian belief. We can also obtain different levels of glory in Heaven, which depends greatly on how much and how well one suffers the trials in this life. We must try to bear suffering without getting mad at God about it, but rather we should thank Him for the great grace that suffering is, and turn it into great riches in Heaven. We should not pass up the chance to suffer well, for this life will end quickly. We only have one chance to do it right, one test to determine where we will be for all eternity and at what level we will be. If you are not at peace with God, then please become so. Confess your sins. Invite God into your life. Unite your suffering to that of Christ for the love of others to save their souls. Think of other people first, rather than of yourself. Be a real Christian, join without complaint in the suffering of Christ, and then you will share in the joy of Christ, the love of Christ and the peace of Christ. You will have picked up your cross and followed Him, as He requested. So since you embraced the cross with joy and a great attitude, then you will share in the glory of the Son of God, as He promised, a joy and peace and reward beyond anything we can even imagine, and that will last forever.

This is our hope. This is the Easter message; first the suffering, then the glory. This is why we can be joyful always under any conditions. For one day our sufferings will be over and we will follow Jesus to heaven above. There we will be given a new glorified body and give Him the glory and praise He earned and deserves. And He in turn will give the greatest reward for eternity to those who have been asked to suffer the most, as all of you here today obviously have been.

Hallelujah! Be happy, be joyful, be at peace, it is your Christian right. And such an attitude is a tremendous help to Jesus to convert others. Because if a person can handle suffering well, he has the answer that everyone is looking for and will lead them to it. After all, isn't that why Jesus is the perfect leader?

So the best suffer the most. Always remember; first the suffering, then the glory.

Thank you very much for letting me share with you today.

"Now, all our peace in this miserable life is found in humbly enduring suffering rather than in being free from it. He who knows best how to suffer will enjoy the greater peace, because he is the conqueror of himself, the master of the world, a friend of Christ, and an heir of Heaven." The Imitation of Christ, by Thomas Kempis

A novice remarked to St. Therese (of Liseux, the little flower), when she was suffering terribly just before her death, *"I do not like to see others suffer, especially saintly souls."* She remarked instantly,

"Oh! I am not like you: to see saints suffer never moves me to pity! I know they have the strength to endure, and they thus give great glory to God. But those who are not holy, who know not how to profit by their sufferings, oh! how I pity them; they do indeed arouse my compassion, and I would do all I could to comfort and help them." St. Therese of Lisieux, *The Little Way: Counsels and Reminiscences*. Taylor

"If we understood the value of our crosses, we would be numb with joy and happiness at receiving them; trials, tribulations, anguish of every kind would call forth songs of gladness and enthusiasm and, spontaneously, we would intone the Te Deum." (Dina Belanger, an Autobiography, p229)

"My brothers, count it pure joy when you are involved in every sort of trial." Jam. 1:2

"I exceedingly abound with joy in all our tribulations." 2Cor. 7:4

4

FORGIVENESS

Father, forgive them, for they know not what they do. (Lk 23:34)

TALK NARRATIVE: Loreto, Pennsylvania is in the beautiful mountain country of North Central Pennsylvania. It is here that Demetrius Augustine Gallitzen established the settlement in 1799 of what was to become known as "Catholic Town, USA" because of the rich spiritual tradition that developed here. The Franciscans also have their headquarters here.

A good man and a few friends are responsible for organizing 14 consecutive Catholic Men's Conferences in Loreto. They contacted me and requested two speeches on "Forgiveness," the theme of the Men's Conference for the year 2011. The first given, the keynote, was very similar to the Men's Conference talk given at Columbus (Chapter 6), but with a further emphasis on forgiveness.

The following is the second talk, oriented specifically to the miracle of forgiveness I received in prison camp, and explaining how to obtain the necessary grace from God to forgive.

Christian Men's Conference
Saturday, June 11, 2011

My name is Guy Gruters and I was asked to speak about my experience as a prisoner of war (POW) in the Vietnam War, particularly how after developing great hatred for my captors, by persistent prayer and a personal confession I was given the grace to forgive them.

I am now going to read you a short story out of a book titled: *Shower of Heavenly Roses*. It is a book that gives several testimonies about the power of prayer with the intercession of St. Therese of Lisieux. I will then discuss what I have learned by experience about the power of prayer to obtain God's grace to forgive.

Shower of Heavenly Roses; Stories of the Intercession of St. Therese of Lisieux, by Elizabeth Ficocelli, pp. 115-119.

Family Forgiveness:

I used to tell God that if He ever answered this prayer, I would consider it a miracle. We have two children, a boy named Simon and a girl named Carly. There are nine years between them and something went terribly wrong when Carly was five, something so horribly unspeakable, it changed our lives for ten long years.

When Carly was thirteen, she confessed to me that her brother had molested her for years, swearing her to complete secrecy. This shocking news threw our fam-

ily into an upheaval of overwhelming pain and misery. It literally tore us apart. Carly mournfully revealed how deeply this situation had affected her mind, how she suffered flashbacks and relived the torture every time she looked at her brother. She told me for years she tried to block out the whole experience, but to no avail. It particularly came to a head one day when Simon had been away for six months, and his sudden return made the memories come flooding back to her to the point where she could no longer bear it.

Devastated for my daughter and my family, I made arrangements for Carly to see a counselor. She refused to allow her brother to attend the sessions, as she could not face him. Before long, she stopped going altogether — the memories were just too painful.

One night, after Simon had been at the house, I went into Carly's room to check on her. When I opened the door, I could tell by the look on her face we were in trouble. We took her to the hospital and had her admitted under a suicide watch. A week later, Carly returned home with an appointment to see a psychiatrist. She was found to be suffering from Post Traumatic Stress and a dissociative disorder in which she suffered from multiple personalities, only in her case they were all her own personalities at different ages.

At this time, Carly had started living at school, and she eventually refused to go to any more therapy sessions. Then, late one night, we got a call from our daughter that she was planning to die. Fortunately, we got to her in time and again she was hospitalized. This time, she dropped out of school and came home to live with us. We could not allow Simon to come home while Carly was there. For ten years he did not come home for Christmas or even call on the phone for fear she might answer. We had to go to him. Mind you, my son was living in the same hell as the rest of us. He was so sorry for what had happened and wanted to heal with his sister, but Carly was not ready or able to forgive her brother. She even called him from time to time, threatening to call the police and have him put in jail. Our family lived in complete and utter misery during this time with no hope of ever escaping the nightmare. No matter how much I prayed for peace and forgiveness to heal our family, the situation remained the same.

Just about the time I was reaching my breaking point, the reliquary of St. Therese was passing through town. My son, through an unusual turn of events, became the driver for the "Thereseobile." He spent three days driving the sacred relics from church to church, and all the time he was with the holy saint he begged for her intercession.

Three weeks later, Carly saw her brother driving on the street and mentioned it to me in passing. This may not seem miraculous to an outsider, but bear in mind Carly had not mentioned Simon's name once in ten years. (She even for a while, when asked if she had siblings, told people she was an only child.) I told my daughter that Simon had seen her as well, but didn't want to upset her by waving. What Carly said next shocked me so profoundly I though I might faint on the spot. She said matter-of-factly that she wasn't angry anymore, it just wasn't worth it, and to tell Simon the next time to wave. Only a month before, she had made one of her threatening phone calls to him!

A few more weeks passed by. Carly and I were at a local hospital to visit someone. Just as we were about to enter the room, Simon walked out. There they stood, brother and sister, face-to-face for the first time in years. I was so scared I couldn't even breathe. Carly told Simon that things were okay, that she was feeling good. I thought I was dreaming. It was truly the miracle I had been seeking.

I am confident that St. Therese had interceded for my daughter and that God graced Carly with the power to forgive. It still brings tears to my eyes whenever I think about that moment. Carly told me later that for years she had out-of-body experiences, which is common with her disorder. She said one day (shortly after her brother had started praying to St. Therese) that she felt all the other parts of her personalities become one. She was so frightened she started crying because she didn't know what was happening. Now we all recognize this as a miraculous healing.

Just so we would never doubt St. Therese's involvement in this matter, we received the proverbial sign of roses. I had asked Simon to get me some of the roses from the reliquary, which he did. I had planned to keep some of the petals and give the rest to my mother. I carefully placed the rose petals in an envelope to save. A few months passed and I forgot all about the petals until my husband went to give Carly something in an envelope. When she opened it, she asked, "What's with all the rose petals?" I looked and realized that it was the same envelope I had used to save the petals. I have no recollection of putting that envelope back in the box. To me, it was St. Therese sending roses from her reliquary that were delivered from my son's hands into my daughter's. It was the ultimate sign of forgiveness.

Today, my children are on very good terms and my daughter is mentally healthy, happily married, and expecting her first child. She is thinking of making her brother the godfather. My children together bought me a three-foot statue of St. Therese, which is one of my greatest treasures. Without this dear saint's intercession and the power of forgiveness, nothing would have ever changed in our family. I am truly blessed. Thank you, St. Therese of Lisieux. — Anonymous

This story dramatically communicates to the reader how prayer can help us to forgive another who has hurt us and how vitally necessary it is to seek such help from above.

It is always a big help for us to reflect upon the power Jesus had to forgive those who crucified Him. Not one of us has suffered like Jesus did and He forgave all those who were responsible for His crucifixion and death. He forgave them before they even repented or said they were sorry and while still in utter agony. He gave a perfect example to us. He does not ask us to do anything He did not do.

As I shared this morning, I turned to God in prayer in order to change my heart and forgive the prison guards. They had tortured one of my fellow soldiers to death. I was very angry and developed hated for them. I turned to God and asked Him for the grace to forgive them and prayed hard for this intention. In time I was given a different perspective and attitude within my own mind.

This was miraculous. Because as you can imagine, I was quite set on hurting my captors in any way I could. I was mad. I was angry. I would have killed them with my bare hands or any other means if I had been given the chance.

The weapons of the jet fighter plane I flew had killed many of the enemy. But this was in the normal course of fighting a war, and there was no hatred in it. Prison camp was more personal and really different. These evil men had tortured my injured buddy until he died for no good reason.

The key point is that I hated them interiorly and was very mad. But because of the power of prayer, I changed and in time actually started to pray for them and desire they get to Heaven some day.

Think about this! Reflect with me! I was in my mid-twenties. I had been fighting in a war for over a year. I was very mad and angry because of what had happened to my friend and the rest of us. But my prayers were answered. I was now a different person who was loving those who were hurting and killing us by praying for them. If this is not a miracle, then what is?

It was exactly like the story I just read. It points out that God is really in control and can change us interiorly if we only request His help.

This fact should give each and every one of us great hope, especially those who have been through a divorce or other circumstance that has given great reason to hate another or hate several people who have hurt us.

How can God do this? How can He change a tiger into a kitten? How can God change one who hates into one who loves?

The answer is that it is with a supernatural gift of grace! Who knows how it all works. But with repentance and prayer, one can receive this gift to forgive. This is a fact. It may not happen overnight. It certainly didn't for me. It may take months to turn completely around. But it can and will happen if a person is sincere and persistent in the desire to do God's Will, which is to forgive those who have hurt us.

Please permit me to explain what I have learned in my reading about grace and what it takes to receive it from God. Whole books have been written on grace. Anyone can read them like I did. But to summarize what I understand about it from them, it can be stated that three things are required to receive grace. They are:

Being humble
Being generous
And praying for grace

A person has to be humble enough to kneel down and ask God for help, as I did. This means to realize that one is incapable on one's own to solve the problem. There are many ways to grow in humility. One can study the life of Christ or read whole books on the subject. Whatever it takes to grow in humility must be done. Holy Scripture states clearly that God does not give grace to anyone who is not humble;

God resisteth the proud and giveth grace to the humble.
Jas 4:6

Humility is the key that lays open the treasures of God's grace, as St. Peter says: *"To the humble He gives grace."*
1 Peter 5:5 From the book, Know Yourself, by Joseph Malaise, S.J., page 160

The second requirement is to be generous. This is a term the spiritual authors use to mean that a person must give up his or her will in order to do God's Will. In other words, a person must say to God,

"I want to do what I know is right, what You want me to do, and not what I want to do."

A person thus has to be generous and give of himself, that part of him that wants to sin or be selfish. It is all part of being repentant. In my case, I knew it was wrong to hate another and it was right to forgive them. So I told God that I wanted to do His Will, i.e,, forgive, and I meant it with all my heart.

The third requirement to receive grace is to pray for help, the grace from God, the interior change required to have the strength to be good, to do right. By praying for help one is really being humble and admitting to God one is not capable of changing on one's own. It is saying to God, "I am a sinner and I need the help to change and give up this sin." In my case, I needed the help or grace to stop hating my enemies and instead forgive them.

So these three things are what it takes to obtain grace.

I have not mentioned going to confession, but notice (and we can rejoice) that this sacramental act is the perfect fulfillment of the process I have just described. A person confesses to the priest sorrow for not doing what is right. In doing this, the person is being humble, admitting the wrong to the priest. This is also an admission of weakness. Naturally, the person wants to change to do the right thing. This is being generous. Then the person tells the priest he will try to not do wrong (sin) again. The person is saying he will make the effort to change. The priest blesses the person by giving absolution. In this way the person receives grace, sometimes right away, to change and to overcome the bad habit or the sin.

So you can see how powerful the Sacrament of Reconciliation really is. It is the great aid that God has given to all Catholics to change and receive grace. The whole process of receiving the Sacrament results in receiving the grace to change for the better.

Now to return to the focus on forgiveness.

I want to emphasize that without God's help or grace, a person is not going to be able to forgive. If the person doesn't, he will be living in a state of serious sin, like I was. When I hated those who hurt me, I sinned, because it was not God's Will for me to hate. Rather, God's Will was that I forgive them. I was not being humble and generous, but prideful and rebellious. I was not being a child of God, but an enemy of God.

And being His enemy, He had turned me over to the devil. This is how God uses the devil to chastise and lead a sinner to repent. And if one doesn't repent, He lets the devil destroy the person.

"The man who sins belongs to the devil." 1 John 3:8

In my case, I was being inspired by the devil to stop eating. I wanted to commit suicide. This was the only way I could apparently hurt my captors, which I was trying to do because I hated them.

It is no fun to be inspired by the devil, to have your life run by him. Holy Scripture clearly states that when we sin, we belong to the devil. The spirit of the devil gets power over us and inspires us to continue doing wrong. It helps our selfish nature to do bad things. In my case, it was inspiring me to hate enough to want to kill myself. I was angry, I was mad, I was negative, I was confused. My interior life was in shambles.

Then after I repented and prayed to God for help, all this changed. My interior life was put back in order. Instead of the devil running my life, it was the Spirit of God. I had peace. I was joyful. I was full of love for those who hurt me.

The positive effects of supernatural grace on the spiritual life are very real. We can utilize this divine assistance in our constant struggle (warfare) to imitate Jesus Christ in our interior spiritual life. This lets our spiritual life grow stronger and stronger, even as our body grows weaker and weaker.

The concrete expression of this fact is to strive to be like Jesus in every way. It is to strive to be virtuous, to form and practice good habits, not bad ones. We are to literally form perfect habits (virtues), the habits of Jesus Christ, the habits of God, divine habits, not worldly ones. Forgiveness is just one of the virtues.

This is a life-long process. Most of us have fallen in many ways and so have many bad habits. The goal is to methodically change these bad habits, our vices, into good habits, the virtues.

The process for changing each bad habit is the same as I went through with changing from hating those who hurt me to forgiving them. I repented of my error or sin. Then I made the effort to change. In time, and after praying for help, God gave me the grace to change. After returning to the USA, I had more changes to make in my life. I began to drink too much. I had to commit to change. I had to go to confession. I had to pray and make the effort and in time, I gave up drinking.

Well, by the grace of God I got rid of my big sins long ago. By the grace of God I keep them away from me. But there are a lot of ways to improve one's nature and become more like Jesus. In doing so it requires receiving lots of grace. This is called growing in the life of grace. It is what growing in our spiritual life is all about.

We have to learn about virtues and then try to form and practice them. We have to do this until the end of our lives. And the more we change and become like Jesus, the more grace we receive.

This is important, for when we take that last breath, the level of change we made determines what place we receive in Heaven. The more grace we have when we die, the more glory we receive in Heaven. This is all because of the fact that the whole process of receiving grace is a process we go through to love God. For this is what we do when we strive to do God's Will, by striving to be like Jesus. We love God. The more we love in this life, the higher we are in Heaven for all eternity.

I hope I have explained in a convincing way how important it is to forgive and get started in the life of grace. That was my goal today.

It takes lots of prayer to do this, lots of doing God's Will, which includes growing in humility. Many spiritual authors of our Faith consider humility the foundation, the bedrock of all virtues that we have to learn.

God has given us the sacraments, and we have all the spiritual books we could possibly need. We just have to do our best and then He will give us the grace to be holy and full of love, which is why God created us to begin with. Nothing else really is important.

I pray that all of you do well in this life and grow greatly in the life of grace. Thank you and God bless!

A few words on Forgiveness in a Marriage;

The following was given to a Diocesan Marriage Preparation Seminar in Indianapolis, Indiana, on January 22, 2012. It was in response to a question after this talk on forgiveness as to, "How does the need to forgive relate to a marriage?"

Built-in Problems and Conflicts

A man and a woman are human. They both have fallen natures. They can and will make mistakes that they will be sorry for. This means that they must forgive each other, because men and women are not perfect.

Also, a man is different than a woman. A woman is different than a man. They have different perspectives. They have different personal goals. They have different values and desires. Both must realize this and try to overlook or accept each other's different ways of seeing things.

In addition, when two people get married, they become one and start a new family together. However, they bring into their marriage the values, habits and ways of doing things of two entirely different families. These differences will often assure conflicts and odd behavior in each other's eyes. This is a further reason to realize that there will be conflicts that will have to be accepted, overlooked and forgiven.

Finally, when a man and a woman, each who has never intimately lived with a spouse before, start to live together constantly, conflicts will arise over various big and small matters. This must be realized, accepted and dealt with.

FORGIVE FOR MARRIAGE SURVIVAL
The above lists many of the ways that problems can start in a marriage. It is obvious that both partners must learn how to forgive for the marriage to be good, peaceful, loving and survive. This generous love can make "lived happily ever after" reality.

THE NUMBER ONE RULE
How can this happen? How can we learn how to forgive another who has hurt us? Well, the number one way is to realize that it is God's Will that we forgive. So to avoid sinning and to please God and show Him we love Him, we must forgive. That's all there is to it. We make an act of our free will to do it.

THE POWER OF THE WORD
Each of us should memorize three scriptural verses so that when we have to face a temptation to not forgive, **we can overcome the temptation by the power of the Word, as Jesus did in the desert.** The Bible verses are as follows:

You must not let the sun set on your anger.
In other words, every day we start with a clean slate.
In your anger do not sin; let not the sun go down upon your anger.
Ephesians 4:26

You must forgive seven times seventy times.

Set no limit to the number of times to forgive each other.

Jesus said to him: I say not to thee till seven times; but till seventy times seven times. Matthew 18:22

If you love those who love you, what credit is that to you?

To love divinely, we have to love those who hurt us and treat us badly in one way or another.

If you [merely] love those who love you, what quality of credit and thanks is that to you? For even the [very] sinners love their lovers (those who love them). And if you are kind and good and do favors to and benefit those who are kind and good and do favors to and benefit you, what quality of credit and thanks is that to you? For even the preeminently sinful do the same. Luke 6:32-33

GET READY FOR THE SCHOOL OF LOVE

Marriage is one of God's testing grounds for us. It is a school of love. Do we love God? Will we do His Will over and above what we think is right in our eyes and fair? Once the honeymoon is over, each spouse will face one test after another. One of the tests repeated over and over again daily is will we obey God's commandment to love. This means we must generously forgive those who hurt us.

DANGER SIGNS THAT WE ARE FAILING THE TEST

If we catch ourselves trying to get back at our spouses because of something they did or said, we must immediately stop and pray. Otherwise, this is the start of vindictiveness. This was my big mistake (sin) in prison camp. If it is not stopped in a marriage, it will grow similarly into hatred and un-forgiveness. Separation will result.

NO LIMIT

There are no words in Holy Scripture that define any limit to forgiveness. It does not say, for example, "If my spouse becomes a heavy drinker, I don't have to forgive him or her for that." The point is to see everything as a test and do our best to pass each test. The harder it is to forgive one's spouse the bigger the test it is. Remember, If you love those who love you, what credit is that to you? (Luke 6:32). If we pass the big tests, then God will bless us in this life and the next. So pass the big tests, get the big credit!

FINAL COMMENT

It has been said that *"forgiveness is to a relationship as water is to the body."* Therefore, let's not let anger or hatred or harsh words or anything else stop us from forgiving the one we have chosen to spend the rest of our lives with.

St. Maria Goretti
(1890-1902)

One of the largest crowds ever assembled for a canonization—250,000—symbolized the reaction of millions touched by the simple story of Maria Goretti.

She was the daughter of a poor Italian tenant farmer, had no chance to go to school, never learned to read or write. When she made her First Communion not long before her death at age 12, she was one of the larger and somewhat backward members of the class.

On a hot afternoon in July, Maria was sitting at the top of the stairs of her house, mending a shirt. She was not quite 12 years old, but physically mature. A cart stopped outside, and a neighbor, Alessandro, 18 years old, ran up the stairs. He seized her and pulled her into a bedroom. She struggled and tried to call for help. "No, God does not wish it," she cried out. "It is a sin. You would go to hell for it." Alessandro began striking at her blindly with a long dagger.

She was taken to a hospital. Her last hours were marked by the usual simple compassion of the good—concern about where her mother would sleep, forgiveness of her murderer (she had been in fear of him, but did not say anything lest she cause trouble to his family) and her devout welcoming of Viaticum, her last Holy Communion. She died about 24 hours after the attack.

Her murderer was sentenced to 30 years in prison. For a long time he was unrepentant and surly. One night he had a dream or vision of Maria, gathering flowers and offering them to him. His life changed. When he was released after 27 years, his first act was to go to beg the forgiveness of Maria's mother.

Devotion to the young martyr grew, miracles were worked, and in less than half a century she was canonized. At her beatification in 1947, her mother (then 82), two sisters and a brother appeared with Pope Pius XII on the balcony of St. Peter's. Three years later, at her canonization, a 66-year-old Alessandro Serenelli knelt among the quarter-million people and cried tears of joy.

COMMENT:

Maria may have had trouble with catechism, but she had no trouble with faith. God's Will was holiness, decency, respect for one's body, absolute obedience, total trust. In a complex world, her faith was simple: It is a privilege to be loved by God, and to love him—at any cost. "Even if she had not been a martyr, she would have been a saint, so holy was her everyday life." (Cardinal Salotti). *AmericanCatholic.org*, July 6, 2013, *Saint of the Day.*

...pass the big tests, get the big credit..."billionaire" in Heaven for ever

5

VOCATIONAL TALK FOR HIGH SCHOOL STUDENTS

TALK NARRATIVE: Very good friends of ours asked for a talk to High School Students considering a vocation as priests in our part of Ohio. The reason was to present considerations in the choice of vocations, whether married, single or religious, and to stress the importance of the decision, because this would be the primary way they would love their neighbor on earth. But to love our neighbor the best in any of these vocations, it is vitally necessary that the love of God must be overriding and take priority, and so the talk stressed this also. I wanted to reiterate the fact that God would be their shepherd in any vocation they chose if they lived it according to His Will. And that this would give them an outstanding quality of life even on earth with deep peace and joy, but much more importantly, lead them to an eternal reward beyond imagining, closest to the Throne.

THE LORD IS MY SHEPHERD

Hello everyone! My name is Guy Gruters. I have been asked to tell my story and how it relates it to your lives at this time of decision in your passage through life.

How can what I went through relate to the decision you are examining now?

Well, what if there was a way, based on your choice of priorities and goals today, to optimize not just your life on this earth but your immortal life in Heaven for countless trillions of years to come?

In fact, there is a way to set up your life for total victory, a total victory of love.

What happened to me may give food for thought and encouragement about your personal decision in the choice of vocations. Because your life ahead is a clean slate, a bit of thought now seems like a very wise thing to do. Why not put yourself in the best "big picture" position to succeed, no matter which vocation you choose? The choice for everyone is the same, whether married, single or religious.

Each of you can choose to go down different routes. The choice or decision you make now or after you graduate from high school determines not just your life during your few years on earth but also your life and the quality of your life for all the endless years of eternity. This is a simple, true and awe-inspiring fact!

First, a few words on my background, the part you can relate to most, because it is what happened to me when I was your age.

I graduated from high school. Because I made good grades and was in good physical shape, I applied for the Air Force Academy and was accepted. I did this because I wanted to become a soldier and defend our country. My father was a soldier in World War II. He spent more than two years away from his wife, my mother, and me defending our country. I guess I wanted to do what he did.

Going to the Air Force Academy meant that I had a chance to become a fighter pilot. You had to get high grades at the Academy and stay in good shape physically to make it happen. Well, this is what I wanted to do and what I did. So in seven years or so after I graduated from high school I was flying in a fighter plane over a country the United States was at war with.

Being a soldier is a vocation of love because a soldier is ready to give up his life for others. Many of my friends did just this. They never came home from the war. Others came home wounded and had to live as a cripple for the rest of their lives. The reason that being a soldier is a vocation of love is because Jesus said the greatest way to love another is to give up your life for them. As I just mentioned, this is what sometimes happens to soldiers fighting in a foreign land or fighting to defend the integrity of their own country against an invasion.

What happened to me is that I was shot down. My fighter plane was hit by an exploding shell from a big gun. This is called cannon fire or anti-aircraft fire. Then I had to eject out of the fighter plane and parachute to the ground. However, God was caring for me all the time.

The place where the cannon fire hit the plane was not where I was sitting. This was the first way God protected my life.

Then there was the fact that the plane did not explode into a million pieces as it was hit. It should have or could have, because a fighter plane is full of jet fuel and also hundreds of shells and rockets that are fired at the ground or bombs that are dropped from the plane to the ground.

I was shot down twice. On the first shoot down God kept me alive because I had time to eject from the plane even though it was on fire and getting very hot. The cannon fire that hit the plane the second time just missed my body but the flight controls of the fighter were shot to pieces. This threw the plane over on its back and toward the ground at five hundred miles per hour.

Then another miracle occurred. My parachute opened and I made it safely to the ground even though I was not high up off the ground at all when I ejected. I had to eject from the fighter when it was diving for the ground upside down from less than 1500 feet above the ground.

You can imagine landing on the ground in a country that you were just flying over shooting at the same soldiers that were now going to capture you. Well, this was the next miracle. The soldiers and civilians did not kill me when they first found me even though they were very mad at me.

In fact, God had me fall out of the sky without a gun so I could not defend myself on the ground at all. If I would have had my handgun with me, I probably would have shot at them first. If I had, I would have been shot and killed by them. There were many soldiers and they all had weapons with many rounds and more powerful ammunition, automatic rifles instead of pistols. Another save by God.

Then I was caught. I was unable to escape and I spent over five years in a country we were at war with, but lived through it. This may not seem like that big of a deal to you, but the fact is that I was one of over 3500 aircrew that were shot down and not rescued. Only about 472 (from North Vietnam) or less than 1 out of 7 men lived. The rest were tortured to death or killed in one way or another by the Russians and North Vietnamese. Some of the pilots were also taken to Russia and tortured to death.

At that time Russia wanted to know all about our nuclear bomb secrets. Some of the pilots who were from headquarters organizations or whose planes could carry the latest nuclear bombs knew much about this. So they loaded these men on airplanes and took them to Russia and there they were tortured to death and never heard from again. Many men were also killed by being tortured to death right in the camp where I was in North Vietnam.

You may be wondering now whether or not I was tortured and the answer is yes. But God saved me again. I will tell you how. The interrogators, that is the enemy soldiers who asked all the questions and tortured us, did this to me as to everyone. As instructed, after a while, pretending to be broken, I gave them a story that was not true and this got me out of some of the initial torture for military information.

But then they started all over again. This time they were going to make me read over the loudspeaker system things that were not true. The result is that those listening would think that the North Vietnamese Government was the good guy and the United States Government was the bad guy. They also wanted us to go in front of the international news media and tell lies that would make their country look good and our country look bad.

I told them I would not do this and they started to torture me again. Then sometime later in the middle of the torture, they asked me why I would not do such and without me even thinking what I was going to say, God spoke through me and said, "because it would disgrace my family." These were probably the only words that I could have said that would have prevented further torture and death. I did not know this, but God did. You see I did not know that the North Vietnamese had great respect for family honor and so when God said this through me, they understood that I was like them in this regard. So they stopped the torture and let me go back to my cell alive. I was the only one I knew of who was spared this way from meeting the delegations sympathetic to North Vietnam from the United States and Europe.

Well, by now I was starting to think that God was in control and I was not, and that God must be caring for me every day. This was surely true. Maybe it was because I had a wife and two children back home and she needed a husband and they a father, or maybe it was because I had always tried to go to daily Mass when I could, or maybe it was because my mother and Aunt were saying the rosary for me every day.

Whatever it was, it became apparent to me that God was in control and He was keeping me alive. This is how I can relate to the scriptural verse that reads: "The Lord is my shepherd; I shall not want." You all know what a shepherd is. It is a person who cares for sheep and the word "want" in this verse means that the shepherd will care for the needs of his sheep. Well, I was just a dumb sheep and God was caring for me every day and keeping me alive even though there were hundreds of ways that I should have or could have been killed or died of one disease or another.

The conditions there were horrible. There were no doctors or dentists. If you had an infection in your mouth from a sore tooth the guard would give you a nail to punch the swelling and let out the puss. The food was full of rat excrement and the water had live things swimming in it. We froze and shivered all day long in the winter and were very hot and covered with heat rash in the summer. There were rats all over the place. They crawled over you at night and there were also giant spiders and centipedes. The centipedes could kill you with one bite and this was all in addition to having the guards walk around beating you and with guns ready to kill anyone, and did if anyone got out of line from the despair.

Needless to say, I became very close to God in prison camp, closer than I had ever been to Him. I was so thankful that He kept me alive against all these odds. Truly He was my shepherd even though I was in a very evil place. But He got me through it and out of it and I came home alive to care for my family and live a full life here in America. My wife and I had five more children for a total of seven, and we have just adopted an eighth and all eight are still alive, many with children of their own.

So how can each of you relate to my story? Well, the fact is that God loves each of you just as much as He loves me. The fact is, the simple wonderful truth is, no matter whatever you choose to do in life, if you stay with God, He will be your shepherd and care for you. There are no exceptions!

I learned much about God in prison camp. Afterwards, when I returned home, I read the Bible to find out more about God. In the Bible it states that we were created to be holy and full of love (Eph 1:4) This is why God made us. He did not make us like He made cows or horses or other creatures. We are not just animals. They have another purpose in God's plan. For us, God's plan is that we grow in holiness and love. This is because someday we are going to leave this earth and get new bodies and live for all eternity in heaven above.

We are all God's children. He is truly our Father and this makes all of us brothers. I know each of you have different mothers and fathers but they only helped God to create the bodies we live in. It was God that created the part of us that will live for all eternity. This part is our soul or spirit. It is what is inside of us and what we think with and why we are different from each other.

This is the part of us that can become holy and great in love. This is our job down here while we live. We have time and a free will to do this. Time and a free will are the two coins that everyone on earth is given to spend in God's test of love down here. This is why we go to church and try to obey God's Commandments. This is why there are priests to help us to progress in our growth in holiness and love.

If we try to do this, then we are doing what God wants us to do. But if instead we try to get the most fun out of life by doing the wrong things, then we will not be making our Father happy at all. In that case, instead of being our shepherd He will be really tough on us. Otherwise He would be a terrible father, one who abandoned us to sin and hell without teaching us why sin is so bad.

What I mean is, if we do wrong, we will be children of His that He will want to keep away from the children that love Him. It is just like your father at home on earth would keep you away from a friend who steals or takes drugs. The point is that we all have to make choices whether or not we do what is right or what is wrong. The right choice is hard to do in many cases because this world we live in makes it easy to do what is wrong.

If you choose to do what is wrong you may get punished. If you choose to do what is right you may get blessed. When I was your age I chose to become a soldier. I truly felt that God wanted me to do this and so I was not doing something rebellious but I was in a way trying to please my God and Father. As a result, He got me through a war alive, even though I had over 400 combat missions and five years in a communist prison hell. He was my shepherd and protected me and saved my life even though I was in great danger all those years and surrounded by very evil people.

Just like me when I was in High School, each one of you are at a time in your life that you will have to choose what you are going to do in life. I chose to be a soldier, but you can choose to do other things. However, whatever you choose to do, it should be something you think that God our Father wants you to do. It should be something that will help you fulfill your purpose in life, that is, help you to become holy and full of love. This is the "big picture" key to not really blowing our one chance down here, our one and only lifetime on earth, to seek to please God greatly and be with him the closest in Heaven forever.

Why should you try to do what you were created for? Well, as I explained above, one reason is because if you do then you will always have a perfect all-powerful shepherd to watch over you. God will care for you even in the worst of situations like He did for me. But there is another big reason and that is so that you can be happy and fulfilled in this life.

You see, God is our perfect Father and He wants what all fathers want for their children. He wants them to always be happy and full of joy. He will give us this happiness if we strive to do His Will and not our own will. If we try to do our own will, then we will end up trying our hardest to fulfill our natural desires. To do our own will results only in short-term pleasure, but in the long-term it will make us miserable and not happy.

We will do selfish things that we think will make us happy. But what will make us happy in this regard will only be a short-term happiness. For example, perhaps we think eating a rich meal with lots of desert will make us happy. It will for a short time but it won't last. Or perhaps we think that getting drunk will make us happy. Well, again, it will for a short time but it won't last. Let's move on. Perhaps we think that having sex with a girl will make us happy. It might for a short time, but not for long either. Or perhaps we think becoming a fighter pilot or something similar will make us happy. Well it is good to fly around in a fighter plane or run a successful restaurant or be a big shot in a company, but this desire being fulfilled will not bring us lasting happiness either.

My point is that God made us for Him and so the only way that we will have lasting happiness in this life is to strive to fulfill the purpose that He created us for which is to strive to be holy and full of love. The sooner we realize this the quicker we will stop pursuing happiness in all the places where it is really impossible to find it. If you realize this tonight, you will not waste years wallowing in the world, the flesh or sin.

I want to read to you a story by St. Augustine. It was a story about when he was young like you and he discovered this truth. Here it is:

We are told how St. Augustine, one of the greatest men who ever lived, stood once upon the seashore watching the waves and gazing also on the sun as it was gradually sinking behind the horizon. Overwhelmed by the beauties of nature he ex-

claimed: "Oh, ocean and sun and nature, can you give me peace!" But he received no answer. The waves continued to rise and fall as if suggesting that all earthly things were like them, unstable and incapable of affording peace to the soul.

St. Augustine then raised his eyes to the cloudless heavens and began to watch the stars as they were shining in the firmament. Again he asked if peace were to be found in their midst, and their reply seemed to be that they, like all other bright things of nature, must fade away after a few hours' radiance and that true and everlasting peace must be sought elsewhere.

And on the wings of thought St. Augustine rose to a still more lofty height. He began to seek for peace among the heavenly spirits around the throne of God. But he was told in reply that these spirits were after all, creatures and that nothing created could satisfy the craving of the soul.

Eventually he turned to God and there he found the object of his heart's desire, and in the exuberance of his joy he exclaimed: "Oh Lord, Thou hast made us for Thyself, and our hearts can never find rest until they rest in Thee." (From the book *Rest A While* by Patrick J Gearon O.Carm. pages 62, 63)

So we can all learn from St. Augustine that we will never be happy and content in this life until we strive to be holy and full of love. Because we must be holy and full of love to rest in God as St. Augustine learned. This is also called being one with God or united to Him. It is also in Holy Scripture that this is what Jesus wanted for all of us. He stated just before he left us:

I do not pray for them alone. I pray also for those who will believe in Me through their word, that all may be one as You, Father, are in Me, and I in You: I pray that they may be one in Us. (John 17:20, 21)

I hope I have clearly given you some advice about life that reflects the best I have learned from the Church, the Bible and experience. Now you know it. The key advice is to stick with God, in other words, do His Will, that is, what is right and good. Then He will care for you as a shepherd does his sheep and you will also experience lasting happiness, joy and contentment no matter what happens in this life. This will occur because you will be living one with our Father or united with our Father as Jesus did when He lived on this earth.

Jesus was holy and full of love and we are all supposed to imitate Him as we grow in age during this life. This can happen if we strive to always do as Jesus would do. He lived all the virtues (good habits) perfectly. This means His habits were all perfectly loving. He always strove to do God's Will and we must also, no matter which vocation we choose.

So each of you may ask: "How can I know what my Father, God, wants me to do in this life?" Well, consider that no matter whatever you do as far as working or how you spend your time in this life the ultimate goal is to become holy and full of love like Jesus was. This being the goal, then it makes sense we should pick something to do that will help us in the best way to attain it.

And what is it that can keep us from being holy and full of love? If we read the Bible it will tell us the three things that get in the way between God and us. They are the world, the flesh, and the devil.

THE WORLD: IN THE WAY

The world keeps us away by filling our lives with distractions. In other words, if we try to be like everyone else then we will try to have a nice car, a nice house and lots of money, listen to the news, watch television, watch sports, play video games, have many friends, and be popular and well liked by everyone and go on lots of vacations to entertain ourselves, etc. If this is our goal than we will spend all our time working for such and we will have no time to study about God and pray to Him. This is a very common way to waste a lifetime and results in a very low place in Heaven, if we are even lucky enough to make it.

THE FLESH: IN THE WAY

The flesh is our body. I like to consider it a personal donkey that our soul has been given to ride around on during our life on earth. As long as we are down here our donkey is always with us. Our donkey has many natural desires for food, drink and sex. If we spend our life trying to fulfill the extra desires of our donkey, then our mind will be so distracted that we won't even want to think about God or make any time for religion. We won't want to go to church. Instead, we will be very busy trying to make our donkey happy by giving it all the animal pleasure it can have. But it is a happiness that is not lasting and we will end up destroying our donkey and being very sad if we go this route. We are not created to give animal pleasure to our donkey but for our souls to be united to God on this earth and forever in Heaven. So we have to tell our donkey, our body, what to do, not let it tell us what to do. We know what food, drink and maybe sex is best for our donkey's welfare, based on our choice of vocations. That's what we give him. Who ever heard of a donkey rider asking his donkey what to do or where to go or what to feed him, etc.? So it is very smart to control our donkey with the reins we are given, that is, our free will. Not to control our donkey is not smart.

THE DEVIL: IN THE WAY

The third way is the devil. I don't think anyone here is going to mess around with the devil, in other words, worship the devil or pray to him. However, a person can invite the devil into his life. This is done by not doing what is right or in other words not choosing to do God's Will. If a person chooses to do wrong, that is, sin, then the devil gets control of the person. The bigger the sin the more control he gets. This is how God uses the devil to punish the person who does not do right. The devil's goal is to take us out, in other words, destroy our life and our family and also have us die early and not make it to heaven. By the way, he also gives us constant misery even during our lifetime on earth; no peace, no joy, no love.

If we start to do the wrong things like eating too much, or drinking too much, etc., then what will happen is that we will become enslaved to doing this. This is how the devil gets control of us. Then we find ourselves wanting to stop doing wrong but we can't. This is the slavery of sin that Jesus came to free us from. If this happens, then the only way to get power over the bad habit (the vice) is to go to confession and tell God through the priest that we are sorry. It is very important to understand that Jesus is the savior in these situations, and we are not. We are not strong enough. That is why He came. With humble confession and prayer, we will get the interior strength (the grace) from Jesus to overcome the runaway desire. It takes both us and God's grace. Then we can get back to trying to be holy and full of love. It is harder after we have fallen, but with this extra help from the Sacrament we can do it.

There is a lot to learn about spiritual life and each of us has to strive to learn it. Otherwise we will fall into one of the many traps that the world, the flesh and the devil have for us and waste our lives by not fulfilling the purpose God created us for. So it is perfectly reasonable to take time to study and learn what we can about the spiritual life. It's very important. The sooner we learn how to become like Jesus the better. It is to learn how to be *"holy and full of love."*

Jesus said that to be holy we have to love God with all of our heart, mind, soul and strength and love our neighbor as ourselves. Well, we have to study and learn how to love God with all of our heart, mind, soul and strength and then do it. We also have to choose a way to serve God by loving our neighbor, that is, choose a vocation and do our best at it.

You can choose to live your life as a single person or a father of a family or become a priest or a monk or another type of religious person. All of these ways of spending your life are ways you can spend loving your neighbor. This is why it is called a vocation. It is what you do in this life to serve God by doing His Will by loving your neighbor.

All this is how we will grow in holiness and become full of love and thereby reach a high level of happiness in this life and also a high level in heaven someday when we pass from this life.

See this life as a school, because that is what it is. And never forget, we all have to grow in holiness and love to make the best grade.

"God will never allow all those who love Him to enter the religious life. He will give some of them the mission of living in the sanctity of marriage, in the midst of society, providing an example of virtue and carrying on an apostolate that priests cannot, bringing the light of Christianity into circles that priests enter rarely or not at all." (*Charles de Foucauld,* by Jacques Antier, p330) You can see Charles realized God's plan for family life, and how important it is that families be holy and witness to other families in society, even when society is sinful and evil. It is to be a Christian, a follower of Jesus Christ, Who lived on this earth for thirty years in a holy family, witnessing to those around Him in the little village of Nazareth.

Thus, we can be holy and full of love in any vocation we pick. But if we choose a vocation that will help us do this, it will help greatly. My point is that if you can do something with your life that will give you time to learn how to love God while you love your neighbor, then this would be best.

This is why the Bible says becoming a priest or a religious is the best choice. It is because a priest or a religious can spend time learning about how to love God while also loving his neighbor at the same time. You can also do this in any other vocation you choose but it is harder because you have to overcome more of the world, the flesh and the devil. There are simply more distractions in the other vocations.

But remember that the holiest people that ever lived were Mary and St. Joseph and they lived in a family. They became holy and full of love. So it can be done in a perfect way in the other vocations. However, it is definitely harder because to have a family you have to deal more with the world and the flesh. You don't have as much time to learn all about how to love God like a priest or a single person does.

The fact is, we must know what we have to do to love God in order to do it. This is not easy, it is not obvious. A priest learns all of this in his schooling. This schooling in love of God is called his formation. He becomes an expert in spiritual life and knowing what to do to become holy by loving God. This is called growing in perfection of charity. It is also called becoming recollected. A priest can spend all his life striving to become truly holy because he knows from his schooling, his formation, what to do. Then he spends his life doing such (loving God) while he loves his neighbor by being a good priest.

Being truly holy is also to grow in virtue. To grow in virtue we have to study and learn all about virtue. The priestly and/or religious schooling and vocation provides this opportunity more than the married and single vocations do. Did you know that the spiritual writers discuss considerably more than fifty virtues? Most people don't realize there is so much to being truly virtuous. It is a rare married or single that studies virtues at an early age. Yet this is the key to becoming like Jesus, that is, to constantly be growing in virtues until we live as He lived. This is tough to do when you don't even know what they are. And they are not all obvious. They must be studied.

My point is that if you choose to become a priest or religious you will have an understanding of both loves that really matter in this life, the love of God and love of neighbor. You will know and understand earlier in your life what it takes to strive to become holy and full of love. It gives you a jump on optimizing your love-life, we might say.

Again, this is the goal for all of us. This is how we will be graded in the end. And this is important because there are levels in heaven and the highest levels are given to those who have become the holiest and most loving in this life, those who become the most like our perfect model, Jesus. These are the levels of the saints. These are the neighborhoods of the saints.

Wouldn't you like to be in those neighborhoods for all eternity? Each of you was created to be a great saint. God does not play favorites. We all have the same opportunity. We all have time and free-will decisions to make every day. How great you are in Heaven for all eternity is strictly up to you, working with the grace of God given through the Sacraments and prayer and your free-will decisions to attain the most perfect virtue possible. So you can see the values and priorities you set now really are vital to you.

This is honestly how it is. This is really what is important, nothing else. The approval of the world, the wealth of the world and bodily pleasures are shallow, temporary and mean absolutely nothing in Heaven, our true home for all eternity. This world is strictly our exile, our school and our test. How much do we love?

I hope and pray that you do well in this school of life that we all have to pass through. I started late in the school of love, but you don't have to. I hope and pray that each of you really attain perfect love, the love of Jesus Christ, and so the very highest level of Heaven for all eternity, the best neighborhood, the one closest to the Throne.

May God be with you and may you always rest in Him.

Thank you for your attention.

"The patient man is better than the valiant, and he that ruleth his spirit than he that taketh cities." Prov. 16:32

*"Eye has not seen, nor ear heard,
Nor have entered into the heart of man
The things which God has prepared for those who love Him." 1 Corinthians 2:9*

6

MEN'S CHRISTIAN LEADERSHIP CONFERENCE

TALK NARRATIVE: A good friend of mine, Mr. Chuck Wilson, has a son who attended Franciscan University of Steubenville in Ohio with my son. Chuck has been instrumental in organizing the annual Catholic Men's Conferences for the Columbus Diocese. I was asked to speak to the tenth annual gathering of approximately one thousand men about what the Catholic Faith meant to me both before and after the POW experience. I also addressed the continuous care that God has given to my family throughout our lives in difficult situations. We believe the "saves" in each instance are due to graces received as a result of attendance at daily Mass.

Tenth annual Catholic Men's Conference held at St. Andrews parish in Columbus, Ohio, sponsored by the Catholic Men's Ministry, Saturday, March 10, 2007.

The Theme:
Answer the call to holiness by knowing the love of Christ through the family.

Doug Lascelles, Master of Ceremonies:

Our first speaker is one of the most highly decorated officers in U.S. military history. A U.S. Air Force Captain, Guy Gruters, of Minster, Ohio, flew more than 400 combat missions during the Vietnam War. Captain Gruters was awarded more than 30 combat awards, including two Silver Stars, two Distinguished Flying Crosses, two Bronze Stars for Valor, two Purple Hearts, the P.O.W. Medal, and more than twenty Air Medals. But it was his faith that carried Guy to victory in the biggest battle of his life. Shot down twice during the Vietnam war, Guy was captured the second time and spent a grueling five years and three months in communist prison camps. Here to share his amazing story of faith and family, please welcome Guy Gruters.

FORWARD AIR CONTROLLER US ARMY SOUTH VIETNAM
After I attended the Air Force Academy and pilot training, then fighter gunnery training for the F-100 aircraft, I volunteered for Vietnam. I served there a total of six years and 15 days. The first seven months were as a forward air controller with the 173rd Airborne Brigade, an excellent U.S. army unit. This Brigade fought in many parts of Vietnam. During the last months of my service assigned to this unit in 1967, it was stationed at the Dak To Special Forces Camp in the Central Highlands. Combat action was continuous because we were the "Fire Brigade," and it was our job to finish up the tough battles.

O-1 Bird Dog aircraft used for Forward Air Controller mission in South Vietnam

MISTY FORWARD AIR CONTROLLER NORTH VIETNAM

While at Dak To, I signed up for an all-volunteer, top-secret unit flying as scouts low level in North Vietnam in the F-100 fighter aircraft. It was called the *MISTY* Fast FACs, or *MISTY* Fast Forward Air Controllers. I was shot down and rescued on one of these *MISTY* missions. I was shot down a second time a few weeks later, captured and spent several years in a communist prison camp.

F-100 FIGHTER USED FOR FORWARD AIR CONTROLLER MISSION IN NORTH VIETNAM

I WAS PRIDEFUL

I want to talk today about what my faith meant to me in combat and while raising a family in the United States. I would like to discuss some aspects of my background that resulted in pride which almost killed me in prison camp. I am trying to convey the truth that pride should be avoided like the plague, and that everything we have or have done well is only due to the grace of God, and is nothing that we should try to take credit for.

I became an Eagle Scout in High School. I averaged 27 hours of coursework each semester at the Air Force Academy. I had a 4.0 GPA in science and engineering for the first three years.

GUY AT THE US AIR FORCE ACADEMY

I was rated a top engineer in my class of 470 and was sent by the USAFA for a Master's Degree in Astronautical Engineering at Purdue University. I was also sent to compete for a Rhodes Scholarship in my senior year. I was on the USAFA Judo team, and we were number two in the nation. I was a good boxer. I was on the Wing Staff my senior year at the Academy. I was number two in my pilot training class out of 32. So I had many academic, military and athletic accomplishments.

83

GUY'S WIFE, SANDY, THE FORMER SANDRA LEE HANCOCK
AT FLORIDA STATE UNIVERSITY

I now understand that the successes were due to my attendance at daily mass all those years. But before prison camp I ascribed these good things happening to my ability, rather than to the grace of God.

GUY AND SANDY WITH FIRST-BORN DAWN BEFORE VIETNAM.
SANDY IS CARRYING SHERI

Despite my pride, I thought I was humble. Jesus told St. Faustina that this was common in prideful people. St. Faustina asked Him why there were so few great saints, and He answered that a person has to be humble to be a saint. St. Faustina said "But there are so few saints. Aren't there more really humble people than that?" and Jesus said, "No." He said pride was widespread because Satan convinces everyone they are humble and so people do not make the effort to pursue humility. And since humility is the basis of all other virtues, prideful people just don't make the big leagues in Heaven. It is tough to fix the problem if we are blind to it.

CHAPLAINS IN COMBAT
The Catholic Church supported us in Vietnam with excellent military chaplains. Even at Dak To, when we were in tents during the monsoon season, the priests would have Mass every morning in the deep mud. It meant a lot to us. We had confession constantly at daily Mass as we were in dangerous action. I had no fear of dying because of that. Many times I was in intense combat under heavy fire with numerous tracers coming by my aircraft all the time, but I was without fear. I thought there was something

wrong with me and I was leery of saying anything about that to anybody, for concern they might think I was mentally disturbed.

PEACE IN BATTLE

But since returning home, I read a book by one of the mystics given insight into the life of Jesus. She wrote that Jesus talked to the Roman soldiers and said that He wanted them to be good soldiers and be satisfied with their pay.

They asked Him, "Well, why do such large crowds come and listen to you out here in the countryside?"

Jesus said, "It is because I give them peace; that's what people are after." Then He said, "I can give you peace too."

They responded, "No, You can't do that, sir, we are always fighting, we go from one place to another. We're always in battle."

Jesus said, "I understand, but I give peace even in battle. Even in battle."

And that's what He did for me. I had peace in battle. In my opinion, that's why Christian soldiers have always been the best soldiers in the world, and I am sure that will be true until the end of time.

Misty FACs 1967

Standing: Bob Blocher, Lt Haltigan, Guy Gruters, Bob Porter, Jere Wallace, "PJ" White, Gene Mooney, Ron "Nape" Miller, Bob Craner, Mick Greene, Don Sibson
Kneeling: Maurice McHugh, Charlie Neel, Jim Mack, Joe Cerito, George Pinney

F-100 MISTY FACS; WE HAD GREAT PEACE IN BATTLE

(Next I described prison conditions and it was similar to the discussion in Chapter 12)

These conditions were a standard part of living in a communist prison camp. We had no pleasure, no break and no relief. The worst part was that it looked like we would never get out and would have to live the rest of our lives in these conditions.

This belief was frustrating and very discouraging. The beatings and torture were extremely humiliating. Since I had developed great personal pride, these led to increased anger and eventually hatred of the guards and interrogators.

SIX OF SEVEN KILLED

They brought each of us in for interrogations multiple times every week. We never knew whether we were going to come back from them or not. More than 3500 aircrew were shot down over North Vietnam and not rescued, according to official US Military records. And our air-sea rescue forces were as good as they could be. We called them the bravest men in the world. They did a wonderful job coming in where nobody should come in to get us. They took such heavy losses that they would come to get us in two-ship flights, because often one of the choppers would get shot down trying to get us out of there. Then the second chopper would rescue the other chopper's crewmen as well as us. But despite their best efforts, more than 3500 aircrew were not rescued, and only 472 of us came home from North Vietnam. This was out of a total POW release of approximately 600 of all services and which included captives taken in South Vietnam. That means six out of seven air crewmen were tortured to death or killed by the Russians or the North Vietnamese, one way or another. Also, some men were not able to handle the conditions, would stop eating, and so they died.

CONDITIONS INCREASED OUR FAITH

Most of the men were able to handle the conditions because almost all the men had basic religious faith, as I did. But our faith grew stronger with God's care in the prison camps. God increases faith in tough situations. I believed in God before prison camp, but had no idea of His complete and absolute power. I'm convinced that's one of the reasons we have trials or crosses on this earth. He is trying to help us develop stronger faith so we will make the effort to try to be good to get to Heaven.

IS GOD UP HERE?

I was pondering our situation one day after a few months in North Vietnam and wondering if God was there in those conditions. I thought to myself, "Well, you can't ask God to be in the middle of evil like this. He probably is waiting for us on the border. He probably will pick us up if we ever get out of here." I mention this because it gives you an idea of my faith in God when I was shot down. I believed that He was there in Heaven, that He was powerful and running the world, but not in the day-to-day details. I thought He just worried about the big things.

GOD WAS RUNNING EVERYTHING

I believe that because of that honest question, over the next year He showed me His power was absolutely infinite in every detail of life. There are no coincidences. Once I understood that, the prison camp experience became a blessing to me in every way, because He brought me so close to Him there that my faith has given me great strength and confidence ever since, especially in bad times.

The first month I was up there, one of the POWs, a good friend of mine, was tortured and beaten to death over a period of about a month in a cell less than six feet from me. He died horribly but heroically. His name was Lance Sijan. It was a source of great sadness, helplessness, heartbreak and anger to my other cellmate and me. Because of his death, others' deaths, and because of being beaten around and tortured, my anger grew. I had never been mad at anybody in my life. By constantly dwelling on the terrible injustices happening, I developed a raging hatred for the guards and interrogators. There is a pleasure in hatred just as in all serious sins. Having experienced it, I believe hatred is the greatest of all sins. God is Love, Satan is hatred.

VINDICTIVENESS ALMOST KILLED ME

I felt like I was a force of goodness and justice against the filthy communists and I would somehow get even with them. It became an obsession. Soon I could not even sleep well at night. All I could think about was how to get even, how to beat these guys, each one of them. This went on for months. To confirm how clever the devil is, the entire time I thought that I was still on God's side. After some months, in the middle of this really intense, all consuming hatred, I started to get thoughts like, "Why don't you just stop eating?" or "Go into the corner and sit on the floor. That will teach them. They can't get you to meet delegations, if you're sitting on the floor and not eating."

The biggest fear in prison camp was to be tortured into meeting a delegation sympathetic to North Vietnam from the United States or Europe, because we had to memorize every question and answer that the delegation would ask us. The communists would give the delegation a list of questions to ask and then we would answer on camera with the answers memorized after torture. Being a POW in a communist prison camp is like being a milk cow in a stall, and the milk is propaganda. We were being milked by torture for a bucket of treason to the United States of America.

THOUGHTS FROM THE BAD ANGELS

"They can't beat you. You can beat them by just not eating. That will let you beat them." These thoughts became stronger and stronger, but I recognized this as suicide. I had been to Catholic grade school and knew that suicide was always wrong. Catholic Doctrine teaches that thoughts come from the spirit world. I realized these very strong thoughts were from the wrong source. I remembered the lesson, "God is Love, Satan is hatred, and so hatred is the worst sin." I tried to stop hating and thinking of revenge. But it was impossible to do so on my own. I could not stop. I finally asked God for help on my knees. "Please help me. Please! I understand I am in trouble here. Please get me back with you." I made endless acts of contrition and prayed the rosary over and over. But it took months to stop hating my captors. I had no powerful graces from Mass or Confession to help me in prison camp.

PRAYER NECESSARY TO FORGIVE

With my constant prayer but only after many months, God finally led me to the point where I was praying for my interrogators and the torturers. I realized they were loved by Him just as I was, and that He also wanted them to go to Heaven. That was very hard to do and a wrenching conversion for me. At the same time He let me see daily that He was totally in charge which gave me great peace and joy. This was miraculous to me at that time and it has been since. The greatest peace and joy I have ever had in my life was in prison camp when praying for my captors. I believe the reason is that I had time to pray and really converse with God all day long.

GOD WAS WITH ME

I would like to quote the 18th Psalm:

I will be a witness to you in the world, O Lord. I will spread the knowledge of your Name among my brothers, Alleluia.

I witness to you that God revealed Himself to me in everyday life in prison camp. Upon reading the stories of the Saints after I came back, I learned that they maintain God will do this for all of us if we open our eyes. Generally, we do not have time for Him and we do not take the time to see Him work in our lives. But in prison camp we had the time to see what was going on. We were able to see His power. People say, "Well, you were just thinking that. It was coincidental." But I knew it was not coincidence. I knew and understood what He was doing and I saw His power daily.

I will give you a couple of instances.

GOD SAVED ME FROM MEETING DELEGATIONS

When the communists wanted us to meet a delegation, the first thing they had us do was read the communist-written news of the day over the camp loudspeaker system. There were speakers in each cell. The news was read for fifteen minutes on certain nights. The news was about the communist outlook on the war, bragging about their great victories in South Vietnam. Of course, it was total lies, completely false, as is all communist propaganda. The standard things the communist military forces did in South Vietnam were to lose battles and die a lot. The only place communists won in South Vietnam was in the media of the United States and North Vietnam. But the communists didn't speak English very well, so they had American pilots read their doctored news. Then after that went on for some time, they convinced us through torture to meet a visiting sympathetic delegation from overseas and repeat their lies.

When my turn came up, they brought me in to read their news on the radio to the other POWs. I told them I would not read on the loudspeaker. They tortured me. After about eight hours of that, they brought me in to see the camp commander.

He said, "Why do you continue to resist? You know that sooner or later, we will have you read on the loudspeaker."

I replied, "Maybe so, we'll see."

Normally, they didn't bring us out of torture until we asked for mercy. Also, understand that I had no idea what questions the camp commander was going to ask. When he repeated his question as to why I resisted, my answer came out of nowhere,

"Because it would disgrace my family."

The camp commander nodded his head and gestured with his hand. "Take him back."

They put me back in torture for a little while, then unfastened me and put me back in my cell. I was the only one I knew of not tortured until I read on the radio. I am sure that they could have tortured me until I gave in and read. I have no illusions about resisting torture under long-term conditions. Their tortures went on 24/7 for weeks at a time.

I am sure God helped me with the words He inspired me to say. He beat their torture with words alone. The Asians have a great respect for family. I was inspired with probably the only answer that could have convinced the camp commander to stop the torture. God saved me from my worst fear, meeting delegations, simply by inspiring me with an answer that resulted in the torture being stopped without effect.

GOD SAVED ME FROM THE HOTBOX

(Please see Chapter 1 for details of the interrogation that tried to convince me that the Communist Government was all powerful through the torture of the hotbox, and how God saved me from it)

It was things like that happening with regularity that let me see who was really in charge in a communist prison camp. And it wasn't the communists.

This kind of thing didn't happen just to me. Remember, we had no help from the US military. We didn't have the United States. We didn't have our families. We didn't have anything supporting us except God. We were one on one with these guys and they had all the physical power. They had all the worldly power. It went on for year after year and it appeared certain it would be for a lifetime. It was very, very discouraging if you didn't have God, but with God, you could make it.

CHURCH SERVICE

To give you an idea that God didn't just reveal Himself to me, when we first were shot down the POWs already there would tap through the wall, or get to us one way or another, that we would all have a church service at Sunday noon. This was when the North Vietnamese sounded the gongs for their siesta. We would all say the *Our Father,* the *Pledge of Allegiance,* and the *23rd Psalm* together. Even though we were alone in our cells, we each knew that everyone was praying together with us.

Later on, about three years into my captivity, very brave soldiers in the U.S. Army Special Forces with other Air Force and Navy special operations units came into North Vietnam and raided a prison camp called Son Tay. This occurred on November 21, 1970. It went well at first. They killed all the guards present, but the POWs had been moved out of the camp about one to two weeks earlier. So our raiders did not recover any POWs.

They felt the mission was a failure and the American people felt it was a failure. But to us, the POWs, it was the most successful prison raid in history. The communists were forced by that raid to take us out of those one and two man cells in many scattered small prison camps and put us together in big dungeons, approximately 45 men each, in Hanoi, at the Hanoi Hilton. And it was wonderful to have 45 men together in those cells. They had to do that to defend us from being rescued by our special operations soldiers.

Our commanding officer, Colonel Risner, was a very good man and a great leader because he was a religious man. Based on witnessing leadership in combat, business and family life, I'm convinced good leaders are sincerely religious men. Colonel Risner was behind the order of the church service at noon on every Sunday. Years later, he was still in command.

Risner said, "Now that we are together in a large group, we can have church services with hymns and we can have a preaching from the Bible. We will have about a two-hour service."

So there was a process to first determine the hymns. Chaplains were chosen in each dungeon and Colonel Risner worked together with all seven dungeons and came up with ten or eleven hymns to sing — starting with The Star Spangled Banner, Amazing Grace, the Battle Hymn of the Republic, and others — hymns that almost everyone knew.

RULE OF SILENCE

It is important to understand there was a rule of silence in the communist prison camps. We were not allowed to let the guards hear us in those cells — we couldn't even talk to our cellmate in other than a whisper. However, sharply at 12 noon that first Sunday in the dungeons, more than three hundred POWs belted out the Star Spangled Banner at the top of our lungs. The guards came in with their machine guns and lined us up — and took the commanding officers out. They left the dungeons and put the commanders into irons in the torture rooms. The next man in charge — as determined by date of rank — took command. We always knew who was next in command when the top man went out, all the way down the line to the last man. We had good order and fine obedience up there and it worked to present a united front to the enemy.

The next man in line stood up and said, "Gentlemen, our service was interrupted, let us start again." We sang the Star Spangled Banner. The guards came in, took the next leaders out to the torture rooms. The next leaders restarted it. They took them. Finally, all the torture rooms were full. We finished the service.

We would monitor the interrogations in the interrogation room about fifty feet away in a different building. When we put our ear on the ground, we could hear the conversation in the next building over. The next day on Monday, when it was my turn to monitor, an Ohio man named Ed Mechenbier was being interrogated by the camp commander.

The camp commander said to him, "You can have no church services. You embarrass us in front of the Russians. You know we have a rule of silence. You must obey the regulations. Torture and death apply to this. You know that."

Ed Mechenbier said, "It doesn't matter what you do including killing every one of us, but as long as one man is alive we are having that church service."

He said it so simply and so coolly and so firmly, that they knew and we knew that there was going to be no compromise. And believe it or not, from then on we had that church service every Sunday, because they didn't want to lose the last guys still alive. We were insistent because everyone was like me. Everyone that had made it this far had made it because they stopped relying on themselves and turned to God. Everyone wanted to give glory to God.

I try to bring that story up in my talks because it's so important. All of life has tough situations and we can get through every single one of them, if we turn it over to Him and try to do what He wants us to do in that situation, which is simply the right thing. If the right thing is not obvious, we can go to Confession and ask the priest and do what he says.

MASS AND CONFESSION

When I came back, we had a beautiful Mass with Confession before the Mass. We didn't have Mass and Confession for the five years in prison camp and I missed them greatly. It was wonderful to have the Sacraments. Ever since that time, I am very thankful for Confession as well as for the Mass and I continue to attend daily Mass and go to frequent Confession. God blesses each day we go to Mass and makes everything work out all right, even when we mess up. As he did for me in prison camp, God somehow lets us see the mistake before it's too late and we wreck our lives. He gives us His grace to overcome our sins and get back on the road.

THE BIBLE, THE CATECHISM, CONFESSION HAVE THE ANSWERS

When I came back to the States, I read the Bible four times during the first year. I knew every word was inspired by God, and I have read it consistently ever since for over thirty years now. In daily Mass, we go through the whole Bible every three years. The Bible is the perfect guide as it is the Word of God, and it gives us tremendous guidance on every issue. We can purchase a good concordance and look up any topic. If there are any doubts, look it up in the *Catholic Catechism*, which I call the book of perfect truth. If there are still any doubts on the right decision, go to Confession and ask a priest. Jesus Christ will give you the right answer through him.

I left the military to raise a family. We had two little girls before prison camp and we had five children afterwards. So we have seven children, plus three miscarriages, so we have three special angels in Heaven helping us go through life here. We have just adopted our eighth child.

HOMECOMING: FIRST MEETING OF GUY, SANDY, DAWN AND SHERI

GUY AT HOMECOMING

INFINITE VALUE OF CHILDREN

I'll mention another thought He gave me in prison camp. One of the problems in the United States is that the only time we ever stop going a mile a minute is during daily Mass. We don't have time to think or pray. We had time to think in prison camp. It is like being a monk in a lot of ways. I know now that all thoughts come from or are allowed by God, based on what the spiritual writers say. That is how He controls every-thing. Everything is controlled by God the Father. And evil is allowed only if it brings about greater good, just like the crucifixion did.

One of the thoughts He gave me was, "What would you take for your wife or your children? Would you take a million dollars for any one of them?"

I thought to myself, "Of course not."
"Would you take a billion dollars?"
"Of course not."

"Would you take a trillion dollars? Would you take all the money in the world for them?"

"No, No."

The thought came, "What would you take for one of their arms? Would you take a million dollars for one of their arms?"

"No."

"How about a trillion?"

"No."

"How about all the money in the world? How about all the power in the world? What if you ran the world?"

"No, I wouldn't take it."

"What about for their finger?"

"No, no, no, no, no!"

"What about if someone were to just slap them around, promise that they wouldn't be hurt? Would you let them do that for all the money in world?"

"No, I wouldn't."

Now that's the truth. I bring that up because I was 26 years old when I had that thought. I think everyone ought to tell their kids that a child is worth more than everything in the world. Yet He gives children to us. What will our children and their descendants be worth in Heaven for the next so many trillion years? How could anyone think that it's not wise to have as many children as we can possibly have in a marriage? It doesn't make any sense when we realize that the real wealth in life is the children in a family. He gave me that understanding and I tried to have as many children as we could, knowing He would let me take care of them somehow, which He did.

NUTRITION

I saw the value of nutrition here. My body was in bad shape from the years of few nutrients. After I came back, we couldn't have children for three years. Finally, we had another child and then others. My wife was 43 and 44 years old for the last two. We were blessed, as I mentioned, with seven children.

(Here I described the parasites and their effect on our lives in prison camp and their effect on our married life and my work life. It was essentially as covered in Chapter 12.)

RECOVER TRUST OF PEOPLE?

As I said, I left the Air Force to raise a family. I joined the Eastern Airlines organization as an airline pilot, but was laid off almost immediately in the fuel crisis of 1973. Although an engineer, I joined IBM and became a salesman for IBM. This came about because after prison camp, I never wanted to talk to another human being in my life. That's how bad prison camp was. I wasn't a salesman, I was an engineer, but I had no trouble talking with people before prison camp. In prison camp, the only person I was talking to was trying to torture me to make me a traitor, so I lost my trust in other people. It took years to get over that feeling. I believed the only chance I had to be able to interface with people again was to take a sales job, where I might overcome my hangups. I was offered two engineering jobs and a sales job by IBM. I wanted desperately to take an engineering job, but I took the sales job. It forced me to interact with customers and eventually brought me out of the disgust with and distrust of people.

Some four years later I said to my wife, "I just wish I had what I had before I went to Vietnam, the total trust in people, because I would be a heck of a salesman."

Actually, I was a good salesman. I closed the biggest sale IBM had ever booked by a single salesman, 48 million dollars, all on my own, not with a team. I was a good salesman, but I didn't have what I had earlier before the war. It was still hard for me to talk to people.

I told Sandy that. She said, "That's all right, Guy, you are doing really well and you still have another year."

I said, "What do you mean, I have another year?"

Sandy said, "Guy, they told the wives that it would take you as long to recover psychologically as you were in prison. You know, based on what had happened in World War II and in Korea."

I said, "Why didn't somebody tell us that? Why didn't somebody tell me that?"

I had been dealing with a situation and I didn't understand why I had real trouble facing people. I think it was something spiritual. Because I sinned with my terrible hatred, I believed I had a disposition towards hatred to overcome. The trouble with sin seems to be that once we sin, it is easier to commit that sin again. There is a weakness in the soul, and it has to be fought for the rest of our lives. In this case, I had to fight to be able to forgive, even for the littlest things. This included my spouse and children; but with everybody else too, so I couldn't let myself get upset with people. I had sinned so badly that it was still with me as a weakness. That's another good reason not to sin seriously.

MY BROTHER BOMBED ME OUT

My brother, Terry, followed me to the Air Force Academy and to combat in Vietnam. When I was captured, Terry resolved to not leave Vietnam until I was released. The Lord let him have his wish to get me out after he had served many tours there and been shot down twice and crash-landed once behind enemy lines.

MY BROTHER AND MY HERO, CAPTAIN TERRY GRUTERS, U.S.A.F.

Terry flew one of the B-52 bombers that bombed us out of prison camp in late 1972 (Operation Linebacker II).

B-52S BOMB US OUT OF PRISON CAMP IN THE CHRISTMAS BOMBING OF 1972

Terry proved to be a true brother as the verse in Holy Scripture reflects: "*A brother is a better defense than a strong city.*" (Prov.18:19). Terry and I were close all of our lives, even though I was three years older than he. I was born in Sarasota, Florida in October, 1942, because my mother was living with her mother while my father was serving in the United States army during World War II, in Southern Europe and Northern Africa. My father who was by then a Lieutenant Colonel was later transferred to the Pentagon in Washington D.C. and Terry was born in October of 1945 in Washington D.C.. After the war was over, my father returned to his previous job as an engineer with Bell Telephone company in New York City, and we lived in Fair Lawn, New Jersey. My father unselfishly commuted an hour each way, each day to work, so that we would not have to grow up in the big city. We moved back to Sarasota, Florida in 1958, when my father retired at the early age of 49. He became a professor at Manatee Junior College in nearby Bradenton, Florida, until he retired a second time some fifteen or so years later.

As children in New Jersey we use to pray, worship, work, and play together. We attended St. Anne's parochial school and were altar boys at St. Anne's church. We prayed family prayers and the family rosary and attended Mass together. We shoveled snow and delivered papers together from the back of a pickup truck. Later we trapped muskrat and were forever exploring the woods and nature. We were both boy scouts and loved learning nature skills and camping. We played the endless games of touch football and capture the flag together with the other neighborhood boys. Games like these and exploring nature and organizations like the boy scouts were very popular in the days before TV became such a dominating influence in American life. Terry had a very happy childhood. He loved the outdoors and sports. He played Little League baseball and was named Boy Scout of the Year in his troop at about the age of 12. Our family moved to Florida when he was thirteen and he fulfilled his scouting promise by becoming an Eagle Scout at about age 14. He also loved to read and frequented the library. He was a very good student and was elected president of the National Honor Society at Sarasota High School when he was a senior. He was also athletic, running the mile for the Sarasota High School track team.

Terry followed me into the Air Force Academy. While there, he was the co-captain of the undefeated (in nine dual meets) Air Force Academy cross-country team which also finished second in the nation at the national championships.

USAFA Cross Country Team, Terry is center, front row
He was an All-American

Had their fifth runner not been unable to compete due to an injury, their coach calculated that they would have easily won the national championship. Terry was also named an individual NCAA division I All-American in cross-country based on his 14th place finish in the National Championship race. He was even interviewed for *Sports Illustrated* and his comments were published in a story about that race.

Terry was also a good cadet. As a senior, he was the first semester squadron commander of the outstanding squadron (top squadron out of 42) and he was also elected class treasurer of his class.

OUTSTANDING SQUADRON AWARD (OF 42).
TERRY (RIGHT) WAS SQUADRON COMMANDER

He was also an excellent student at the Air Force Academy and graduated with honors with an engineering science degree. He later served on the Board of Directors for the Air Force Academy for the years 1971-1975.

While at the Academy, he also went to the U.S. army's Fort Benning parachute training school and received the coveted jump wings. After graduating from the Academy and finishing pilot training, he took an assignment that allowed him to get to Vietnam the quickest. He became the pilot of an O-1 aircraft and served as a forward air controller directing air strikes for the airborne division of the Army of the Republic of Vietnam (ARVN). He was stationed all over South Vietnam at many remote sites, and participated greatly in the invasion of North Vietnamese occupied Cambodia in 1970. His goal was to do what he could do in order to get his brother (me) back home to his family. One time, when Terry was checking out a new pilot, Chip Deems, in the O-1 aircraft, their only engine quit and they had to crash land in a bomb-cratered field. Fortunately, they landed well and were rescued by helicopter.

TERRY WITH THE SOUTH VIETNAMESE AIRBORNE UNITS (ARVN) IN O-1 AIRCRAFT

After the first one-year tour was over he volunteered to return again in a fighter plane to Vietnam. He also volunteered for a special CIA unit that was trying to help the prisoners escape from their North Vietnam prisons. However, he was not given either of his choices, but instead assigned to fly B-52's. After completing B-52 training, he immediately volunteered to return again to Vietnam in the B-52. He flew out of Guam to Vietnam during that tour. After finishing the first tour, he immediately volunteered for another one. This time he was stationed in Thailand and flew missions in Vietnam on an almost daily basis. He had now been flying in Vietnam for quite some time. He quit counting his combat missions after he reached 500. It was during this second B-52 tour that Nixon decided to bomb Hanoi (Linebacker Two) to get the prisoners out and force an end to the war. It was on one of these missions while attacking a Mig airfield near Hanoi that the plane he was co-piloting was hit by a Sam (Surface to Air Missile). I have included Terry's description of the resulting damage, struggle for survival and successful ejections at the end of this talk's transcript.

B-52 CREW AFTER RESCUE: (L TO R) WILLIAM NORTH: NAVIGATOR;
JOHN O. MIZE: AIRCRAFT COMMANDER; DENNIS ANDERSON: ELECTRONIC WARFARE
OFFICER (EWO); WILLIAM ROBINSON: NAVIGATOR; TERENCE GRUTERS: CO-PILOT;
PETER WHALEN: GUNNER

During this bombing operation, the North Vietnamese officers and politicians were so afraid of the bombing that they went into the American prison camps to be sure they would live through it. Shortly after the Linebacker II operation finished, it was announced that the North Vietnamese had decided to give up and release the prisoners, and begin peace talks. Unfortunately, the peace talks dragged on and America did not press its advantage. Terry ended the war with two distinguished flying crosses, a purple heart, and many other medals.

After I came home, Terry left the Air Force and went to work for IBM. He married Stephanie Gruters, the daughter of a Lieutenant Colonel who was also stationed at Ellsworth Air Force base in South Dakota, which was Terry's home B-52 base. Terry and Robin (Stephanie's middle name) have been married 39 years as of 2013, and they have six wonderful children. Their names are Kelley Michele, Joseph Ryan, Jacqueline Mary, Timothy Ross, Sally Rose and Stephen Terence. All six attended St. Martha's elementary school and graduated from Cardinal Mooney high school. Three of his children were presidents of their high school class (Joseph, Timothy and Sally). The other three did not run. Three of his children were all-state athletes, Kelley (tennis), Jackie (cross country and swimming) and Timothy (cross country). Kelley and Jackie got athletic scholarships to college (Chaminade University in Hawaii for Kelley and Villanova University in Pennsylvania for Jackie). Timothy and Stephen both graduated from Franciscan University in Steubenville, Ohio. Joseph graduated from Florida State University and Sally graduated from Ringling School of Art as she was very gifted artistically. Sally also attended many classes at Franciscan University while concurrently attending Ringling school of Art. Four of Terry's children have advanced degrees. Kelley and Jackie have master's degrees and Joseph and Timothy are Certified Public Accountants.

Four of Terry's children are married, all in the Catholic Church (Kelley to Stephen Pierce, Joseph to Sydney Spence, Jackie to Theodore Caouette and Timothy to Ashley Petruzzi). One of Terry's great joys is that all of his children have retained their faith and attend Mass. Terry currently has five grandchildren under five years old. (Tyler Joseph and Samantha Grace, children of Jackie and Theodore), (Stephen Mako and Chloe Michelle, children of Kelley and Stephen), (Spencer Joseph, child of Sydney and Joseph) and another child is scheduled to be born in July of 2013 to Timothy and his wife Ashley. Hopefully there will be many more.

After working a few years for IBM, Terry and I left IBM after purchasing a very small existing software company, whose software was obsoleted and needed to be rewritten into a new computer language. The two previous owners had decided to go out of business. Terry started out as the only employee of the new company and started re-writing the software into the new language. He has been with this company from 1978 until the present, although the name was changed to keep current with the market-place. Its current name is P.C. Software Accounting, Inc. I joined the company about six months later, and stayed with them for many years, while I was also a co-pilot and then a pilot (Captain) with Eastern Airlines before Eastern Airlines went under. After that, I had some excellent corporate world jobs which I will discuss in brief in a few moments. By the way, the company that we re-started, and God has repeatedly blessed, has done very well over the last thirty years or so. For example, for the last seven years it has been rated second in the Reader's Choice survey in the Client Write Up Software category of the CPA Practice Advisor magazine. These results are based strictly on the number of votes received, which obviously favors the big companies. The survey results from 2011 really highlight how well P.C. Software has done. It fin-ished second that year and was the only company that finished in the top four that was owned by a company with less than a billion dollars in annual sales.

IN THE CORPORATE WORLD

In 1991, I became the director of MIS for Pearl Vision in Dallas. And then after that, Vice President of MIS for McCrory's stores, overseeing their going from 750 stores down to zero.

It was the owner's idea to liquidate the company. He wanted to end his involve-ment in retail operations. I went through a number of years of that. We would be choosing people to layoff every few months. This is really a lot of fun, if you haven't done it yourself — saying goodbye to your associates who have become good friends, as you are letting them go. Not! I tried to set everybody up as best I could.

Then it was my turn. I went from a salary of over $200,000 to $30,000 over-night. I had brought my family from Dallas, Texas, to Yorktown, Pennsylvania. Mean-while during these years I had been hooked by the sin of avarice, again without realiz-ing what was going on. I had a big beautiful home, a 7,500 square foot mansion on ten acres on a lake just outside of Dallas with beautiful furniture. I made money, and would spend it on things, the house and the children. My children were getting every-thing that I never had. With this kind of poor parenting we were becoming a spoiled family, where the kids thought the world owed them a living. So God took care of that perfectly, by putting the family on $30,000 annually with seven kids.

CONFESSION STOPS ANY BAD HABIT

Also during that time, when it got tough I started to drink a bottle of wine a night. This went on for three or four years until eventually all I was looking forward to was a bottle of wine. The Lord let me realize that was dangerous. I had successfully stopped smoking earlier in my life. I had stopped temporarily a number of times, but never was permanently successful. But then I put it in God's hands and went to confession every week, once a week, until I stopped smoking.

I did the same thing with drinking. I put it in God's hands. I said, "I agree I can't stop drinking. I don't have any power Lord. I am going to confession until You lick it. You're the Savior, Lord, please save me. I'm a slave." That is what I said. "Save me. Please beat this for me, Lord, as obviously I can't beat this problem by myself." He beat that for me, just like He defeated the hatred in prison camp.

THEN TO OHIO

My youngest brother, Peter, who lived in Ohio, asked me to help him. Peter feels he has been called to a special mission to save, strengthen and rebuild the family. He was working with a group of families to formulate a plan to do just this. I accepted his invitation and have been helping him on "The Team," as he calls it, to accomplish this mission.

Peter suffered from a horrible divorce, but he got through it. He gave his life to God, and decided to serve Him by trying to do what can be done to help other families to not have to go through what his did. This mission is continuing. One day soon, the plan is to seek approval for a *Religious Association of Christian Faithful* in the Church per the normal channels the Church has established for such.

We are all excited about being a part of something that may someday have very positive results. Time will tell. With God, nothing is impossible, and we all know how much help families need.

ST. BRIDGET PRAYERS

I have had great devotion for the last twenty years to the St. Bridget prayers in the Pieta prayer booklet. I say those every day. I also have devotion to the rosary and daily Mass. I say the prayers that Sister Teresa of Calcutta called the miracle prayers, which are the Memorare nine times in thanksgiving and then nine Memorares in petition for Mary's intentions for our children, for our family, for our Church and for our country. They are miracle prayers, because by now at 65 years old, I know it is only a great miracle that gets us through one day at a time with life's challenges. We also pray the "Chaplet of St. Michael" in the *Pieta* booklet for our children.

Our children are doing well by the grace of God and no other reason. They have gone to college. But the most important thing is that they are Catholics still attending Mass.

What I do is concentrate on avoiding the seven sins, the seven great sins: pride, avarice, impurity, anger, gluttony, envy and idleness.

WHY AVOID SINS?

The best answer is to honor God, our Creator, Who has given us so many, many gifts, including the Ten Commandments to make it easy to do His Will. This is to do everything we do out of love of God and neighbor.

But in my case, holy fear also plays a strong role. To help me avoid those sins, many of which I have fallen to in my life, I visualize that I am in a car, and that I am going down the interstate on the right hand side of the road. My family is with me in the car. When I commit one of those sins, I know by experience what happens. My car goes across the lanes, across the median island. Now I have the oncoming traffic to dodge. Sooner or later, I get the living so and so kicked out of me and try to get back to the right side. I have to make an act of contrition, go to confession and stop sinning which gets me back on the right side and the family out of danger.

Then I start to think, "Well, I really want to do this sin again." But then I just imagine the oncoming traffic, the way it was. I know God's power is perfect, His love is perfect, and hence His discipline is also perfect, and the oncoming traffic is going to be there if I sin seriously. So I try to stay on the right side without ever going to the left side. I try to avoid the serious sins completely. The thing that helps me avoid sins best is that I know the family is in the car with me. It's bad enough for me being beat up so much, but I hate even more to see it happen to my wife and my children.

God, of course, says it best;

He who hates the law is without wisdom, and is tossed about like a boat in a storm. (Sirach 33:2)

So I have found and believe the key to a happy, healthy, and peaceful family is avoiding those seven sins and doing the opposite, which is what God wills, which is His Law, which is the *Ten Commandments, the Beatitudes, the Corporal and Spiritual Works of Mercy, and the Christian Virtues.*

If we look at each of the sins, just look at the opposite virtue and that's what God wants. Pride is Satan's pride and joy. Pride is the very worst sin, and I try to always remember I have it big time, especially when I don't think I do. Humility is what God wants from us. Rampant impurity is for animals like dogs and pigs. He wants us to be better than that and have faithful marriages. Satan wants us to have avarice for worldly possessions. God wants us to take care of our families, a primary job, but he also wants us to be generous with any excess wealth we have, rather than getting more and more expensive things. Opposite to anger is forgiveness. He really wants us to forgive instantly. I have to fight this very hard. Whenever we sin seriously, it is just that much harder to fight it the rest of our lives. Again, this alone is a reason to never sin seriously. I have to fight gluttony too. I think we are all brought up to eat because of taste, instead of eating for health. I'm trying very hard to turn myself and my family around. This involves, as St. Basil so clearly taught, eating for good health, not taste, and so getting rid of all the processed food or artificially taste-enhanced food. I didn't have too much trouble with envy, and we're supposed to be joyful when other people are doing well and have things. We are not supposed to be sad about it. That seems obvious, but I understand it must be hard to change if we fall. Idleness, of course not, we have to work hard. Again, my trouble a lot of times was working too hard with no time for God, and that is a mistake too.

THE CATHOLIC FAITH IS OUR STRENGTH

In summary, I believe the real strength of our lives is our Catholic Faith. Then we can rely on His mercy for His little ones, which we all are, and never on our own power. This makes God our shepherd. This is what the great Saints say, that we have no power to do good and it is all God's glory when we do anything right. Scripture says it best,

Without Me you can do nothing.
(John 15:5) (Jesus)

Let him who would boast, boast in the Lord.
(2Cor. 10:17)

But we have to learn what to strive for by reading good spiritual books. These good actions, good habits, to strive for are called the virtues. Then we pray and try our best but give all credit to God for any success. We should always be reading the Bible and the *Catholic Catechism.* I also think fine books to read for confidence that we can do it is the *Divine Mercy Diary* of St. Faustina and the books on St. Therese the Little Flower. They became very great saints because they understood they were little people, learned sincere humility and trusted in God to become holy.

That's us too, we are the little people. We can do the same as they did. God loves us as much as He loves them. He also wants to make us and each member of our families into great saints. He wants to save us; He came to save us. He has all the power to save us, if we tell Him we trust in Him. It doesn't matter if we are single, married, or religious. He really will make us saints if we just give Him permission. We must try hard but rely above all on His grace.

GOD'S COUNTERATTACK

Remember Pope Leo XIII was told by Satan in the late 1800s that he had been given the world for one hundred years. Many theologians believe those hundred years were the 20th century. Well, now those hundred years are up, God's counterattack is underway and we are all soldiers in the front lines of the spiritual fight to retake the world. Look at the holy leaders God has given us: Pope John Paul II and Pope Benedict XVI. The greatest fight is the spiritual fight now in progress for our souls and the souls of others. We can be spiritual warriors in this fight by trying to be virtuous in every way and leading our families to practice the same conduct.

For the family men among us, we have the primary duty to evangelize our families. In our family life, we move in circles that priests and religious never reach. One of the great helps in the re-evangelization of this world is to pray for and strive our hardest to have a truly holy family, living according to God's Will in every way. The example of our families' conduct can conquer souls. There is nothing better than a large, holy family to convince people the Catholic Faith is the answer, just as there is nothing better than the absolutely disastrous families of atheists and atheistic nations to convince people that atheism (Communism, Socialism, Naziism) is not the answer.

GUY AND SANDY At POW REUNION

TYLER'S WEDDING TO CAROLINA

GOD WINS

We have God's assurance that the counterattack will be successful. The Catholic Church will spread over the entire world and all people will do God's Will on earth as in Heaven. We can be an important part of the victory. It will bring us great peace and joy right now during our time on earth and rejoicing for all eternity. So let's seize the opportunity.

Thank you.

NARRATIVE: Following the transcript of this talk, I am inserting some questions and the response to those questions by my brother, Terry. These questions, and others like them, were posed by an author who was writing a book about the Linebacker II bombing missions. These questions were directed to crewmembers that had taken part in the Linebacker II missions, and particularly to those crewmembers that had experienced out-of-the ordinary experiences, such as being hit by a surface-to-air missile (SAM). The Linebacker II missions took place over North Vietnam over an 11 day period during the last days of 1972. These missions have also been referred to as "The Christmas Bombing," or "The 11 Day War." During the first eight days of this effort, the B-52's hit various targets in North Vietnam but few if any B-52 missions attacked the Hanoi area itself. This all changed on day nine, when a number of Hanoi targets were also attacked. Although all of North Vietnam was well defended for air attacks, Hanoi was extremely well defended by many Russian-made SAMS and an incredible number of antiaircraft guns, as well as by MIGS. By the last day of the 11 days, the SAMS and ground fire had been effectively silenced, and North Vietnam was virtually defenseless against future airstrikes. Linebacker II was credited with ending the Vietnamese war and bringing the North Vietnamese back to the peace talks.

Terry was the co-pilot of a B-52 crew during these missions. He received a Distinguished Flying Cross for his part in this effort. The pilot and commander of his B-52 crew was John Mize, who received the Air Force Cross for his heroic performance. It is quite notable that despite severe damage to the B-52 that they were flying, which eventually crashed into the jungle, all six crewmembers parachuted from the B-52 and all were rescued.

What did it look and sound like as you approached Hanoi on the ninth day?

Hanoi was blacked out just as the briefer had told us. There was also an immense amount of antiaircraft fire (flak) that lit up the sky. When the SAMS launched, they looked very similar to a NASA space launch. They, too, emerged from a fiery launch, and had trailing exhaust flames as they came up through the sky. The big difference was that the SAMS were not being launched into a clear morning sky, but rather they were being launched at night into a flak-filled sky. I also remember seeing a huge fire-ball at about our altitude as we were coming in which I surmised was one of our B52's that had been hit and exploded. All in all it was an immense fireworks display that was quite overwhelming. There was also a lot of chatter on the radios, and some of the voices were excited which further magnified the drama.

What impact did the losses in the first eight days have on all the missions? When did you realize it was the same way every day? What did you and the others think?

The losses got your attention. Invariably you knew some of the individuals who had not returned, and you wondered whether they were killed or captured and how their families would be affected. Each mission was very dangerous and we quickly realized after the first or second mission, that all of the missions over North Vietnam would be this way. Based on the danger, you had to seriously consider the fact that you might get killed or captured on any mission. My response to this was to make sure that I was on good terms with God. Since I was a Catholic, I prayed and I went to confession. Many people had similar feelings. My personal joke at the time was that it seemed like even the non-Catholics were going to confession.

One of the positive effects of the losses was a significant increase in morale. The crews that flew the dangerous missions were also drawn much closer together in trust and camaraderie. There was also a much closer relationship between the crews and the maintenance personnel. Whereas on the normal B-52 missions, the ground crews just routinely got you out, on these missions they were giving you sincere "thumbs ups" and other significant gestures of support.

You were hit three times during those nine days. Tell me about the first time

I don't remember noticing the hit the first time. I remember seeing missiles that I thought might hit us, but I did not feel anything as far as an impact of a hit. On either this first mission or the second mission that we were hit, I remember that there was also talk about the presence of MIGS, but I saw nothing of those and, once again, physically felt no hits. I do remember seeing the holes in our aircraft after we returned to our base and had landed. I thanked God and I also realized what a nice machine the

B-52 was. (Note that the first two times that we were hit occurred during the first eight days. The third time that we were hit occurred on day nine when our target was SAM site VN-243 near Hanoi.)

Tell me about the time you were shot down on night nine.

I will relate my recollection of what happened that night. Many years have passed since then, and some of my memories may not be exactly correct, as far as the details go. But, I can say that my main memories of that time are still very vivid in my mind.

I was very excited to be going into Hanoi itself because I knew that that was where my brother was and I had great hopes of seeing him get out of there. I also knew some others who were prisoners of war that I had gone to the Air Force Academy with, particularly Tim Ayres, and I had similar hopes for them. I was also filled with compassion for all of our prisoners and disgusted that we could not, or more accurately, would not take the steps to get them out of there. I was also excited about helping to win this war which I felt was critical to the long-term welfare of the free world and eventually to our very survival as a nation. I knew that bombing Hanoi at this level would get the enemy's attention.

Our crew realized that this target would be the most dangerous one that we had so far, and we were concerned that we might be shot down. Because of this, John and I discussed our options before we took off. In particular we discussed what was the best course of action to take if our plane were damaged to the point that the crew would have to bail out. We agreed that we did not want to go down in or near Hanoi. We agreed to "push the window," to get as far away from Hanoi as we could before we bailed out. We realized that there would be a certain risk in flying a seriously damaged plane, but a greater risk in going down in or near Hanoi.

I was also very focused on doing whatever I could do to make sure that we exactly hit the target for obvious reasons. It is my recollection that this mission took off at about midnight with the scheduled time over target a few hours after that. We were flying out of U-Tapao Air Force base, which was located in Thailand about 90 miles southeast of Bangkok, near Sattahip on the Gulf of Siam. Thailand borders Cambodia and Laos to the west and both Laos and Cambodia border Vietnam to the east, so we were fairly close geographically.

The night really began at the briefing. By the time we got there, we were already expecting that we would be told that tonight's targets would be in or near Hanoi. We expected the Hanoi targets because a rumor that we were hitting Hanoi had spread like wildfire that afternoon, and the rumor appeared to be confirmed. When the briefing started, we were all startled because the commanding General came in to talk to us. This had never happened before. Another very unusual thing was that it was huge because there were about 100 crews flying at the same time (instead of the normal 10 or 15).

The General came in and told us that we were going to hit Hanoi. It was a patriotic speech, and he was right on the money when he said that it was about time that we got a chance to win the war or words similar to that. By this time, one of our pilots had been a prisoner for something like nine years and I had long since realized, as had everyone else, that the "limited war" concept was not working and had little chance of bringing a resolution to this conflict. I firmly believed that we would have to physically send in troops to Hanoi and take it if we wanted to win the war on our terms. This appeared politically unlikely, but all in all I was thrilled and thought that any major escalation was a step in the right direction.

After the General finished, a Lt. Colonel came in to brief us on what to expect in air defenses. He told us that Hanoi would be blacked out and he said that there would be a lot of flak (with accompanying tracers) in the sky. However, he said that we would be flying so high that the antiaircraft guns would not be a factor. (We were flying at an altitude over 50,000 feet.) He was right about the city of Hanoi being blacked out and he was right about their being a lot of flak and tracers in the sky. He also warned us that there would be enemy fighter planes, (Russian made MIGS), but he elaborated on the strong fighter support that we would have. That was all fine.

The next thing he discussed was how to avoid the SAMS. I listened to his words quite intently, as we all did, and I was quite satisfied with what he had to say. Later, after combat over North Vietnam, I remember literally laughing at his words, and I have been amused about them ever since whenever I think of those missions, because they described an ideal situation that did not correspond to reality.

The Lt. Colonel told us that the SAM's launching would look like a missile launch that we saw on TV when we watched a space program launch. He said that you would first see a ring of fire and then a stream of fire coming from the missile as it rose into the sky, just like you saw when you watched a space launch. He said not to worry when you saw a SAM launch, just to note the time on your watch. He said that it would take about 35 seconds for the SAM to reach your altitude so you had plenty of time. He then explained that there were different types of guidance systems on the SAMs such as heat seeking, radar guided, etc., and that the key to a successful mission was to react correctly but not to overreact. He instructed us to ignore the SAM for about 10 to 15 seconds, and then to note the position of the SAM in the windscreen. (i.e. 10 bolts up and six bolts over) Then he said to make a slight turn and turn back on course again. Then he said to look at the position of the SAM in the windscreen again. If it was still in the same relative position, then you should take your evasive maneuvers or drop chaff etc. However, if it was not in the same position, then that SAM was not tracking your plane and you should just press on, as there was nothing to worry about. Of course, he also mentioned that during the last 90 seconds before dropping bombs, the plane had to be on a fixed course and that no evasive maneuvers could be made during that time. This was because any deviation in course in the last 90 seconds would cause the plane to miss the target. This all sounded quite reasonable to me until later that night.

We took off. I remember the "thumbs up" and the other gestures of support from the ground personnel. They definitely knew that we were going to Hanoi, and they were being very compassionate and supportive. This touched me.

The flight was uneventful until we turned in over the Gulf of Tonkin to North Vietnam. I remember seeing the first SAM of the night. It was just like the briefer had said, and we followed the instructions correctly. We waited the recommended time and then we carefully noted the position of the SAM in the windscreen. Then we made our turn and returned to course and noted the new position. The SAM was in a different position and John and I agreed on that and held steady. The next thing we knew it looked like we were going to be hit, but the SAM missed us and we felt much better. I believe this same sequence of events happened a few more times on our way to our SAM site target near Hanoi. So far so good, just as briefed.

However, when we got closer to the target area, it is my vivid recollection that about 35 SAMS went off at once, or at least so many that the windscreen was full of them. That is when I literally laughed at my stupidity in not asking the obvious question during the briefing, which was, "What do you do if more that one SAM is fired at the same time?" I thought, "So many college graduates and we are all stupid." In any case, we were soon locked on target and could not do anything anyway. It is my recollection that we were hit shortly after bomb release.

The SAM exploded under the wing on John's side. It rocked the ship and almost immediately three of the engines on that side went out. A fourth was still running. We could not restart any of those three engines, and we went through emergency procedures to shut them down properly. We began to lose altitude and we both had to apply rudder to fly on course. John was also adjusting the remaining engines to try to maintain our altitude. There were intermittent fires on that wing most of which went out after the emergency engine shutdowns. We went through the other emergency procedures to shutdown other affected systems on that side. John had also been hit with some shrapnel in his legs and was bleeding, but he said that he was okay and seemed fine. Everyone else on the crew reported okay and the intercom system was functioning. We lost cabin pressure, but we all had our oxygen masks on anyway. The one remaining working engine on John's side had a fairly significant fire. I shut it down and we started losing altitude faster and also had to apply full rudder to keep straight. Our navigator gave us a course to try to get to Laos. We could not risk turning around and heading for the sea. John made this decision and it worked out well. We were worried about getting hit again but it did not happen.

I kept turning on the remaining engine on John's wing, and running it until it would cause a fire. It would take a while for the fire to start and meanwhile the plane flew much better. Then I would shut it off and the fire would go out. This went on for quite awhile. I kept John informed. We knew that we were taking a major risk in not abandoning the plane at this time, and by "playing with fire" on an engine that was mounted on a wing full of jet fuel, but we did not want to go down in North Vietnam if we could possibly help it.

I remember thinking that our plane, still tens of thousands of feet up in the dark sky, could explode at any moment. This was the case because of the fires and the damaged electrical system and all the fuel that was still in the wing tanks. Additionally we were still over North Vietnam and we could easily be shot again, either by ground fire since we were at a much lower altitude by now, or by MIGs or SAMs.

What a strange feeling it is to realize that you might soon be dead. This is a feeling that touches your spirit to its depths. There I was looking out over the darkness, hearing all the noise of the plane, watching the fire, and thinking life might soon end. Well, as you can easily imagine, I had God on my mind. I knew that I was in His hands. In fact, I knew that all six of us were in His hands and that He was in total control of this giant airplane that was holding together by His might and Will.

What invisible forces must have been at work. How many angels were supporting the wing of the airplane that had been hit by the SAM missile? Who was keeping the fuel in the tanks or that was flowing out of them from exploding from the heat of the fires or from the electrical system sparks? Why didn't the fuel explode when the SAM missile first hit us and the explosion had taken out a portion of the wing? Our God lives! He is in control and it was not my time to go yet. These had been my thoughts up to that moment.

Somewhere along the line the fourth engine on John's wing went out for good. We kept losing altitude, but slowly, and we got to Laos. I think that we were at about ten thousand feet at that time, and this would have been a good altitude to bail out from, since we had a number of crew-members to get out. The trouble was that the terrain in this part of Laos was terrible. Our navigators confirmed this on their maps. It was full of Karst (rugged rocky landscape) and cliffs. We could easily be killed on landing. There were also many enemy soldiers in Laos and bailing out in bad terrain into enemy territory did not seem too bright if we could avoid it. John made the decision to try to get to Thailand. There was obviously no way that this plane would make it to the base much less be able to land so that was out of the question. We were well aware of the plane, that also had four engines out, that had tried to land a few nights earlier. That plane had crashed and four of the six crewmembers died.

We kept losing altitude. We were now in contact with rescue helicopters. We had also been talking about bailing out for some time. I had gone to army parachute school at Ft. Benning, Georgia, but no one else had ever jumped from a plane. My major contribution to the conversation was to tell everyone to use the normal delay, not the zero delay, on their parachutes. We also kept reminding each other of the training adage,

"When you bail out, put your back in the position that you want it to be for the rest of your life."

And now thoughts of bailing out into the night over a thick tropical jungle filled our minds. I was the co-pilot and I would be in the plane until almost the very end. The commander and I had to keep it flying until the rest of the crew got out. This was the pilot's and copilot's job just like holding course for the last 90 seconds of the bombing run was. We got hit because we had to do our job and make the run to bomb the SAM site and now I might die because it is the commander's and the co-pilot's job to be the last to abandon the airplane.

A strange sense took possession of me. I realized that my life was expendable. I was a soldier, and I was very possibly about to die for others. This was how I was loving my countrymen who are in God's Eyes, my neighbors. Risking one's life for one's country is an act of heroic love. My family and my close neighbors were all safe and secure back in Florida. They were probably watching TV or sleeping or shopping at the store and here I was at four A.M. in the morning, flying over a jungle in a giant plane that might soon crash into the ground with me in it, if all did not go just right. I had already been saved from death many times this night, would I be saved again? I realized that our whole crew was totally in God's Hands.

We did make it to Thailand, although by now our altitude was getting dangerously low for bailout. Because of the lost engines, we had gradually lost altitude since being hit near Hanoi. It was still the middle of the night and we were over forested terrain. We followed the recommended order of bailout. This order allows those in the most precarious positions, such as the navigator and radar navigator, whose seats are in the lower portion of the plane and who must eject downward, to get out first. The pilot and copilot are the last to go because they have to control the plane.

We were letting the rescue helicopters know what was going on, and they were right with us. Everything seemed to go okay for the gunner, the electronics warfare officer and the radar navigator. However, the navigator's hatch did not blow, as Bill Robinson, the navigator, informed us over the intercom. We were now down to about 3500 feet. The navigator told us what had happened and said that he would have to jump out the hole where the radar navigator's seat had been. John told him to go ahead. We waited a little while and heard nothing else on the intercom. We waited a little longer.

Then John and I talked over the situation, and we both felt that Bill had gotten out by now.

John told me to go ahead and go. I pulled my roof ejection switch. The roof blew off just like in the movies. I remember being quite delighted, as I knew that if my roof hatch had failed, there would not have been enough time to get out safely, since I would have had to go to the lower portion of the plane where the navigator's and radar navigator's seats were. Those seats ejected downward not upward like the pilot's and copilot's seats and therefore one could only jump down into the sky from one of those ejected seats, like the navigator had to do.

I told John I was going. I pulled my trigger. I was out in the night. I remember laughing as the seat fell away from me and my chute opened. I was quite surprised to be alive but was delighted to be free of the din of the aircraft and floating down towards the ground which was black and indistinguishable.

I remember what a beautiful night it was as I drifted down in my parachute. It now seemed very likely that I would live. The worst was over. I was no longer sitting in the plane waiting for it to explode. Tears of joy were in my eyes. I was filled with a spirit of gratitude. I felt like kneeling down and praising God, and thanking Him for my life.

Another awesome type of feeling enveloped my being. I was overwhelmed with the feeling that God is, that God exists and that God loved me. I knew somehow that God cared for me and that God's hands were upon me. I knew that God was controlling my parachute and was making sure that I was okay and would not die as I descended from the plane to the ground below.

However, I did realize that it was still possible that my life could end, since it was very dark and I would soon be crashing into the jungle. I could not even see the trees below me. But, by now I had a strong sense that God had saved me and I would land safely and be rescued. Later I thought about many other things that could have killed me as I parachuted down towards the jungle, but my overwhelming feeling at this time was joy and gratitude to God.

Some of the things that could have happened follow: I could have landed in such a way that I broke my back or my neck, especially since I was landing in the jungle. It was also possible that an enemy soldier or soldiers might be down in that jungle and having heard or seen or plane, they could have killed me when I landed. This was a remote possibility since we were landing in Thailand, but who knows what can happen in a jungle. Or I could have landed in a lake or river and possibly drowned. I could even have landed on or near a cobra or other poisonous snake. All in all, there were still risks as I floated down towards the earth. But I had no doubt that God had saved me so far, and I was not worried. I was realizing God's saving presence in a very big way by now.

Then I saw our plane crash into the ground some distance in front of me and explode into a huge fireball. I wondered if John had gotten out okay. I prayed for him and all the crew. I then realized that I was very close to the jungle below, and I prepared for a tree landing as I had been taught. I crossed my arms protecting my face. I kept my legs tightly together and shortly thereafter I began crashing through the trees. I ended up in the pitch-black forest, hanging in the air with my parachute caught in the trees. I did not know if I was 100 feet up or just a few.

I pulled out my light and shined it towards the ground. I was about 4 or 5 feet from it. I laughed and released myself from the chute. I again thanked God. I pulled out my radio and brought up the rescue helicopter. They worked with me until they found me. They asked if I was okay and I told them I was fine. They dropped the jungle penetrator. A jungle penetrator is a folded up metal seat attached to a cable in the helicopter. The seat is very compact, but can be unfolded and sat on. The jungle penetrator was only about 20 feet from me and I saw it immediately. They offered to send someone down to help me. I told them not to. I opened the prongs and sat on the seat and signaled I was ready. They hauled me up through the trees and started moving away and pulled me into the copter.

Once again, I was delighted and thanked God. I realized that it was God alone Who had saved me, as our plane could have easily blown up with the fire on the wing filled with jet fuel. Or our plane could have been uncontrollable with four engines out on one side. Or my seat or my parachute could have not worked, or it could have been too late to bail out at all, by the time the other crewmembers were out. Or our plane could have been hit before bomb release and some of our bombs would probably have exploded, when the SAM hit us. Or we might have been forced to bail out in enemy territory, and I might have been killed or captured. I realized that I had truly lived through a near-death experience. Whenever I relive this mission in my mind, I can not help thanking our wonderful God.

All of our crewmembers were rescued, most of us by different helicopters, and we were taken to various bases. The rescue crews did a great job and we thanked them. We were each quickly informed that everyone on the crew had been rescued and all were in good shape. This was evidently quite unusual and a cause of great celebration. What a joy! The cliché "happy to be alive", now had real meaning for us, and it would always have real meaning for us for the rest of our lives.

When our crew was reunited the next day, we shared our thoughts. We relived our collective experience and told of our individual rescues and collectively expressed our thanks that the helicopter crews that had rescued us were so dedicated and professional. But we all acknowledged that God had saved us, because it was so farfetched, based on our circumstances, that we had all survived. Either then or later, John expressed his belief that God had saved us by saying that there was a "Seventh Man" on board, meaning Jesus Christ.

We were a united crew, a crew of six men who had just experienced one miracle after another as happens over and over again in war. God had used us to battle the forces of hell that night. In fact, He had been using us to do this as part of the US Military because the forces of hell were using the evil politicians of that country to control the people and keep them from practicing their basic freedom to worship God. This was exactly similar to the actions of Hitler and the Nazi Government in WWII.

As all know, a communist government will not let their people worship God. They don't believe in God or perhaps the God they worship is not the true God (they make a god out of their socialist government). North Vietnam had become very evil and needed to be forced to their knees to stop the war they were waging against the people of South Vietnam, who did not want to be controlled by an evil government.

God uses soldiers to fight for freedom, and this means that we were working for God directly. The commander of our plane was a God-fearing man. He prayed and was doing what he felt God wanted him to do. He led the crew into battle under the banner of the cross. His intentions were good. His goal was to stop evil from spreading. God chose to save us that night, really that morning, but others had died over Hanoi in the thick of battle and fell out of the sky to the ground. We were thankful that our lives had been spared and so, too, were our families.

I have put this event out of my mind, for it happened many, many years ago. I sometimes reflect back on it when I realize how much God blessed me by letting me live. I realize how much He blessed me when our family and extended family gets together at Christmas or at other family gatherings. In fact, I realize how much He blessed me even when I do something as simple as talk with one of my children, or do something with them or their families. I have the same feeling when I pick up a grandchild or "race" with them in the park, or hear one of my grandchildren say blessing before meals or their bedtime prayers. I realize how much I have been blessed when I spend time with or talk to my beautiful wife, who will always be beautiful to me.

I live. I was saved that night, and it was all God's doing. What a loving Father I have. My God is a wonderful God. He decided before time began that I would continue to live long ago on that ninth day of the Christmas bombing of 1972. He saved me so that I could have a family and serve Him with my life further in this way. Amen.

(Note by Guy: Remember that Terry volunteered to fight in Vietnam over and over again. No one with a brother in Prison Camp in Vietnam was forced to go. According to official sources, Terry was awarded numerous medals including the Distinguished Flying Cross with 1 Oak Leaf Cluster, the Purple Heart, the Air Medal with 13 Oak Leaf Clusters, the National Defense Service Medal, the Parachutist Badge, the Republic of Vietnam Campaign Medal with Palm Unit Citation, the Presidential Unit Citation, the Republic of Vietnam Staff Service Medal, the Air Force Outstanding Unit Award with 1 Oak Leaf Cluster, the Vietnam Service Medal with 2 bronze service stars, the Small Arms Marksmanship Ribbon, the Air Force Longevity Service Award, and The Republic of Vietnam Cross of Gallantry with one Bronze Star.)

"The true soldier fights not because he hates what is in front of him, but because he loves what is behind him." G. K. Chesterton

7

LEADERSHIP IN THE HOME AND FAMILY

TALK NARRATIVE: In early 2005, I was introduced to Mary Lou Warren of the Seton Homeschool Organization (__www.setonhome.org__) by Judy McClotsky of Catholics in the Military (__www.missioncapodanno.org__). Mary Lou is responsible for organizing the National Homeschool Conference and the Regional Homeschool Conferences for Seton Homeschool. Mary Lou asked if there were any leadership implications for the family from my mili-

Good morning. My name is Guy Gruters. I have been asked to talk to you today about leadership in the home and family. I am a Catholic. I have been a father since the age of twenty-two. I have seven children and raised them up in the faith. Five of them have gone to Franciscan University of Steubenville, Ohio, and all are still going to church on Sunday and practicing their faith.

I believe the reason that my children are strong in their faith is because of the grace that God has given me to lead my family all these years. I would like to convey to you what I have learned about leadership, which is so much a part of the vocation of fatherhood.

The word "father" all by itself speaks of leadership. All who grew up in an intact family had a father. We have a "father" that we listen to in our parish church, that is, the priest. We have the Holy "Father," the head of our Church, and we have God the "Father." In all cases, the word *father* denotes leadership and authority, someone that we have to listen to and obey. In today's society, the traditional role of "fathers" upheld by the Church throughout the centuries has deteriorated.

In any organization, there must be a leader. A family is no exception. This is especially true when there is a large family. I will try to briefly summarize some of the key points that I think are important in accepting that the father of the family must play the main leadership role.

Before I begin, however, I would like to simply define what the leadership role means. To be a leader means that in addition to witnessing to an organization, or in this case the family, with goodness and a virtuous life in all respects, it also means that the buck stops here. In other words, the leader of the group or family is one that must take the responsibility on behalf of the group for the decisions that need to be made which affect the group.

The analogy to military leadership is clear to everyone. In the most difficult fight I ever participated in while imprisoned many years in a ruthless Communist Prison Camp, we never would have survived without obedience to our leadership. The chain of command is clear also in the Church. The Pope makes decisions, and the Bishops obey them. The Bishops make decisions, and the parish priests obey them. The parish priests make decisions, and the families obey them. In the corporate world, if you are the CEO of a company, you are the man or woman that makes the decisions to lead the company. Everyone else must follow your leadership. It is important to realize that without leadership, there is no order, necessary tasks cannot be done competently, people cannot get along. This is why all must follow the leader in any organization.

There must be order throughout an organization so necessary work can be accomplished efficiently. One can reflect that in an organization that does not have strong leadership there is dissension, disorder, and a lack of cohesiveness. Effectively, there is chaos.

Every city or house divided against itself shall not stand.
Matt. 12:25

God has established authority on this earth, as mentioned, for all organizations, including the family and the Catholic Church. St. Augustine calls this "the order of love."

FIRST REASON

But I feel the most important leadership that He has established is embodied in the father of each family. The first reason is because if children learn about obedience in a family, this respect for authority will be carried with them throughout their lives. If they are brought up to listen to their "father," they will listen to teachers, they will listen to policemen, and they will listen to government officials. Even more importantly, they will listen to the parish priest (the "father" of the parish), our Pope's (the "Holy Father") directives and decisions, and finally to God the "Father's" Commandments. This means they will strive to do God's Will as clearly taught by the Catholic Church. Love follows agreement and so God wills order, i.e., leadership and obedience to leadership's will in all organizations for the sake of agreement and hence love.

Obedience is learned best during the impressionable age

This is because children have an impressionable age. It is in these young years that respect for authority must be taught. If children do not grow up with a solid basis of respect for authority, then throughout their lives they will have problems. If they do not listen to their teachers, they will not learn and progress in school. If they do not listen to their employers, they will be unable to keep a job. If they do not listen to policemen or to the government, they will become criminals. The country will not have an effective military to protect it if the soldiers do not obey their commanders. If they do not listen to their parish priest and the Holy Father, they will be vulnerable to occasions of sin and bad companions. They will do their own selfish will instead of God's Will, as manifested by their parents, teachers, bosses, government, and Church. And so parents have a God-given and vital responsibility to teach their children respect for authority, especially in their younger years. All other organizations in human society rely directly or indirectly on this parental responsibility being fulfilled well.

This is why leadership in the family is so important. This is why both the mother and the father must make teaching their children respect for authority an overriding priority. This is why the father of the family must be the respected leader in the family to the point that his decisions must hold firm and not be questioned. Certainly the mother or older children in the family can make decisions and lead, when necessary and in many ways. My wife had to make all the decisions for our family during the six years that I was in Vietnam. But when able, the head of the family, the father, must make and take responsibility for the big decisions and resolve disagreements in the family. He must not dodge his duty. In this way the children learn from a young age about authority, about obedience, about respect for authority.

I believe that the most important thing that a mother of a family can teach her children is just this: the lesson of how to respect authority. I believe the best way she can do this is by her own example in always respecting the authority of her husband as the father of the family. It is very clear in Scripture that wives are to respect and obey their husbands.

It is not explained in Scripture why respect for authority in the family is so important but it is clear to me why God has made sure that it is mentioned in Holy Scripture. If the Church is to practice perfect obedience to the Church hierarchy, and all other organizations such as the military, police and emergency services, business organizations, etc. are to practice obedience so as to insure order, peace and effective competence, how in the world can we possibly think that in the first unit established by God and the most important organization of all, the family, there would not be the necessity for leadership?

Logically, the leadership of a family must be either by the husband, the wife, or the children. God has clearly said in Scripture it is to be by the husband. He has clearly indicated this in the natural order as well. That is, the husband is the biggest and strongest physically, and he does not have all the tremendous responsibilities that come physically and mentally with the bearing and raising of children by the wife and mother. He is free and able to lead without strong diversions and at times, strong physical and care-giving limitations, for example, those of the sickness of children, late-term pregnancy, and recovery from childbirth.

As far as leadership by the children, only TV sitcoms and the media show this disordered situation as reasonable. The difficulties that ensue are not sought by rational families. Can you imagine the children making family decisions? Yet this can happen today. One all too possible way is by the father abdicating his role and having the mother lead the family, because a mother's tender, loving heart can be incapable of resisting her children's desires and she can effectively turn over the leadership to the children.

Leadership also involves setting an example; in other words, the father of the family must be a good leader. By far the most important characteristic of leadership is good character. So the father must be a virtuous man who strives to have all good habits, such as praying for guidance for the family, being a good protector, being a hard worker, etc. For it is tougher to look up to someone who has many bad habits. But even if the father does have bad habits, his position as father of the family must be respected in order to teach the children respect for authority. It is his position as father that must be respected, not he himself individually, and therefore he must be listened to and obeyed. Of course, as with all authority, any decisions that counter the Will of God are not to be obeyed. This is exactly the same as respecting and obeying teachers, the commanders of military units, the CEOs of companies, leaders of countries, parish priests, the Pope, even though the individual leader lacks virtue in one way or another. For our example, Jesus obeyed and counseled obedience to the Pharisees, who had serious moral problems. *Respect and obedience must be rendered to the position, not the individual. Otherwise, since all leaders down here are human and not God, there would be no leadership and hence no order possible on earth.*

The father's strong decisions should only be made when there is an obvious need for them, such as family disagreements or decisions affecting the livelihood or well being of the family. If his wife, the second in command and the mother of the family, takes clear exception to his directives or notices a problem with them that her husband may have missed, she should speak to him privately about her concerns. She should never question his authority in front of the children. If she does, the children will immediately learn how to do the same and they will question the father's and mother's authority, they will then question the authority of teachers, of policemen, business leaders, the parish priest, the Pope, and they will question the authority of God Himself. We will not have children with a strong Catholic Faith if the respect for authority is not taught by example within our families.

Thus, it is impossible to overemphasize the importance of clear leadership in the family and how it affects the child's future obedience and well-being. His or her entire life both in society and in the Church will be directly affected by it. Someone who has not learned habitual respect for authority in his or her younger years will be at a disadvantage, will be crippled at everything he or she attempts and will have a consistently tougher, more difficult life than necessary. But most tragic is their possible disobedience of God.

SECOND REASON

The second main point I would like to share about leadership in the family is that it is necessary for family love to truly flourish.

When two people disagree, love seems to go out the window. Arguments do not bring greater mutual love.

We as Christians, followers of Jesus Christ, must make our priority putting love first in our lives and in our families. There should be no disagreements within the family, for without disagreements there will always be love. To repeat, when two people are in a state of disagreement, love suffers. Thus, the father of the family must put love first and the wife and mother of the family must put love first.

The father must face up to and take the responsibility for firm family order. He must be the leader of the family at all times no matter what happens in the family. He must not give up his responsibility to lead because it is difficult. Making decisions under the pressures of daily life is tough. At least half of them can always be second-guessed and may seem wrong with the passage of time. But this must not discourage him. He must keep praying for God's guidance and keep trying to do his best. The mother should also support his decisions to present a united front with minimal disruption in family harmony. With this agreement, there is increased ability to love. This is why it can be stated that love is the fruit of obedience. This is true in family life, religious life and in society as a whole. For example, this is why the strict obedience of military life results in such tremendous love between soldiers in a unit.

God has established authority on this earth and all legitimate authority must be obeyed. Of course, this also means that any authority giving orders or commands against God's rules or commandments is not legitimate and is not to be obeyed. I am describing legitimate authority here. There is a key overriding reason why it is His Will that all respect and obey such God-given authority on this earth. It is so all can love. Order results in peace, harmony, and love. Love follows agreement. If the wife surrenders her will to her husband's will, as Jesus and the Holy Spirit surrender their Wills to God the Father's Will, there is only one will in the family and hence perfect agreement and perfect love just as there is in the Trinity. This is the reason why the wife is enjoined by the Bible to give obedience to her husband as the Church obeys Jesus Christ. It is for love, it is to have the agreement necessary for love to flourish.

THIRD REASON

I would also like to mention the importance of the father's leadership in the family from a perspective of protecting his wife in ways other than physically. All expect the father of the family to protect the family if a thief breaks into the house. No one questions this. He must be ready to give up his life to protect his wife and children. But this situation is rare.

However, it is also the husband's responsibility to protect his wife in all other ways as well.

For example, he must protect her from disrespect by or disobedience from the children. To question her position of authority and respect is to question God's family order which must not be allowed. The honor due father and mother is the fourth Commandment of God, the first and most important of the Commandments for Love of Neighbor, according to the *Catholic Catechism* (The first three Commandments are the minimum essential commands for loving God, the second seven the minimum for loving neighbor).

This daily and constant protection of his wife must include that of his wife's interior life. All know that the mother is considered by Catholic teaching to be the heart of the family. The mother is the treasure house of God's love, Divine love, in the family. It is the mother who cares the most, gives the most, and sacrifices the most. She is full of God's Divine (giving, caring, sharing) Love to the ultimate degree. She raises up the children after having kept them in her womb, nurses them on her breast, changes their diapers, cares for their every need, and nurtures them in so many ways through their entire childhood. Really, her love and care for the children will never cease for her entire life. This is true love. I am confident the mothers of families can be sure they will live very close to God's throne in Heaven. One of the Saints said that the closest to the Throne of God in Heaven are the mothers of large families.

The father of the family must protect his wife's interior life so that this constant motherly love is maximized. Understanding that true love is found to the greatest degree possible in the focused loving heart of the mother, then the father must protect the mother from the world about her, from all the problems, concerns and threats of the world.

Why is this important? The mother's interior life can be destroyed the quickest by worry. Therefore, the father of the family must do his best to protect his wife from being worried, especially about financial matters.

He must provide a secure home. He must provide for all her needs and those of their children. He must protect her from anything else that would cause her to worry. I believe the greatest way to destroy a mother's heart is to load it up with financial burdens and problems. Hence the father of the family, who is also the provider of the family, must take full and total responsibility for financial matters in the family.

If he turns this over to his wife and there are difficulties with the finances of the family, for example, there is not enough money to pay the bills, etc., the mother will suffer great interior stress. But there will always be tough financial problems and difficulties. There will never, ever be all the money that seems necessary. There will always be priorities to ponder, establish and meet. With these concerns, she will not be able to be as loving a mother as she might be otherwise, one of all love, care and thoughtfulness.

Therefore, the father must be the responsible leader and care for his wife, the mother of the family, by protecting her and freeing her from worrying about financial matters and anything else that may upset her interior life. She must be free to love. She must be content to love. God's Divine Love must pass through her to the children and to her husband so that the family becomes a nest of God's Divine Love.

Then the children will grow up full of confidence and trust in God's Love. With her love and loyal support, her husband will become confident and competent in all his duties. So God's blessings will overflow for the family. They will have a very productive, disciplined, holy life on this earth and, hopefully, live for all eternity close to our Creator, the God of All Love.

SUMMARY

To recap, I believe three key reasons for God's establishment of the father's firm leadership in the family, the first and most important organization on earth, are:

Teaching obedience by example to the children in their formative years so they in turn will have the virtue of obedience to societal, organizational, and the Church's laws, which will make their life productive, happy and holy.

Establishing agreement in the family by a single source of decision making, thereby eliminating arguments and dissension, so love can flourish. Love follows agreement.

Protecting the mother's heart, the conduit of God's Divine Love to the family (giving, caring, sharing), from any worries or concerns, especially financial.

Thank you for your attention.

This page blank

8

MANHOOD

TALK NARRATIVE: The following is a talk given to the men of the student body of Franciscan University of Steubenville in 2002. My five youngest children all attended Franciscan and I believe the University is a special gift of God to the Catholic community of this age. You might consider researching it and recommending it if you know of some young person about to attend college. Good religious formation during college years is so important for a happy, holy life without horrible mistakes.

A MAN IS NOT A WOMAN - A WOMAN IS NOT A MAN

I have been asked to talk on manhood. I will be generally talking today about the married vocation, since this is my experience of almost fifty years raising seven children.

Manhood is an important topic because it is a topic that all men should be focused on. To be a man is to live a calling, for all men were created as men, not women. A man is significantly different than a woman in so many ways. Only in spiritual equality before God are they exactly alike. These differences are a source of constant wonder to both the husband and wife in a marriage. As a result, there is no boredom in marriage.

A man is called to care for and protect a woman. This is natural law. A man is thus created with a body that is usually bigger and stronger than a woman's body. A man is called to be a soldier on the front lines in time of war and risk death and mutilation constantly day after day. Believe me, although war is necessary, it is truly brutal. War movies are a joke. They cannot convey war's viciousness and brutality in any way; or the length of time the brutality lasts; or the conditions in the trenches or prison camps. Hopefully, our nation will always protect women from having to do this.

A man is called to work in an occupation for the most hours of each day and of his life, either inside or even outside in the weather. But because he has a beard if necessary for the cold, he is better able to do this, even through all seasons. His body is also built to take harsh treatment. He has strong arms and shoulders and in general is fit for a life outside the home in any conditions encountered. He is perfectly capable of self-defense in dangerous situations or locations.

This contrasts to a woman. For many reasons, she is better suited to be somewhat protected physically from both the weather and criminal elements by living a life for most of the time in a home caring for children and doing all that women like to do most, because it is natural and best for a woman to do these things. Although a woman can compete with you in almost any job, you cannot do what she can so in establishing a warm and loving home for you and your children. God's love comes primarily into your family through your wife's heart, not yours. She is the heart of the family. So the children and you will suffer greatly if the woman you marry is not concentrating on being a warm and loving homemaker. Her job, not yours, is the most important job on earth.

I suggest, I beg, I plead, I pray, I hope with all my heart and soul that you make the decision to allow your wife to focus on raising your children, and this means live within the income you make, no matter how much or how little it is.

Your priority must be the family, not the career. I have been a "career" man in both the corporate world and my own business, and I can attest, as you too will find out, that the "corporate" ladder of success is pathetic to hold up as the goal of life. It is simply a necessary evil to endure and work hard at in order to provide for a family. If you want to be a fanatic company or small business career man with career or money as your priority, I advise you to stay single and not put your wife and children through the life that will result.

If you choose the marriage vocation, then you should love God and your closest neighbors, your wife and children, by concentrating on your family life.

I believe a good, loving, large, holy traditional family is the correct goal for a married man or a married woman to have. To accomplish this goal, as well as putting the welfare of the family first over worldly material goals and approval, it takes the sense of values that only a strong spiritual life can give. There have never been more successful families than good Christian families, because Jesus Christ showed us the way to a perfect family life with the example of the Holy Family He lived in for thirty years of His life on earth. The Church has held this up as the ideal for two thousand years. To the extent we follow this example, we will have the approval and blessings of God. To the extent we don't, we won't. God never changes the rules.

JESUS WAS A MAN IN ALL WAYS

With this introduction we can see why men can relate more to Jesus, who was the perfect man, just as women can relate more to Mary, who was the perfect woman. Jesus is a man's example, bar none. He spent his life working in a wood shop and at times outside. We can assume this, because he knew much about farming and animal care. This is discussed well in Holy Scripture. He used parables about growing wheat, and caring for animals and fertilizing fruit trees, etc. Jesus was a man in all material or physical ways, as all men should be, but even more importantly, Jesus was a man in interior ways also. He showed all by his witness and with his words that he was not focused on pleasing his fleshly body, but on caring for his spirit.

THE IMPORTANT FOCUS

In today's world little is mentioned about these two natures each of us have. But we must reflect upon the fact that because of the sin of Adam and Eve, each of us was cursed with a selfish nature. Of course, Jesus had no selfish nature, but he still had to face life and always do what was best for his spirit. A real man, one who strives to imitate Christ, will always be focused on his spiritual life. And what is spiritual life, except the nurturing of one's spirit and at the same time the denial of one's selfish nature.

THE BASIS OF IT ALL

Jesus made this clear when he stated that to be a follower of his one had to deny his very self. It means to overcome one's selfish tendencies. It means to put God first, not pleasing one's body or one's ego. Holy Scripture is packed full of examples of what a person has to do to be a good person and also what is wrong or bad in God's eyes. In all cases, to do what is right, or God's Will, as Jesus always did, we have to overcome or deny our selfish nature.

STAY ON THE RIGHT TRACK

For example, to eat for the glory of God we have to eat for health of body and mind, not for pleasure or enjoyment. The same holds true for our sexual desires. We have to use our body when it is needed to nurture the love we have with our wives and procreate new children. Our sexual urges must not be used for selfish reasons or purposes in any other way, whether before or during marriage. This is to be chaste and pure, and means we have to deny our bodies what they crave and desire most. This is why fasting and chastity have always been so valued as essential mortification for the denial of the "self." It is so that our spiritual life can be primary and strong.

LIVING A LIFE OF THE SPIRIT

Overcoming our egos is another example of the practice of self-denial. Every person has a desire to be the greatest in the eyes of others, or at least to put themselves first and others second. It is to have pride. Jesus called us to be humble and meek, like He was. This is contrary to our selfish nature, and so again it takes self-denial to be a real man. But with the practice of self-denial, our spirit will grow strong and when it does, we will grow greatly in love. This is the case because our spiritual nature unites with the Spirit of God, Who is always dwelling within us if we are living in a state of grace. This means we will shine with the divine attributes of God; His Love, His Joy, His Peace. Holy Scripture defines also what a fleshly person reflects in all that he does in life. These fleshly traits are described in the New Testament in the letter to the Galatians.

NOT OF THIS WORLD

A real man is a man because he strives to be a perfect husband and father. This, too, is contrary to what is found in the world. The news media and the world about us has perverted fatherhood and put down being a husband. Thus, to be a real man, one has to stand against the world and be separate from it. God's Kingdom is not of this world. This is made clear in Holy Scripture. A real man can imitate St. Joseph in this regard. He was not of the world. He did not choose to live a worldly life in the big city of Jerusalem, but he raised his family in a country village of Nazareth.

CALLED TO LEADERSHIP

He was the head of his family, because he knew this was what God willed him to be. This role of leadership for a father is made clear throughout Holy Scripture. A real man is the leader of his family, but at the same time is ready to die on the cross for his wife. Holy Scripture states that he is to love his wife as Christ loved the Church. And to what extent did Christ love the Church? He loved it to death on a cross. We must love our wives to the extent of death on a cross. That means each one of us here. This is God's command to us, God's Will for us.

LEADERSHIP HAS A PRICE

In today's world this means that a husband and father must always do what is right in God's eyes, even if his wife does not agree with him. In many cases, doing such means much suffering in his family and sometimes divorce. If the latter does occur, then he must stay pure or chaste until he is reunited with his wife. This is a real crucifixion for a man who once lived in a married state and enjoyed a sexual union with the one he loves.

HOLD FIRM

A real man is thus focused on doing God's Will and this means being a leader. A leader also has to be a lonely man at times. This is the test that God puts all men through, as he did with Adam, for a woman at times can be very focused on doing what she thinks is right, but if the man has prayed about the matter and knows that in God's eyes it is wrong, he must hold firm. The key is that the man has prayed for guidance from God before making the decision. Since the man is the head of the family, he must lead and hold firm until his wife sees the light.

An exceptional leader famously said;

"Be sure you're right, then go ahead." Abraham Lincoln

Do you think this is easy? It never is. Yet this is what a leader must do.

GET THINGS STRAIGHT FIRST

Most of you here today are not yet married. I certainly advise each of you to be sure to discuss the leadership role of the man in the family before you propose to your wife to be. She must understand that you are determined to lead the family, and run the show based on God's Laws and what is best for the family. At times, it will mean financial restraint, eating for health, living within the income that is available and saving funds for emergencies. Doing what is best for the family sometimes means driving old cars, if necessary, and not spending money to keep up with the Joneses or for pleasures or entertainment in excess. Your wife's agreement makes this much easier.

This attempt to run the family according to God's Will and with financial prudence should be a comfort to your prospective partner, not a problem.

DECIDE WITH PRUDENCE

Many decisions have to be made in the daily life of a family and God has divined that the man make them. Either the family has one head or two. It is best to have only one head. But this means we must accept the responsibility and duties of leadership. We cannot run from it. We cannot complain when they are tough to make. We must protect our wives from worry. And we are to be servant leaders, not selfish leaders or leaders putting any member above the welfare of the family as a whole. And so being a leader does not mean to make the decision based on what we want selfishly, or feel is best from our standpoint, or on doing what will please our wives or children, if pleasing ourselves or them will jeopardize the future stability/welfare of our families. Each decision must be based on prayer and what is right for and best for our families.

Of course, being a man in the family also means being the provider of the family. It means working hard to care for our families our whole lives. Most men will do this. But some will not put their foot down and insist that the family live within the income the father has available. More families in my eyes break up because of overspending than any other factor. The man must insure that this does not occur.

GOD'S WAY OR NO WAY

To do this means saying no to the purchase of items that cannot be justified or are not needed. It means possible conflict, and this is why I'm advising each one of you to discuss this thoroughly with the woman you would like to marry. If she does not agree with you being the leader and a real man in the family, then don't marry her, for you must be a God-fearing man, not a woman-fearing man. You must put God's Will first, not the will of the world, which infers that the woman should run the family.

Having the woman as the leader of the family does not work because it is not what God wills. It is clearly God's Will that the man lead in the family, as is stated over and over again in Holy Scripture and by the Church for two thousand years. This will never change. God does not will two-headed families and does not will woman-headed families, except in emergencies or if the man becomes inoperative, i.e., a worthless drunkard or drug addict.

It doesn't matter what the world thinks or says or how many times it is tried, such families will always be dysfunctional. There must be God's order in the family to have peace and love and strength, and this means it must be headed by the husband.

God will not bless a family that does not do his will. The family will end up in divorce, as so many have. All this must be discussed before you marry. You will all be called to lead your family, and you can do this very well if the woman you marry has the goal to be a holy, Catholic wife, like Mary was. If she does not, then do not ask her to marry you. You cannot make your wife obedient and respectful to you, which is so necessary for your support because of your leadership role. It is up to her. She must value obedience as the tremendous virtue it is and the wonderful source of humility it is. You must also. The world and the worldly run from obedience, yet it is a great virtue and absolutely necessary for humility.

You must be obedient to God and your boss or customers. Your wife must be obedient to God and to you. Your children must be obedient to God and to each of you. This works. It is the order of love. It is because obedience destroys pride and selfishness. Prideful and selfish people cannot love or be loved well. The spiritual writers call obedience and humility sister virtues. You, your wife and your children become humble through the self-discipline of obedience. Humility is the basis of all virtue and love. So your obedient, humble, virtuous, loving family is then blessed by The Love.

WE HAVE A PERFECT MODEL

Jesus came to this earth and lived in the Holy Family to give all an example. He was a perfect man and so was St. Joseph, as Mary was a perfect woman. At least we can assume that Joseph and Mary were near-perfect, since they lived with Jesus and are the holiest Saints that have been proclaimed such by the Church. My point is that as the father of a family, you can model your life after St. Joseph, because he was God's perfect example for all time of a father of a family. He was the true protector, provider of, and leader of his family.

ONE WILL

This is made very clear in Holy Scripture. We can say that part of the reason that St. Joseph was a true leader of his family was because, as Holy Scripture also reflects, Jesus and Mary always did what St. Joseph decided was best; one will, St. Joseph's will, the father's will, just like the Trinity. Remember, Jesus and Mary were both far superior to St. Joseph, yet they respected his position as leader, because God wills the husband to be so. Again, this point needs to be made to your wife to be before you propose to her. Be sure to do this. It is very important. It is how you can be a real man, like St. Joseph, and she can be a real woman, like Mary. It is how you both can do God's Will and have a family for the Lord that is functional, with agreement and hence love, and not a family for the world that is dysfunctional, without agreement and hence without love.

FAITH, A REQUIREMENT

But being a true leader of your family also means much self-denial and sacrifice. God wills you to be a real man as a father of a family and this will mean a life of hard labor raising a large family, if you are blessed with such. It means having faith in God to provide the work you need. In fact, it means having faith in all areas of your life. It means that you will have to give and give and be a man like Jesus, Who was holy, and like St. Joseph, who was holy.

IT'S ALL INTERIOR

To be holy, you must be virtuous, and to be virtuous you must be a man who nourishes his spiritual life, not his fleshly life. I cannot emphasize this enough, for being men like Jesus and St. Joseph were is not an easy task at all, but one each man can only become with the grace of God. However, God demands you make the effort to receive His grace. This means you will have to overcome temptation and pass all the tests you are given. This is what it takes to grow in manhood, and believe me, it is all interior.

There will also be many things in our lives, big and small, that we have to do we will not want to do, but we must do them with a smile and with joy to be real men. Children may whine and complain when they have to do things they do not want to do or when they suffer. As men this is not acceptable, not even in our minds. A smiling, joyful man gives joy and courage and confidence to his wife and children, his fellow workers and anyone else he interacts with. As Mother Teresa said, *"Everytime you smile at someone, it is an action of love, a gift to that person, a beautiful thing."*

THE TEN CHARACTERISTICS OF MANHOOD

Let me summarize now by giving you what I believe are ten characteristics of a real man;

(1) A real man is one who always puts others first, thus, is a loving person, not a selfish person.

This characteristic seems right and good, but it is not easy to live by. It means to place the other person's good before your own. In a marriage, there is lots of giving and sacrificing. It is a daily occurrence. You work and work and then come home and have to work more with no reward or pleasure at times. Then you have to get up the next morning and do it all over again, with a smile on your face.

Can you do it? And my response is, "yes," if you depend on God's grace to get you through and if you don't seek pleasure in life, but to do all for the love of God. To have this perspective is the key to succeeding. It is to be motivated to please God by doing His Will, not be motivated to please your selfish nature. The latter will not work, for your selfish nature cannot be satisfied. So, be a man and put others first and your "self" last.

(2) A real man is one who strives for perfection in all he does, especially in the mundane tasks of his daily duties.

Holy Scripture is clear. It states that we are to strive to be perfect as our Heavenly Father is perfect. The Catholic Church defines perfection as the perfect fulfillment of the two commandments of Jesus: *To love God with your whole heart, your whole soul, your whole mind and all your strength, and To love your neighbor as yourself.* This, then, is the goal of all real men.

To love God with your whole heart is to place God first in your life over everyone and everything. To love God with your whole soul is to strive to not sin. In other words, do everything you know is God's Will. To love God with your whole mind is to do as Holy Scripture states, which is pray without ceasing. It is to strive to be a full-time contemplative and practice contemplative prayer. This is the ultimate goal in this regard. To love God with all your strength is to love God in all these ways, with all the effort and might you can possibly give. And to love your neighbor as yourself is to practice your vocational duties as perfectly as possible. This is because our vocation is given to us so that we have a way to strive to love our neighbor perfectly.

If you are a husband and father, you must try to be a perfect husband and father. If you become a priest, you must try to be a perfect priest. If you stay single, you must live a holy, pure and chaste single life helping and loving others as Jesus would, if He were you.

I mention that it also means doing mundane tasks perfectly, which include one's daily duties. The spiritual writers call these our *"sacred"* duties. This is because of the fact that these are the hardest things to do. This means doing all we have to do to be perfect in our work life both at home (maintaining it and improving it for our wives and children) and where we are employed (eight hours work for eight hours pay each and every day), working to provide for our family's livelihood. It takes great self-denial to be perfect in this way, but with God's grace it can be done.

(3) A real man is one who lives a life of poverty in the midst of plenty, and a life of poverty in the midst of poverty.

The world we live in is a material world. The emphasis is on acquiring things, on accumulating wealth, on having much of everything. This is not the life Jesus sought after. He was born in poverty and lived a life of poverty. This was obviously done to show us that this is what is best. It is best to control your spending and live within your means. Otherwise you spend all your life working and never have time to read and learn about your spiritual life, or have time to practice devotional practices that help you grow close to God.

A real man puts his interior, or spiritual, life over the material life. This is what is important, for all know that this life will one day end. When this happens all that you have accumulated will pass on to others. All you can take with you into the next life is the advancement in your spiritual life, and your life's activities of loving your neighbor. So don't sin by avarice. It is a capital sin. Live as God showed us all how to live, which is to just "get by" down here so that we can grow spiritually and have treasure for all eternity.

(4) A real man is a friend to all, and if married, a real lover of his wife, as is defined in Holy Scripture. He cares for her as he does his own flesh.

To be a good friend you have to love your friend. You have to give of yourself, not be selfish. It all comes down to putting the other person first in front of your wants or desires and sometimes your very needs. As a husband and a father, your best friends are your wife and children. The same principle holds true in this relationship also.

A real man loves. This means to not think of yourself, but of the one you love. It means to give and sacrifice. Holy Scripture defines the way to love the greatest as giving up your very life for your friend. This is the ideal. Few will ever be asked to do such, but the point is to be a real man, you have to be a perfect lover and give and give and give.

(5) A real man is humble and meek, like Jesus desires us all to be. It was Jesus Who said; *"Learn of Me, for I am meek and humble of heart."*

This is a fact. And since Jesus was the ultimate Man, a boy must grow up and become humble and meek to be a man.

To be humble is to not be prideful. To be meek is to control your anger. Both of these virtues are hard to practice. They are mostly interior practices, the type of practices that are the hardest virtues to form and practice. A humble man does not spend his life trying to build up his ego to try to impress others. He quietly does the work assigned to him, and does it to please God, no one else. A humble man does not talk about himself, his accomplishments, his achievements; he keeps the conversation focused on anything else except himself. A humble man does not give his opinion. He tries to search out for the truth and then presents it. A humble man is a very spiritual person. He prays much, studies much and practices all the religious devotion he can. He knows that it takes grace from God to grow in humility, so he goes to the source to obtain as much grace as he possibly can. A humble man is also one who practices self-denial, self-control and self-restraint. He knows that to obtain grace, a person has to be generous. This is a spiritual term that means a person has to generously give up or deny what he wills in order to do God's Will, and this means to deny one's own human nature, which is naturally selfish.

A humble man is also meek. These two virtues correspond to each other. This is a fact, because, as just mentioned, to be meek one has to control one's anger. To do this, a man has to deny his desire to fight back, or save face, or rule and control. All takes self-control. This is what it takes to be like Jesus; being humble and meek of heart.

"Whosoever is a little one, let him come to Me." Proverbs 9:4

(6) A real man is not vain, but realizes that all is passing and thus is not ruled by the desires for material wealth and security.

A man who wants all to look up to him, a man who is proud, is a vain man. It is similar to being prideful. Most men don't care how handsome they are. They are vain in other ways. They strive to gain material wealth and be secure and in this way think they are better than others and seek the praise and honor from others for the same.

To be motivated to become rich and secure in this life is the wrong path to travel. Taking this route is to be lost to the world. It is to want to climb the corporate ladder, to be better than others, to have lots of nice things so others think you are great and really something. Well, a real man has true wisdom. He knows where he is going in this life. He knows what is up ahead and that what means most in this life is pleasing God. This is because he knows this life will end one day, and all the worldly praise and honor will count for nothing. He knows that what will matter then is how much he has grown in perfection of charity, as mentioned above.

A real man, however, is a good worker and will advance in his work life and may become rich. But he is motivated to do well in his career only so he can do well providing for his family. His only motivation is to fulfill his vocational duties or requirements as a father and provide what his family needs to live and survive each day. A real man also knows, however, that the greatest gift he can give to his family is his time. This fact keeps him from becoming a workaholic. He only works as is required to fulfill the job requirements. His motivation is family first always, not the company.

(7) A real man does not let an opportunity pass that he can help another in some way, like giving up his seat in church or opening a door for another.

We know that Jesus was always courteous. He always put others first. So a real man tries to also follow in the footsteps of Jesus in this way. To give up your seat in church or open a door for another is being a man. It is to think of another first, not of yourself. It is to love your neighbor. It is to care for them at the cost of your time and comfort. It is to help another in small ways when possible. It is, as I said, another way to imitate Christ, Who was the ideal Man, par excellence.

(8) A real man is always one of peace and prayer, close to God, or at least focused on trying to be at all times.

A person talks to God when he or she prays. The only exception is when a person prays in a contemplative way. When praying in a contemplative way, a person is so united to God that he or she loves God heart to heart. This type of prayer results in God doing all through the person. In other words, it is to be transformed into Christ.

So either you are always asking God by praying in the usual way what to do, or God is doing all through you when you pray in a contemplative way. To be a person of prayer then is the ultimate goal for all Christians or should be. It is then that Christ lives, not you. It will be a life of union with God.

We know that Jesus was such. He always did the Father's Will. He was one with God the Father and He willed that all be such. This was His final prayer to the Father before He was tortured and crucified.

A real man, then, is a prayerful man. And to be prayerful, you have to be peaceful. This is just how you have to be to pray, for you can't be anxious and disquieted and pray well. Nor, by the way, can you make a prudent decision when you are in a non-peaceful state. God is a God of peace and He will run from a person who is anxious and disquieted. It is not easy to maintain peace and calm through all this life's ups and downs, or when your wife or children are mad at you. But a real man controls the human side of him to accomplish this feat. He is cool, calm and collected. He lives a recollected state interiorly and thus can pray well. And if given the gift of infused contemplation, practices contemplative prayer always, as we know Jesus did.

(9) A real man is one who cares for his body by eating right and exercising it. He protects it from harm, so that he can give God his all for as long as he can while he lives on this earth.

Holy Scripture is clear. It states that whether you eat or drink, you are to do all for the glory of God. To control how and what you eat is very important, because it will result in you being healthy in both body and mind. This is also the case for getting sufficient exercise, especially if you have an office job. A real man is smart enough to know that his body needs to have all the essential nutrients and different food types, i.e., minerals, fats, vitamins, proteins, carbohydrates etc. to maintain his health. He then strives to make sure he consumes a sufficient quantity of the same. He eats for health, not for pleasure.

Having this knowledge and applying it is really the key to maintaining your health. This is especially true in these times, because the commercial food system has been corrupted. Its focus is profit, not food quality. It is run by people trying to sell the population what tastes good and offers the most pleasure to the body. A real man sees through all this and is smarter than these profit motivated companies. A real man thus eats what is necessary to have and maintain good health.

He also knows that God created man to work in a physical way. By working hard a man can get sufficient exercise. But as time passes and a man advances in his employment and his position requires little manual labor, he still knows enough to exercise daily to maintain good health. A real man will at least take the time to do push-ups and sit ups, and run up and down the stairs as a minimum. He does it because it is essential to take time out to exercise daily to maintain health, so that he can be a real man and provide for, protect and love his family in all the ways he must in these times.

(10) A real man is above all a man of joy, realizing that being a joyful man means being a leader who leads others to Christ.

God is infinite Joy. The closer one gets to God the more joyful one will be. Divine joy is a deep-seated joy, a lasting joy, a joy that is present even when carrying many burdens or experiencing many trials. A real man thus has a focus on striving to be one with God, full of His Spirit, united to the Trinity full-time. He knows that the Saints were always joyful, so he tries to imitate them in all ways. So he tries to practice virtue in a heroic way. This takes much self-discipline. But he knows that the Saints did this, and as a result they conquered their selfish nature and were able to then let Christ run their lives. This included filling them with holy joy all the days of their lives.

"Tell the just that all is well." Isaiah (3:10)

A real man is a "happy cross carrier." He knows that Holy Scripture states that God is in control, and that He makes all things work out for the best for those who love him. He also knows that Holy Scripture commands a follower of Christ to rejoice in the Lord, always. A real man thus does just this. He does it by striving to be aware at all times of the Lord in his life. He strives to realize that God loves him at all times. Doing this and knowing that God is Love, means that he can rejoice in the love God has for him all day long. Doing such keeps a real man joyful always. This is because of the fact that he knows that if God loves him and is in control, no trial or cross or anything else can separate him from the Love of the Lord. This fact is also made very clear in Holy Scripture.

CLOSING STATEMENT

I have tried to give you what I believe a real man consists of. I have given you what I believe is the ideal to strive after. Now I will end my talk, but I will continue to strive to practice what I preach. I hope each of you spends your life striving to do the same. You all probably have another sixty years or so to live. I hope as the years pass, you all become real men and can say with St. Paul, *"I have fought the good fight. I have finished the race. My crown of glory awaits me."*

Amen.

"The glory of God is man fully alive."
St. Irenaeus

"You will catch more flies, St. Francis used to say, with a spoonful of honey than with a hundred barrels of vinegar."
"Were there anything better or fairer on earth than gentleness, Jesus Christ would have taught it (to) us; and yet He has given us only two lessons to learn of Him: meekness and humility of heart."
St. Francis de Sales

"Be thou God's House, and He will be thine; let Him dwell in thee, and thou shalt dwell in Him."
St. Augustine

Our Perfect Model:
"In hours of manual work (including gardening), St. Joseph is the perfect model for contemplatives. His attention was centered on God alone amidst all his exterior duties. Work done simply with hands, with the heart set on God's presence is not an impediment to contemplation. St. Joseph's contemplation was reached, not by an intellectual effort, but by a simple attachment to the Divine Reality, to the life-giving, love-giving presence of God. We are apt to think of exterior activity, the work that life itself brings to us, as in opposition to the contemplative life, but in St. Joseph we find just the contrary. The work that life brought him in exterior duties to support the Holy Family did not keep him away from God, nor from having his heart set on God, nor his mind from contemplating God. For contemplation, if it is true, simplifies and focuses the soul on God - on the one thing that should be in our lives." Strong Friends of God, by Father Albert Bourke, O.C.D., page 39

Becoming a contemplative (constant union with God interiorly) will make us the greatest lovers of God and neighbor possible, including our closest neighbors, our wives and children, because it will be God Himself (Jesus Christ) loving though us.

9 LANCE P. SIJAN
MEDAL OF HONOR

TALK NARRATIVE: I gave the following speech to the USAF Academy Class of 2002 on November 13, 1999. This class chose Lt. Lance Sijan, a USAF pilot who earned the Medal of Honor in Vietnam, as their class exemplar, someone for the members of the class to model themselves after. I was asked to address the class because I was with Lance in North Vietnam during the last days of his life and told his story to the Air Force when I returned. I have expanded the original talk with some experiences while a MISTY pilot.

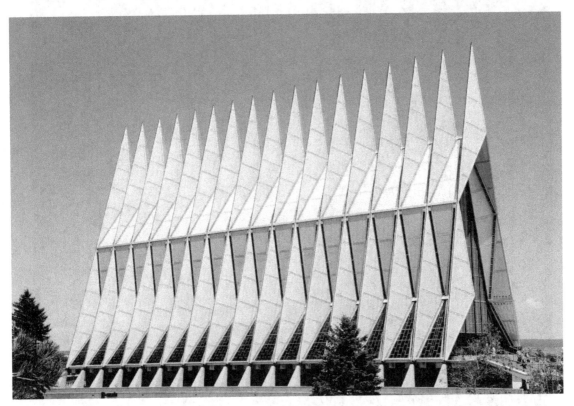

US AIR FORCE ACADEMY CHAPEL

The Medal of Honor

The President of the United States in the name of The Congress takes pride in presenting the MEDAL OF HONOR to SIJAN, LANCE P. Rank and organization: Captain, U.S. Air Force, 4th Allied POW Wing, Pilot of an F-4C aircraft. Place and Date: North Vietnam, 9 November 1967. Entered service at: Milwaukee, Wis. Born: 13 April 1942, Milwaukee, Wis.

LANCE SIJAN, USAF, MEDAL OF HONOR

Mall of Heroes
United States Air Force Academy
Colorado Springs

Life size bronze sculpture

Sculptor: Mark Austin Byrd &
Jenelle Armstrong Byrd

Commission by the Association of Graduates of the US Air Force Academy as a
gift to the USAFA

Citation: While on a flight over North Vietnam, Capt. Sijan ejected from his disabled aircraft and successfully evaded capture for more than 6 weeks. During this time, he was seriously injured and suffered from shock and extreme weight loss due to lack of food. After being captured by North Vietnamese soldiers, Capt. Sijan was taken to a holding point for subsequent transfer to a prisoner of war camp. In his emaciated and crippled condition, he overpowered one of his guards and crawled into the jungle, only to be recaptured after several hours. He was then transferred to another prison camp where he was kept in solitary confinement and interrogated at length. During interrogation, he was severely tortured; however, he did not divulge any information to his captors. Capt. Sijan lapsed into delirium and was placed in the care of another prisoner. During his intermittent periods of consciousness until his death, he never complained of his physical condition and on several occasions, spoke of future escape attempts. Capt. Sijan's extraordinary heroism and intrepidity above and beyond the call of duty at the cost of his life are in keeping with the highest traditions of the U.S. Air Force and reflect great credit upon himself and the U.S. Armed Forces. PRESIDENT GERALD R. FORD

A FIGHT WELL WORTH FIGHTING AND A FIGHT WELL FOUGHT

I would like to thank each one of you for gathering today to honor the memory of Lance Sijan, and also for choosing Lance as the Exemplar of your class.

Lance had tremendous moral strength and strength of will. I believe these were built on three pillars: first, his faith in God; second, his love for his family; and third, his Academy training.

I especially salute the Sijan family here with us tonight, who merited such love from Lance and gave him strong faith. I also salute the dedication of those who prepared him at the Academy—the officers, the instructors, and the staff.

I first met Lance at the Academy in 1963. We were both in the 21st Squadron, and everyone regarded Lance as a good, reliable, and competent cadet. I believe he learned here the lessons of military discipline and completing tasks to the best of his ability, without excuses or complaints.

LANCE SIJAN AS A CADET AT THE US AIR FORCE ACADEMY

As an aside, if you really want to be a leader in all circumstances, make the "No excuse, Sir," and "no complaints, always positive" teachings here your own like Lance did. And this means even in your mind.

I will begin by reviewing the background leading up to my meeting with Lance in Vietnam. I was in an all–volunteer unit flying as scouts (Forward Air Controllers – FACS) over North Vietnam to find targets for the strike fighter–bomber flights. We were called the *MISTYs*. The founding commander of the *MISTYs*, Colonel Bud Day, named it after his and his wife's favorite song, *MISTY*.

While searching for targets we flew low–level, turning and twisting to avoid being shot down at speeds between 450 and 600 miles per hour. But even with these tactics we had a high loss rate because of the long time we were airborne and the low altitude flying in heavy ground–fire over North Vietnam. Missions were generally about five hours long, since we refueled twice in the air during each flight. We were a very close group of fourteen pilots and every man was a dedicated fighter pilot. We all normally flew single-seat, single-engine fighters, the F–100 Super Sabre. We flew the two–seat version for the scouting mission, alternating front and back seats, one man flying and one man on maps, camera, and radio.

Misty FACs 1967

Standing: Bob Blocher, Lt Haltigan, Guy Gruters, Bob Porter, Jere Wallace, "PJ" White, Gene Mooney, Ron "Nape" Miller, Bob Craner, Mick Greene, Don Sibson
Kneeling: Maurice McHugh, Charlie Neel, Jim Mack, Joe Cerito, George Pinney

MISTY FAST FORWARD AIR CONTROLLERS (FAST FACs)

At the end of a typical day of flying, we would gather together in the Officer's Club for conversation to discuss the missions of that day and the following day. With perhaps five to ten men at the table, we sometimes had lulls in conversation. These pauses might last up to twenty or thirty minutes, and yet no one felt uneasy. Awkward attempts to restart the conversation did not occur. I have never experienced this before or since. I believe this was an indicator of peace with God, with ourselves, and with each other. We were under heavy fire each mission and all knew there was a good chance of not coming home. A man under stress is typically restless and distraught but none of the *MISTYs* were.

What brought this peace? We had confidence we were fighting for a good cause. We were there to do what we could to win the war, for many were dying each day. A whole country was being attacked by a ruthless enemy who thought nothing of killing innocent women and children. The daily missions with all their risks were just a part of doing this job. We prayed each night and thanked God for getting us through another day. We were trying to save lives and protect a nation. Our motivation was love, the love that is found in war, the love of neighbor. In this case, it was protecting the families in the villages of South Vietnam. So we lived and slept in peace.

Lt. Lance Sijan was shot down in early November of 1967. My first shoot-down was just a few days before his, after more than four hundred combat missions and about eight months in Vietnam.

(Please see Chapter 1 for an account of this action if you have not yet read it.)

After being rescued by two separate helicopters, Charlie Neel and I reunited with great joy when the choppers landed. We were immediately taken to the hospital at Da Nang. We were happy we had been brought out and were not seriously injured. My wrist had been shattered and I needed an operation and cast for my injury. I stayed in the hospital for a couple of weeks and then managed space–available travel back to the States for Thanksgiving with my family.

Meanwhile, during all the time from my first shoot down until I was shot down again, that is, for forty–six days, Lance Sijan, with a badly injured leg (compound fracture, bone sticking out of the leg) from landing by parachute in rough country, was pushing and dragging himself along with his hands in the jungle, trying to reach a clearing for rescue.

BACK IN THE AIR

After returning to *MISTY* in December, 1967, Major Bob Craner in the front seat and I in back were flying recon. We had to stay under a cloud ceiling of 1500 feet in order to see and avoid the mountains. We were the only flight in North Vietnam that afternoon because of the weather. The roads were full of enemy trucks. Bob had already shot up a number of them with low-altitude strafing. For our last job, we were trying to locate a group of gun batteries that had narrowly missed hitting a number of *MISTYs* in the past. We were circling their well–camouflaged positions to draw fire so we could plot them on our map for attack the next morning. Our friends would return to take out the gun positions we had located. We wanted to make it a little safer for future flights.

F-100 WITH TWO MISTY FACS SCOUT MISSION

Believe me, ladies and gentlemen, a war demands great sacrifice and those who participate in it must be ready to give up their lives. Each of the *MISTY* pilots were men of this caliber. The men I knew were focused on their mission to help a little nation's fight against a stronger invading army trying to take away their freedom. Bob and I both felt this way and it motivated us to give our best efforts.

Suddenly we were hit by flaming 57mm cannon fire and the plane was thrown upside down with all controls gone, lurching for the ground 1500 feet below. I ejected upside down towards the ground and so did Bob. Just after the chute inflated I heard the gongs sound in the little farm villages, which indicated, "Go get the pilot coming down in the parachute." I slipped the chute into a small patch of woods in the middle of the farming valley, made two *Mayday* emergency calls and burrowed my face and hands into the ground. Because I had obtained permission for an earlier–than–scheduled return to flying, Personal Equipment had not returned my .38 revolver. The lack of a weapon saved my life, because if I had tried to use it, I would not have had a chance against the ten-man squad that found me and covered me with AK-47s after about forty–five minutes. I rose slowly to my feet. They brought me to a village, stripped me of all my clothing and equipment, and gave me black pajamas to wear.

After capture I was calm. This was probably because as was the case with all of us who were shot down, I was convinced that escape would be possible and constantly looked for the opportunity. This was not to be, although one *MISTY*, Major Bud Day, the first commander of *MISTY*, who had been shot down and captured before us, succeeded in escaping and making it back to South Vietnam to the outskirts of a U.S. Marine Base. There he was ambushed, shot twice, recaptured, and then tortured terribly for many months. He was an inspiration for all POWs in North Vietnam and was awarded the *Medal of Honor* for his incredible resistance.

All of us who survived the shoot-down and initial capture now had to fight a different war of even greater sacrifices, maintaining our fight in very difficult conditions without any physical weapons, instead relying on God, our character, and each other.

We were in the hands of people who had been lied to by their leaders. They did not know that their country was in the wrong.

A new phase of the war started for me that moment, a time of my life that would draw me closer to God than I had ever been. He was there with me that day. He decided to leave me on the earth a while longer by insuring I did not die in the crash and that I did not have my sidearm to try to defend myself. He never left me for the entire time of my captivity.

Meanwhile, Bob Craner had been captured as he hit the ground in an open rice paddy. They had him covered with rifles as he landed. In the village, he heard trucks and tanks heading south all night long, as part of the preparation for the *Tet* offensive of early 1968.

Back in Phu Cat Air Base, when we failed to return, the rest of the *MISTYs* wanted to immediately go north at night knowing how critical the first few hours on the ground after shoot-down were. It would have been suicide in those weather conditions. I learned later the commander had to post guards on the fighters to keep our friends from coming up. I believe God puts His Love in good soldiers to care for others and the *MISTYs* were as good as they come.

The following day, the NVA brought Bob Craner in shackles to each of the thirty–six gun positions (six batteries of six guns each) which had shot us down. He stood in front of each gun crew as they gave their special cheer. This tour of the gun positions took all day. Bob was an expert on and had written position papers for the *MISTY* unit on the air defense guns of North Vietnam. He noted that each crew was manned by a crew of eight men for the 37mm guns and ten men for the 57mm guns, which was the regulation manning. This was important information, because it meant that, with over 150,000 active guns our intelligence had located in North Vietnam, more than one million men were tied up in antiaircraft defense. This is out of a nation of only seventeen million total people. This would correspond relatively to the United States having fifteen million men on antiaircraft guns. This information alone was an overpowering reason to never stop the bombing of North Vietnam.

As they were leading Bob back to the village, his guard was playing with his survival radio and accidentally put it on transmit where it put out an emergency beeper. When the guard heard the emergency beeper, he flicked the switch and by chance put it on receive. Jim Mack and Jim Fiorelli, two airborne *MISTYs* looking for us heard the beeper and then silence. Jim Mack transmitted, "I got you, *MISTY*, where are you?" The guard was holding the radio and looked at it with a puzzled expression. Bob motioned to him that he would help him with his problem and the guard handed the radio to Bob. Bob Craner was a Fighter Weapons School Instructor and an extremely brave, able and cool man in any tough situation, but I have often thought that this action of his in obtaining the radio had to be one of the coolest moves anyone ever made anywhere. Bob, after the guard handed him the radio, transmitted that he had been captured, he loved his wife, and to tell her he would see her at the end of the war. He also said I was alive and had been captured. Actually, he was not sure of this but wanted to comfort my wife. Jim Mack asked him where he was and Bob said up what we called the Ron River Valley. Jim put the F-100 on the deck and headed up the valley under the weather. Bob told Jim the details of full manning of the guns and the tremendous traffic he'd heard on the roads.

COLONEL ROBERT CRANER, USAF "BOB CRANER, USAF FIGHTER WEAPONS SCHOOL INSTRUCTOR, POW FOR MORE THAN FIVE YEARS. BOB WAS ON THE DESIGN TEAM FOR SPECIFICATIONS FOR THE US F-16 FIGHTER AIRCRAFT, ARGUABLY THE BEST AIR-TO-AIR FIGHTER IN THE WORLD UNTIL THE F-22. A PERFECT CELL-MATE FOR TWO AND ONE-HALF YEARS IN A COMMUNIST PRISON CAMP. THE HUMBLEST, COOLEST, AND YET MOST COMPETENT MAN I HAVE EVER KNOWN IN MY LIFE. A MAN WITH TRUE LOVE FOR GOD, HIS COUNTRY, HIS FAMILY, AND HIS FRIENDS. BOB WAS A TRULY MORAL MAN, A PERFECT FIGHTER, A PERFECT FIGHTER PILOT AND A MAN THAT EMBODIED ALL THAT IS BEST IN MANHOOD." GUY GRUTERS ON HIS WEBSITE; GUYGRUTERS.NET

Meanwhile, Jim was thinking only one thought - rescuing Bob. So Jim asked him to let him talk to the guard in French and Bob gave the radio back to the guard. Jim told him in French that "We will take you to Saigon and give you much gold." The guard understood the word "Saigon," and pointed with glee to the radio. He thought he was talking with somebody in Saigon. Jim Fiorelli in the back seat of the F-100 patched together a call with an airborne Vietnamese in South Vietnam and tried to memorize the Vietnamese for, "We will take you to Saigon and give you much gold."

Eventually, the F-100 came around the bend in the river to the valley where Bob and the guard were and the guard realized that he had been talking to Bob's fellow pilots in the air. He became very angry and almost shot Bob. A little later he offered Bob a chance to escape into the jungle with sign language, but Bob didn't bite. Later on, we found out a number of other pilots were offered an opportunity to escape by their captors in North Vietnam. Their orders obviously allowed them to shoot a prisoner if he attempted escape. I believe many men were killed after capture by trusting their guards in this regard.

Meanwhile in the air, Jim Mack and Jim Fiorelli and the other *MISTYs* looking for us ran into a major flak trap that had been set up in the valley, but never stopped looking until all hope for rescue was obviously gone.

The air–sea rescue people in Vietnam were outstanding, and everyone supported them the best way they could. I had been rescued after my first shoot-down and many pilots were rescued over the course of the war. However, this time the rescue attempt failed, an incident repeated many times in the war. More than three thousand, five hundred aircrew-men were shot down over North Vietnam and not rescued. Four hundred and seventy-two survived the shoot-downs and the camps and were released in 1973. Of these 472, a little more than 300 were the relative old timers in prison with me four to seven years, and one man, Navy Lt. Everett Alvarez, nine years.

Very few knew the risks that had been taken in these failed air-sea rescue attempts to get the pilots out. The "Sandys" in A-1Es provided suppression of the enemy flak and the "Jolly Green" helicopters provided the extraction capability, usually under extreme ground fire. They were the greatest heroes for any downed airman.

But we knew what had been risked for us and we were humbly thankful. I hope you will believe me and try to understand when I say how much it meant to us and the others, who, when shot down and captured, knew that there were men and women who cared for us. We knew men and women like those involved in this rescue attempt in the air and those supporting it on the ground back at the air bases were doing what they could to get us out safely and alive.

This knowledge contributed immensely to the difficult task of trying to live day by day in prison camp when everything appeared hopeless. We believed that many men and women in the United States were keeping faith with us and doing all they could to get us out. As the years passed, this was a concrete way God helped us with the motivation to live out each horrible day rather than quit. It helped us to believe that against all logic we would make it home.

In the village, Bob and I went through initial torture sessions for military information. After a day of this, we each gave a cover story to get out of the ropes and have a chance to escape at night in the small village we were being held in where our chances were the best. On Christmas day, we were taken to a small holding prison near the town of Vinh. The cells were about six feet by six feet and made out of bamboo. We called it the bamboo prison. We were in separate cells and in leg irons and handcuffs day and night.

They brought Lance Sijan to this bamboo prison shortly after we arrived there. He had been injured on shoot-down and further injured in the trek across very difficult terrain and was in extremely poor physical condition. After shoot-down, an immense RESCAP effort (rescue attempt) had been made to get him out with *MISTYs* overhead directing the effort, during which seven aircraft were shot down or badly damaged. The war stopped when a pilot was shot down. His friends all tried to rescue him. Clearly the attempt to get Lance out did not fail due to lack of effort or courage on the part of the rescuers. Lance had suffered a severely broken leg which was a compound fracture (a bone sticking out of his leg), a concussion, and a badly mangled hand. When finally captured, he had been ten days without water and forty–six days without any real food. He looked like a living skeleton and was a mass of raging infections. I saw this when I peeked in his cell while being led past him to go outside.

We heard him being clubbed unmercifully on his wounds under interrogation in that cell multiple times each day, but in accordance with the code of conduct, he refused to give anything except his name, rank, service number, and date of birth. We were not allowed to communicate between the three cells at all, but at certain times we were able to whisper to Lance and we both advised him to please give a cover story as we had done to stop the torture. But he said that he could handle it so far. This lasted for several days and so Bob Craner and I started screaming like maniacs whenever they hit him and complained every chance we had to the officers. His body was in no shape to take beatings like that.

Occasionally they allowed us to take him outside and clean him up. He had a heavy cast on and was hard to handle for the Vietnamese. When I had seen him in his cell he looked like a small man because he was so thin. But when we first picked him up and put one of his arms around each of our necks, he was as tall as we were. I said to Bob, "This guy is really pretty big." Lance then said, "Aren't you Guy Gruters." I did a double take and said, "Yes, who are you?" He said, "Lance." I said, "Lance who?" He said, "Sijan, Lance Sijan." I said, "No, oh no, not Lance." Although he had been a squadron mate of mine at the Academy for three years, I did not recognize him because he was so emaciated.

He had dragged himself through the jungle with his arms due to his leg being so badly broken. The jungle and the rock outcroppings cut his whole body to ribbons. He was reduced to a mass of infected wounds. But even after 46 days without food, a North Vietnamese officer told me Lance knocked out his guard after capture and it took an entire village the better part of a day to recapture him. The interrogators continued to beat him with clubs while asking him questions, but he never gave them any information.

We were then transferred to Hanoi. It was a long and bumpy ride to the Hanoi Hilton, which was the main welcoming prison camp in North Vietnam. We rode in a two and a half ton 6X6 military truck over bombed out roads so rough that going ten miles an hour threw us all over the back of the truck. Bob and I took turns cradling Lance between our legs with his head and shoulders on our bellies and chests, holding him tightly to our bodies. The other man would keep the fifty–five gallon fuel drums from crushing the two. The ride was very difficult for us. But in the state Lance was in, it was a brutal beating. Lance never complained and against all expectations survived that trip.

When we arrived at the Hanoi Hilton we were kept in solo interrogation cells and between interrogations were told to care for Lance. This was a chance for us to get together to corroborate our stories, and Lance did a tremendous job in fostering the necessity of our care for him between interrogations.

After about ten days of interrogation and torture, all three of us were finally put in a cell in the main cellblock. There was one to two inches of standing water in the cell. We each had one blanket. The blankets were wet. It was extremely cold in that cell.

As an aside, I would just like to testify that under virtually all the conditions during my time with Lance in North Vietnam, he was always calm. He was simply a sincere, honest soldier doing the best he could to do what he understood to be right. He told us details of his push through the jungle and about how he knocked out the guard, but only when we asked him. We had to pry the information out of him. We never would have known about it if it were not for the North Vietnamese. He simply wanted to escape. He knew it was the right thing to do in accordance with the code, and Lance always tried to do the right thing without excuse and without complaint. I think he is looking down on us right now, and I'll bet he is embarrassed to see us giving him this kind of attention.

COMMENT

The martyrs are heroic examples of what God's power can do. It is humanly impossible, we realize, for someone to go through tortures such as Lance had and remain faithful. But it is equally true that by human power alone no one can remain faithful even without torture or suffering. God does not come to our rescue at isolated, "special" moments. God is supporting the super-cruisers such as Sijan as well as children's toy boats.

QUOTE

"Wherever it was that Christians were put to death, their executions did not bear the semblance of a triumph. Exteriorly they did not differ in the least from the executions of common criminals. But the moral grandeur of a martyr is essentially the same, whether he preserved his constancy in the arena before thousands of raving spectators or whether he perfected his martyrdom forsaken by all upon a pitiless flayer's field [as Lance did]" (*The Roman Catacombs*, Hertling-Kirschbaum).

The last two paragraphs were taken from *AmericanCatholic.org*, January 22, 2013.

In the harsh conditions of the cell, even though Lance started to deteriorate from pneumonia on top of all the infections and injuries he had already suffered, he always maintained a good attitude. For example, every so often he would growl at the guards when they raised the little door to look in our cell just to get us to laugh, because they would quickly lower it when he did. This was because in the bad condition he was in he didn't look like a normal person anymore.

Unfailingly polite and respectful to the two of us, he asked us to help him exercise to try to increase his strength. It is hard to exercise when the muscles have almost all disappeared from hunger. About the only muscles he had left were some in his upper arms and shoulders because he had used those to survive and move in the jungle. He would try to eat the best way he could. But his body was in such a condition he had trouble accepting any significant amount of food. He never stopped trying to live even as he became weaker and weaker. Bob, Lance, and I knew that his condition was worsening. We would pray the *Our Father* together. When I asked Lance if he had made his peace with God, he said he had and that he was fine. I found out later he had been given his strong faith by the way his family raised him.

As he became so weak that he lost the ability to speak well, he started mouthing one word at a time, then one letter at a time and then finally a blink code (one for yes or two for no). His mind would also go blank from time to time as if the body were trying to conserve the little energy it had left. During this entire period, he never displayed any theatrics and there were no complaints. It was the most incredible thing I have ever seen in my life. When he was finally taken away, with his last strength he called for his father. His death broke our hearts, but his example inspired all of us to try to do the best we could.

As POWs, we were ordered to live by the American Fighting Man's Code of Conduct. I would like to read it to you tonight to demonstrate Lance's compliance. These were the standing orders for American military men in our situation.

Article I: I am an American fighting man. I serve in the forces which guard my country and our way of life. I am prepared to give my life in their defense.

Lance gave his life in their defense.

Article II: I will never surrender of my own free will. If in command, I will never surrender my men while they still have the means to resist.

He was found while unconscious, forty-six days after being shot down. Lance did not surrender of his own free will.

Article III: If I am captured, I will continue to resist by all means available. I will make every effort to escape and aid others to escape. I will accept neither parole nor special favors from the enemy.

According to unsolicited testimony by a North Vietnamese officer, Lance did manage to escape once when he was all alone even though he was seriously injured. He did not stop trying to escape and to convince us of its possibility, even in a high security prison, as his condition deteriorated. As far as parole or special favors from the enemy, it is inconceivable that Lance would ever even consider accepting something like that.

Article IV: If I become a Prisoner of War, I will keep faith with my fellow prisoners. I will give no information or take part in any action which might be harmful to my comrades. If I am senior, I will take command. If not, I will obey the lawful orders of those appointed over me and will back them up in every way.

Lance was a perfect companion in Prison Camp. He made it possible for Major Craner and myself to better resist interrogation. He was always obedient to Major Craner, the senior officer in our cell.

Article V: When questioned, should I become a Prisoner of War, I am required to give name, rank, service number, and date of birth. I will evade answering further questions to the utmost of my ability. I will make no oral or written statements disloyal to my country and its allies or harmful to their cause.

Lance did this perfectly, despite unbelievable pain and suffering. The great French General, Napoleon, was famous in military studies for his ability to effectively motivate and select men for special units. Napoleon said that *"the first quality of a sol-*

dier is the ability to endure hardship." If this is true, and it is tough to find a better judge than Napoleon, then Lance is one of the greatest soldiers in history.

Article VI: I will never forget that I am an American fighting man, responsible for my actions, and dedicated to the principles which made my country free. I will trust in my God and in the United States of America.

Like Job in the Bible, like Jesus on the cross, Lance trusted God even though he was given a bed of thorns, not a wreath of flowers. Lance never complained of the hardships and sufferings presented to him. He kept the faith. He died a peaceful man. He was a soldier to the very end and an example for all time.

Lance was a true soldier, a true American and a true friend and brother to me. He gave his life for all of us sitting here tonight. We are this country. You and I are this country. This is the sacrifice all soldiers are ultimately asked to be ready to make, to die for the people of our country. Lance came from a faith-filled family, and that is what made him what he was. We can all learn from his example. He did everything as perfectly as he could because he was striving to do what was right. And who defines what's right? What is morally right is what God wills.

Ladies and Gentlemen, this is my personal recommendation to you. Do not fall below the standard that Lance has set. Do not think that you can live as you want to. Instead, follow Lance's lead and always live for others. Always do what is morally right. This includes being the best soldier you can be, for you all have been called to serve God in this way in your life. If you do, you will have the strength to persevere through any tough circumstance. It makes everything possible. If you do not strive to always do what is morally right, as Lance did, you will fall by your pride or by bad habits. These will destroy you.

As you know, the book *"Into the Mouth of the Cat"* by Malcolm McConnell has many details about Lance's conduct in prison camp.

To summarize what I saw Lance do in the prisons of North Vietnam and to give some specifics of Lance's exemplary actions, I would like to submit for your consideration what I call "Sijan's Code." These are the ten principles he practiced. Please consider them his legacy and guidance for us.

Then I have a few comments on your time here.

First, Sijan's Code:

NUMBER 1: Be committed and determined to always do what you believe is the right thing. Abraham Lincoln said it best; "Be sure you're right, then go ahead."

NUMBER 2: Be dedicated to your vocation as a soldier, as a fighting man or woman. Your dedication is proven above all by obedience to your commanders. Anyone can follow orders they agree with, but it's tougher to follow them when you don't, or when you think you have a better way. This is when your obedience counts. The Air Force is a key part of the military shield for this country. I sincerely believe it is the finest fighting organization the world has ever known. One factor for that success is the excellent obedience up and down the line.

NUMBER 3: Be a gentleman or a lady. This means someone who is always polite and affable to everyone, someone who is a pleasure to be with.

NUMBER 4: Develop a sense of peace that can be recognized by those about you. This will come with good intentions and not trying to do anything selfish. Put everyone else first, yourself second, even to giving your life for others, as Lance did.

NUMBER 5: Live your life respecting and helping others on a daily basis. Consider all people your brothers and sisters. Treat everyone well, and that includes enemies. Lance didn't hold grudges against or hate his captors. Make forgiveness your middle name.

NUMBER 6: Have the habit and attitude of always being positive. Negative things come up, but look for ways to handle them, overcome them and turn them around. Meanwhile, keep a good attitude and relish the challenge.

NUMBER 7: Build trust with your brothers and sisters by not lying. Stay honest your whole life. It results in solid friendships. People will be able to count on you. Lance refused to answer questions with lies to stop the interrogation and torture.

When we asked him why he wouldn't make up a cover story, he simply said, "I don't lie."

NUMBER 8: Maintain close relationships with your family: your mother, your father, your brothers and sisters, your relatives. Find opportunities to thank them for all they've done for you, especially your parents. Don't allow any grudges in your mind or heart. Always stay open and maintain communication with your family. This is the foundation to build your life on. And, in turn, pass on to your children a solid family life for their foundation.

NUMBER 9: Practice your faith always. Attend church regularly. Pray often. Be serious about your religion. This is by far the most important thing you can do. It is much more important than being strong physically or mentally. Sincere spiritual strength allows superior performance under any circumstances. It was the basis of Lance's triumph.

NUMBER 10: Finally, be joyful and happy regardless of circumstances. Maintain a cheerful mind and heart. Smile always. Who wants to be around a complainer or a whiner or a gloom and doom type? Would you want your men to behave like that? Or your commander? How about your wife or husband or parents or children? Lance never complained even once. Be happy no matter the situation to make this world better for those around you. Consider this a moral duty.

Conclusion:

Now a few thoughts about the situation here of each of you.

YOUR TRAINING IS LIKE LANCE'S

Lance graduated from this school. He played on the football team. He walked the halls and attended classes in the same classrooms you do. He was a normal cadet just like you are.

Then he graduated, became a fighter pilot and died in prison camp after an outstanding resistance. He first escaped and was recaptured, then refused to jeopardize his fellow soldiers by giving the enemy any information at all. He died as a result of severe torture and was awarded the *Medal of Honor* for his bravery.

It takes self-discipline and integrity to live up to this standard. It takes fidelity to do your best at all times. He was only in his twenties when he died. He was obedient to Major Bob Craner, our commander, and gave his life for all of us during seventy-five days of terrible pain and suffering. This proved his character like nothing else ever could. It was heroic love of friends and country.

Few of you will ever be tested like that. But you should all be as ready as he was. If you are, you will have great confidence in this life. You will never be worried about anything. You can take anything in the world if you are prepared.

The training starts here. The motivation is to defend the families of this country. Your goal should be to uphold the honor of being a military officer.

YOU ARE RESPECTED

Your situation is similar to being the captain of a police force in a city. As an officer, your conduct will have a great influence on many lives. People will be looking up to you for the rest of your life, like it or not. There is no possible excuse for not fulfilling the responsibilities the nation honors you with.

Even in adverse circumstances, everything can be done correctly. Being tired or hungry or in pain and letting it affect performance is wrong. Life is not about excuses. Everything should be done with the best effort and patient perseverance through difficulties. You are tested in training here and the tests will continue in normal life and during combat. You must react well consistently. Your responses in tough situations will mirror the responses you learned in training. And don't ever stop being positive or ever complain or ever let a smile leave your face.

The officers and cadets responsible for training at the Academy are developing military officers in a way proven to result in both the best combat leaders and the best leaders in peacetime service preparing for the next war. It is important the response to them is with your max effort. Trust them. Do exactly as you are told.

Learn well, because the way you train is the way you will fight.

I believe you will do your job well in war and for the rest of your life because the training here is outstanding. It will be instinct. You won't even have to worry about it. It comes with the habit of performing well as expected here. Rejoice, you're already a lot tougher than you realize.

Remember, the most important character trait that everyone must have to be a good follower or a good leader is doing the right thing day by day. Whether or not the world recognizes it, you will know you have done your best and will have the peace that results.

Lance had it, and you can too.

Please accept my kindest regards for each of you and your families, wherever they are. I am sure I am speaking on behalf of Lance and his family when I ask you to know that Lance's life was not wasted. He knew what this life was meant for, and that is to love and serve his fellow man by being the best soldier he could be.

Thank you in advance for your service. I sincerely hope and pray that God blesses it in every way.

Thank you all for coming to remember this special soldier that I will always love.

Good night.

10

HEROIC LOVE OF COUNTRY

Bud Day, Leo Thorsness at Goodfellow AFB, San Angelo, Texas, May 7, 2010

TALK NARRATIVE: Very few men have been awarded the Medal of Honor by the United States of America. If you read about their exploits, it is obvious why so many have been awarded posthumously.

It was my great honor to personally know three of these men, Lance Sijan, Bud Day and Leo Thorsness. The story of Lance Sijan is in Chapter IX. Colonel Bud Day was the founder of the MISTY Fast FAC F-100 Unit and was a POW in North Vietnam for more than five years. He escaped from his captors, was shot twice, recaptured, and severely tortured.

COLONEL GEORGE E. "BUD" DAY, U.S.A.F., MEDAL OF HONOR

Colonel Leo Thorsness was one of the now legendary "Wild Weasel" pilots who pioneered the airborne fight by fighter aircraft against and the destruction of ground-based SAM (Surface to Air) Missile Units in North Vietnam. This deadly cat and mouse game attracted many of our finest fighter pilots. His heroic rescue of his wingman while fighting off more than five MIG fighters single-handedly and shooting down two of them deep in enemy territory is still a model of courage today.

COLONEL LEO KEITH THORSNESS, U.S.A.F., MEDAL OF HONOR

The Air Force made the decision to dedicate two buildings on Goodfellow Air Force Base (AFB) in San Angelo, Texas, to these men. One was to be called "Day Manor" and the other "Thorsness Manor."

This speech was the keynote given in San Angelo to more than five hundred Military Officers from Goodfellow AFB and Faculty members of San Angelo University at a dinner in honor of Bud Day and Leo Thorsness.

It gives me great satisfaction to talk tonight about:

Heroic Love of Country

Long ago there was a war on the other side of the world.

There brave men fought and died to keep America free.

It was a war of an odd kind, for our country had not officially declared war.

It was part of a much wider struggle of resisting communist aggression throughout the world.

Our soldiers were there to resist, not to win. Many died obeying rules of fighting designed to avoid a new and much deadlier worldwide nuclear war with the entire communist block, led by an evil Soviet Empire, the U.S.S.R.

It was just a civil war, so the communists said, and according to them the United States and everyone else should stay out of it.

The country of Vietnam had been divided into two parts, a north and a south zone.

The northern zone, North Vietnam, was ruled by a typical communist government.

The southern zone, South Vietnam, was free.

The northern zone was aggressively trying to invade and conquer the southern zone to force communist rule on them.

America chose to try to defend the south from the unwanted enslavement.

The communist countries of the entire world were all united in supporting North Vietnam in their aggression every way they could.

The United States, however, stood almost alone against this onslaught with very little help from anyone for over ten years, if you include the special operations war that started in the early '60s. This means that none of the countries of Europe helped us. We had some help from South Korea and Australia, and that was about it.

This undeclared war continued with millions of soldiers fighting on each side year after year. Many died daily.

Two of the soldiers that were part of this war are here today. They were men of exceptional valor. They sacrificed and risked everything for the freedom which our country enjoys.

These two men were pilots fighting in the air. They flew fighter planes that fought enemy fighters piloted by the best Russian and East German pilots of the Soviet Empire. In the first year of the air war, virtually every North Vietnamese fighter pilot was killed by our Air and Naval forces. From then on, we were fighting the cream of the crop of the Russian and East German fighter pilots. The language of the North Vietnamese air defense forces, both on the ground and in the air, was Russian.

They also contended with literally hundreds of thousands of anti-aircraft guns and missiles manned by the very best soldiers the communist world could array against them. When I was in Vietnam, our intelligence said there were between 150,000 and 180,000 radar-directed anti-aircraft cannon of 37mm caliber or higher. These air defenses included the latest Russian Surface to Air Missiles (SAMs) with the best Russian military crews servicing them.

These men we honor tonight were among those dedicated to resisting the communist aggressors with all their hearts and skills.

Both men were shot down. Both men became prisoners of war. Both men were tortured extensively for years and without any apparent end in sight. Junior officers were generally tortured far less than the senior officers as senior officers possessed more sensitive information. It was the junior officers that sometimes were put into cells with other POWs, but rarely the senior officers.

These men here tonight were kept in solitary confinement and severely tortured over and over again. Both men spent over five years in this communist prison hell.

These two men were each awarded the highest medal our country has to offer for their heroic efforts in this war for freedom.

One can read their stories and reflect on their incredible performance against all odds. But no one can relive or really understand what these men went through to be awarded the Medal of Honor by our county's President on their return. This knowledge and understanding is theirs and theirs alone.

The Medal of Honor is very special indeed. In fact, most service members who have been awarded it for their brave actions in combat did not survive to receive it. They proved their love of country with the gift of their lives. The greatest love is to give up one's life for another. Both men risked their lives many times over for love of us so that we could be free.

It is one thing to let people shoot at you for an hour or a day, but it is a different game when it is a constant battle over many months or years. These men honored here tonight were professional soldiers in extensive combat. It is not the pretended action of a movie set that lasts for an hour or two. Between them they fought in four wars and they were under heavy fire on numerous occasions to complete their missions.

Men of love

Men of Heroic Love

This is fact, not fiction. These two men thought only of defending our country, and were always willing to go with their lives on the line.

I'd like to ask how many in this audience today have fought in combat? Please raise your hands.

How many have been shot at?

How many have been wounded or have been taken prisoner and tortured by the enemy because of obeying the military code of conduct?

Well, we can see there are only a few. Really, there are relatively few people in the entire country with those experiences.

Now, of these few, how many were awarded the *Medal of Honor* for serving their country in an exceptionally outstanding way, confirmed and witnessed by their fellow soldiers?

There are only two here, Bud Day and Leo Thorsness. We are fortunate that they are able to be with us this evening and we are honored to be in the presence of these living legends of patriotism.

Let us all give these men a round of applause showing our thanks and appreciation.

Freedom! This is why these men fought. This is why these men suffered. Freedom! This is why these men risked death day after day.

We have freedom today because these men did what they did long ago in that far off land and because of all the other soldiers who fought there and around the world for the same cause.

Our country is free. The Vietnam war lasted many years and many gave up their lives. It was a part of the war of resistance to world-wide communism and in this regard it was a war well fought and it was a war won. Communism was defeated in Vietnam and held at bay worldwide for all the years our military fought there.

The Vietnam War was a terrible financial drain on the Soviet Union, the leader of the communist world, the real threat to the United States of America and the citizens of our country. This effect is rarely appreciated even today and was unknown to us during the fighting of that war.

Who knows what our lives would be like now if the Korean War, the Vietnam War and the special operations war against the Russians in Afghanistan had not been waged half way around the world for more than twenty-five years?

Who knows what would have happened if our men and women had not been stationed in great numbers in Europe and many other places at forward military bases, well-trained and poised to fight hard if the communist armies moved even a mile into free territory?

What was the result of all this resistance over thirty years?

Well, does the Soviet Union still exist? No, it does not.

Are we still standing free? Yes, we are.

Studies by the best Soviet Communist experts since the fall of the Soviet Union and our victory in the cold war are very revealing. They have shown that the weakening of world-wide Communism was directly due to the financial drain and subsequent financial bankruptcy of the Soviet Union caused by the fighting in Vietnam and Afghanistan. They simply had to give up. They couldn't stay with us. And so they dissolved their empire.

We should never forget this truth; that the open struggles in Korea and Vietnam by our regular military and the clandestine fight in Afghanistan by our Special Operations Forces were in large part responsible for the dissolution of the Soviet Empire. It was a great victory in the fight against communist slavery worldwide.

That fight still goes on, but communism has been greatly weakened.

These two men here tonight were a part of all those fighting forces who have defended our country in far-off lands to keep our country free. We are free only because of the great price paid by such men.

The same bloody currency is being paid now and will always be necessary. There are still communist countries and many other ideologies after our country's land and wealth. This fact will never change. We must always have brave soldiers willing to defend our shores and keep us free.

"BETTER DEAD THAN RED" was an old saying that everyone used to know in this country.

These two men believed it, they lived it, and they fought in numerous wars so that our own country could remain free. They have been true to this fight to this very day, fighting effectively in different ways during peacetime. Their entire lives testify to their character and commitment.

They stood out because of their heroic love, so great and unselfish that they were ready to die and nearly did die many times for love of our country and its citizens.

And who are we?

We are America.
We are all brothers and sisters in this regard.
We are the American family.

There is no other family like this one on the face of the earth. For we really and truly love our freedom to the extent of being ready and willing to die to keep that freedom.

These two men are our American brothers.
They show us the way to be, the way to live.
They suffered through very hard times to protect all of us.
They resisted enemy tortures in those dark prison cells, not for a day, but for endless painful years. It seemed they would have to do so until their death twelve thou-

sand miles from home and family, with little hope of ever returning. Yet they still chose dedicated resistance rather than treason or any compromise.

They endured terrible tortures rather than give the enemy any information about their fellow soldiers, or any propaganda for use against our country.

They lived each day with the purpose and motivation of keeping our country free.

And they succeeded because they returned to this land and have lived here ever since then with their American family in freedom. And this was due in significant part to the sacrifices they themselves made. Can you imagine the peace of mind they must have?

These men excelled in love of country at least as much as anyone who has ever served in the military forces of the United States of America.

They deserve the honor that is given to them today.

In my book, they deserve any honor they receive.

For as long as America stays free, these men should be honored for their contribution.

We can all be in awe of their heroic love.

We can learn from their example to always be ready to sacrifice for our American brothers and sisters to preserve our freedom.

So that we and our descendants are also free to live in this great country and:

So we can freely raise our families here
can work where we want to
can live where we wish to
can worship as we choose to
can speak as we'd like to
can pursue happiness
and so we can be free to love others as these men have.

May the God who has raised up these two men and instilled in their hearts this great love,

Who has given us all our freedom by his Love,

Be thanked and honored by the beautiful witness and wonderful love of these two men now and for as long as our country flies the flag of freedom.

AMEN

Postscript:

Lance Sijan, the Wild Weasel pilots like Leo Thorsness, the *MISTY* pilots like Bud Day and the other Air Force, Navy and Marine pilots I fought with, the Naval and Air Rescue Forces that saved my life, the US Army Special Forces and the Airborne Infantry of the 173rd Airborne Brigade were the finest men and groups of men I have ever known in my life. First in combat and then in prison camp, I believe that the sentiments expressed in *Sijan's Code* were lived almost perfectly by these men. It was their character which impressed me so much, and I had many years as a POW to reflect on this. Nothing in my life since has changed that opinion. I thank God for the honor to have been associated with such men. I am confident that in Heaven, God will give them His approval for *a fight well worth fighting and a fight well fought.*

COLONELS BUD DAY AND LEO THORSNESS AT SAN ANGELO, TEXAS, DURING THE DEDICATION CEREMONIES OF BUILDINGS IN THEIR HONOR AT SAN ANGELO AFB.

Thorsness Manor, San Angelo AFB

Day Manor, San Angelo AFB

BUD DAY'S WIFE OF MORE THAN FIFTY YEARS, DORIS DAY.
BEHIND EVERY GREAT MAN....

LEO THORSNESS' WIFE OF MORE THAN FIFTY YEARS, MAYLEE THORSNESS.
BEHIND EVERY GREAT MAN...

Some People Dream the Dream...
Some People Live the Dream...
Some People Defend the Dream...

GOD BLESS THE DEFENDERS!
Erich Anderson
http://www.veterantributes.org/

I like to see a man proud of the place in which he lives,
I like to see a man live so that his place will be proud of him.
Abraham Lincoln

"Review the great scenes of history: you will find mankind has always been obliged to pay dear for the blessings they enjoyed... The struggles of a great people have almost always ended in the establishment of liberty.... Such a people are spoken of with admiration by all future ages...." "Their souls glow with gratitude for the virtue and self-denial of their forefathers. They consider them as patterns for their own conduct on similar occasions and are continually pointing them out to the reverence and imitation of their children. These are the glorious effects of patriotism and virtue. These are the rewards annexed to the faithful discharge of that great and honorable duty, fidelity to our country.... I pray to God that the fair character I have described may be that of America to the latest ages."
James Iredell, May 1, 1778

James Iredell was one of the first Justices of the Supreme Court of the United States of America, appointed by President George Washington.

This page blank

11

RELIGIOUS FREEDOM RALLY

TALK NARRATIVE:
The Capital, Upper Senate Park, Washington, DC.
June 8, 2012

Good afternoon, ladies and gentlemen. My name is Guy Gruters. I have been asked to give a few words on religious freedom because of the fact that I was a POW more than five years in North Vietnam. I was a fighter pilot with more than 400 combat missions. My plane was hit numerous times, I was shot down twice and captured the second time. I was tortured. I was beaten. I was treated very harshly.

There was no religious freedom there. I was even tortured when they caught me praying on my knees in my cell. I know the absolute evil of atheistic socialist government by experience.

I fought in Vietnam. I fought for this country's freedom and the freedom of the wonderful people of Vietnam. Now I am fighting for the religious freedom of our country here with you in our Nation's Capital. I would never have believed this was ever going to be necessary when I was in prison camp long ago.

Many other air crewmen were shot down and not rescued, over 3,500 of them. But only 472 of us returned from North Vietnam. The rest were tortured to death or killed in one way or another by the Russians and North Vietnamese Communists. Six out of seven died there. They gave their lives for this country so that we could be here today speaking freely of our beliefs and rights.

We went to war to fight socialism, also called communism, a movement in the world that has the goal of making the world one. They call it a "One World Order," or the "New World Order" or the "International Brotherhood of Man" or the "Comintern." To establish this one-world dictatorship, they know that all religion must be eliminated. This is because they can't have one government for the entire world with ruthless immoral policies if people have religion. To have a religion, a person has to believe in what his or her religion stands for or believes is true. This will not work from the one world government's standpoint. Religion cannot be accepted by such a government, because all must accept the one-world government itself as god and as being all-powerful and able to torture and kill and imprison anyone or anything else it wants to do.

So you see, we must realize that we are still fighting the same enemy that I was fighting when I was in Vietnam. We are fighting communism, i.e., socialism. Today they don't call it that, because communism and socialism have been too greatly discredited. So they have new names for it, i.e., "modernism" or "democratic socialism," or "internationalism" or "being progressive" or the "new world order," etc. It is all the same pure evil, a one-world all-powerful dictatorship by a ruthless, atheistic or agnostic ruling elite. It always gains power by promising to take care of the poor or workers or the downtrodden or the middle class or all groupings or citizens with cradle to the grave care by its "benevolent" government socialism. It promises everything to everybody. The citizens of nations don't realize its tyranny and horror until it is too late.

And its first step in each country it takes over is always to eliminate religion.

But remember, our country was founded because of religious persecution just such as this. Most of the immigrants came here because of religious persecution in their own lands. Human nature is such that people want to control others and if a person has their own religious beliefs then the person is hard to control. Ruthless dictatorships have always hated sincere believers. This is nothing new. It has been going on since the beginning.

Having faith is having certain beliefs, for this is what faith is, that is, to believe in what you personally believe is true and factual. This is why a Christian is different than a Jew, and both are different than a Muslim. God has allowed many religious beliefs to surface in this country and around the world. This makes it hard for those who desire to control and rule as tyrants.

Our Country is different than most. It is focused on freedom and liberty for all. This is especially the case in regards to how one believes from a religious standpoint. Our country has lasted and endured based on this key principle of freedom for over two hundred years. It is so important that it is even the very first of the *Bill of Rights* guaranteed to all citizens of our country.

There are some who want to change all this and so they have put pressure in a deceptive way to accomplish this. We must not let these steps be taken. If we do, our freedom, the basis of our country's government, will be shaken. Our country as we know it will fall.

Any law that results in a person's religious rights being taken from them is a law that should not be passed. Any politicians that try to underhandedly pass laws against religious freedom are not Americans. They have other motives. They have goals other than the goals of the people of this country.

What are we to do? We have to keep doing what we have been doing for the last 40 years or so in regards to the killing of unborn children. We have had to protest and speak out and tell all that abortion is wrong. We can't let down our efforts in this regard. The Bishops will tell us what we have to do about the new laws. The Bishops are our leaders. We must support them completely. This includes praying for them all the time as well as perfect obedience. We have to stay united and fight this war that is waging right here in our country. For as Holy Scripture states, a Christian has to be the salt of the earth and it also states that a Christian has to be the light of the world...

We must speak out now. We must fight for our freedoms in any way we can here in our country with our words and protests, and on foreign lands when necessary with our weapons and lives.

Let us defend our freedom. Let us make our words heard. Let us fight the wars we must. For we have our rights that if not defended, will be taken from us.

Our Forefathers knew this. We must return to their beliefs, not adopt new beliefs of so-called "patriotic" politicians of these times. Many of these so-called politicians desire something that is not what the American people will to have. Our government seems to think it is better to be part of a one-world government than to be a free and independent nation. This is what they appear to be working towards in every sneaky and underhanded way they can. This is why they must crush religious freedom in this country.

Again, the whole approach of totalitarian socialist rule is to have all subservient to the government, the exact opposite of what our forefathers willed. They established our Constitution between the government and the people, delegating only limited powers to the government and reserving important, key rights for each citizen. It is what we fought for in Vietnam and all our other wars.

The Constitution states that the government is to be ruled by the people, not that the government is god and can do whatever it wants to.

The Constitution states we are to have religious freedom, not forced atheism, or forced worship of the government bureaucracy.

The Constitution states that we are to be one nation under God, not one state under a one-world government, i.e., the United Nations or some other such pathetic Tower of Babel.

We must see the light. We must expose the truth. Our country is in danger of losing its freedom by trying to become a part of what is called the "new world order," which is just a new way of speaking about the "international brotherhood of man," in other words, a communist world dictatorship.

Everyone thinks communism/socialism has fallen with the fall of the Berlin Wall. Very clever, these socialists who now call themselves by any name except communists or socialists. Well, clearly it has not. To believe this, we only need to consider that we are here speaking about religious freedom because our government is trying to take it away. And the reason is so that our country can become more a part of the all-powerful new world socialist dictatorship.

The government is not God. The government is not above the people. The government is below the people. The people don't serve the government. The government serves the people. We are one nation of fifty states. We are not one country of the "new world order." we never signed up for that. It is not in the Constitution. There is no consent of the American people for a world government.

The problem is that the present government is stepping out of its bounds. It wills domination and power over the American people. It does not want to serve. It wants to be served. Our government wants to reduce the people to obedient servants. Our government wants everyone to always do what the government wills. But this will never work if the government's will is against what a person believes, especially one's religious beliefs. People will resist.

So our government is now making laws that conflict with religious beliefs because it wants to rule and have absolute power. It wants to rule our very thoughts, lives and souls.

Again, it is stepping over its bounds. The government exists to serve us, to insure the freedom for each citizen to believe in what they will to believe in, especially from a religious standpoint.

When the laws our government make conflict with religious beliefs, they are un-patriotic laws. They violate the constitution that has established the government in the first place.

They violate the constitution that allows them to exist, to govern us.

They better be careful. We might just fire them for their arrogant power-seeking and replace them with those that serve us as we wish them to.

I stand here today as a man that represents all veterans of past wars. I stand here to speak for all those men and women who gave up their lives or were wounded in wars. I speak for each of them to say:

"You leaders of our government, you listen to us, the people. We value our free-dom and we want our freedom back and we want it maintained. We don't want laws passed that take our freedom away. We want America to be independent of a ruthless international government. We believe in what our constitution states. Not in some new world government plan.

Our land is below our feet. Our land is God's Country. Our land has been kept free by the soldiers who have fought for freedom from the very beginning. They have all fought for our rights and one of those rights is to believe in whatever religion we de-sire to believe in.

So everyone in our government, all you political leaders out there, especially those who are one-world dictator wannabes in sheep's clothing, listen and listen well:

If your proposed laws conflict with religious beliefs, then they are wrong. They are unconstitutional. They are against our country. Therefore they must not be made into laws of our country. Do not justify them just to bring our country under the domi-nation of internationalism. We don't want it in any way, shape or form.

This is the same proposed one world government that Stalin and Lenin proposed. That's why you don't dare tell the American people what you are up to.

We are Americans. Don't tread on us. We are free and we desire to be free now and forever. We desire to be one nation with one flag, the one we fought for, the one that uniquely stands for freedom. None other. And that's it to my right. Its colors are red, white and blue.

You politicians who dream of a world government where America is just one part of it, you go ahead and leave the country. You are not Americans. You are power-hungry idealists. Go live where you will. But do not impose your will on us. For we are Americans. We are united with and to our brothers and sisters of this nation and we desire religious freedom and all the other freedoms that our constitution guarantees us."

Thank you, and may God bless America.

"No one can rejoice more than I do at every step the people of this great country take to preserve the Union, establish good order and government, and to render the nation happy at home and respectable abroad. No country upon earth ever had it more in its power to attain these blessings than United America. Wondrously strange then, and much to be regretted indeed would it be, were we to neglect the means, and to depart from the road which Providence has pointed us, so plainly; I cannot believe it will ever come to pass. The Great Governor of the Universe has led us too long and too far on the road to happiness and glory, to forsake us in the midst of it. By folly and improper conduct, proceeding from a variety of causes, we may now and then get bewildered; but I hope and trust that there is good sense and virtue enough left to recover the right path before we shall be entirely lost."
George Washington, June 29, 1788

"To the kindly influence of Christianity we owe that degree of civil freedom, and political and social happiness which mankind now enjoys. In proportion as the genuine effects of Christianity are diminished in any nation, either through unbelief, or the corruption of its doctrines, or the neglect of its institutions; in the same proportion will the people of that nation recede from the blessings of genuine freedom, and approximate the miseries of complete despotism."

"All efforts to destroy the foundations of our holy religion, ultimately tend to the subversion also of our political freedom and happiness."

"Whenever the pillars of Christianity shall be overthrown, our present republican forms of government, and all the blessings which flow from them, must fall with them."

Jedediah Morse, 1799

Jedediah Morse was an excellent geographer whose textbooks became a staple in the United States. He was known as the "father of American geography." He was also the father of telegraphy pioneer and painter Samuel F.B. Morse. (Wikipedia)

12 PRISON, LEADERSHIP, TEAMWORK

Previous Page: Colonel Robbie Risner, Commander, 4th Allied POW Wing, North Vietnam, on his release from Prison Camp in 1973. Official USAF Photo, Edwards AFB Photo Gallery.

TALK NARRATIVE: On a trip to visit my son, Ryan, in Virginia, I met a VMI faculty member in Lexington, Virginia, Colonel R.C.L. The Colonel was in charge of a ROTC program at VMI and asked if a speech would be possible on the conditions and torture experienced in prison camp and the combat leadership I had witnessed. On a beautiful day in November of 2003, after a wonderful tour of the VMI campus and the monuments to General Stonewall Jackson of the Confederate Army, I addressed the VMI Cadets. The picture on the cover of this book was taken during this talk.

VIRGINIA MILITARY INSTITUTE

In the military services, VMI graduates hold a special place of honor and respect. It's a pleasure to be here.

I will address three aspects of the POW experience; conditions, torture and leadership.

Part 1. CONDITONS

IN THE CELLS

We were confined in small cells with concrete walls, tin roofs, and barred, solid doors without windows. There was no way to see outside except through the crack under the cell door.

There was no exercise and no leaving the cells. The door only opened briefly to take in food twice daily, to put the waste bucket we called the "crap bucket" or "honey bucket" outside in the morning, when taken for interrogations, and when taken once a week for washing ourselves to another cell with a concrete tank of water.

POSSESSIONS

Our beds were sawhorses with five boards across them. The cells had concrete floors. No way to sweep or dust. We were able to wash out our cell one time in five years. We had a one-liter water container and a metal cup made out of the aluminum from a U.S. fighter plane. We had a small hand towel, the same one for five years. We were issued a little bar of soap about every six months. It was only enough to clean key body parts when we were given a bucket of wash water once a week. The sawhorse bed, the cup, a toothbrush, a tube of pathetic toothpaste, the liter container, the towel, two pair of pajamas, a pair of "Ho Chi Minh" sandals made from tires and the soap were the substance of our possessions in prison camp.

Everything was filthy; the cell, our body, the towel and the clothes. We tried to rinse them as best we could when we were taken to wash each week. We lived in dirty conditions.

FOOD FILTHY WITH LIVING THINGS

The food was two little loaves of white flour bread a day. The bread was sometimes as hard as a rock and full of mold. The loaves were riddled with rat droppings. There was a rat dropping in almost every cubic centimeter. They could not be remeoved. So to eat the bread it was necessary to eat the rat droppings. Unfortunately, many different parasites are in rat droppings. There were also all kinds of worms and weevils in the bread. Some of the weevils or worms were very tough and fairly large. We would bite into the bread and the worms would bite us in the inside of the mouth. They would bite hard. Then we would bite the worms and kill them and eat them. I did not mind that because I knew enough to know that white flour was not enough to live on. Some kind of nutrition was necessary. I knew the worms had a lot of different things in them so I was happy to get them.

ALWAYS THIRSTY

We had a little jug of water which was filled twice daily. This was two liters of water daily. The water was boiled, but there were hundreds of dead worms that could just barely be seen. We drank worms every time we took a drink. We were very thirsty, especially in the summertime. I think the extreme thirst was the worst aspect of the living conditions, even worse than the constant hunger pains.

SICKNESS

Due to the extreme deprivation and unsanitary conditions, we had a number of illnesses. For example, like everyone I knew of, I suffered with dysentery for two and a half years. I also had *Dengue Fever*. It was so painful that it was worse than torture. After the first day or two of that disease, I thought I was going to die. After the third, fourth, fifth and sixth day, I thought, "Now I can understand why sick people say they want to die. It is because the pain is so bad." My head felt like it was going to burst, not for an hour, but for days in a row. There was wicked pain throughout my entire body. They call *Dengue Fever* the "broken bones disease." It feels as if every bone in the body is broken and the body is exploding from the inside out. It didn't kill my cellmate and myself, but it came very close.

TOILET PAPER A JOKE

We were told to use a rough brown paper for "toilet paper" that simply did not work. More importantly, my cellmate and I were only given about one sheet a month, so we never had enough, especially with our constant diarrhea. Later on an interrogator let slip that our guard was stealing most of the toilet paper allotted to us. Our only choice was to use our fingers. But we had no water except two liters of drinking water each day, which was not even enough to satisfy our thirst. This meant the only way to clean our fingers and hands was to wipe them on the concrete walls. So it was impossible to clean our hands adequately and we had to eat bread with them twice a day.

It turned out there were a lot of parasite eggs both in the rat droppings in the bread and in our own excrement on our hands.

BUCKET OVERFLOW

Our bathroom was a bucket of limited capacity. The bucket was used all day and night and emptied each morning. The guard would come and take the locking beams off the door. Then they would open it and the POW(s) would place the bucket outside. The guard would close the door. They would do that for all the cells in whichever camp we were in, whether in Hanoi or somewhere else. Then the POW(s) in one of the cells would be let out to go around and gather the buckets and carry them down to the old French-built latrine. This was really just a hole in the ground. The buckets would be emptied and the empty buckets would be placed back in front of the cells. Then the guard would come around again, open every door, and that cell's POW(s) would fetch the bucket and put it back in the cell.

Procedures such as these insured that each cell was kept absolutely isolated, which the communists desired to make sure we never saw, talked to or were friendly with another POW in the camp. This made interrogations more effective and resistance more difficult.

In the wintertime in our cell, and in many of the cells, the bucket would overflow because the waste would exceed its capacity. It was large enough in the summer, but in the winter it would overflow for months. We had no way to clean it up. We were allowed to clean the floor of our cell with water one time in five years. We lived with raw sewage on the floor. This was in addition to the worms and bugs we ate and the rat droppings in the bread. The rats were pervasive up there.

ENDLESS RATS INSIDE AND OUTSIDE THE CELL. USED WITH PERMISSION FROM *Prisoner of War*, BY MIKE MCGRATH

So little creatures started living and reproducing in us.

PARASITES

After a couple of years, parasites became visible, including tapeworms of over twenty feet long coming out our bottoms.

WORMS CRAWL FROM MOUTH

After three years, one day I was talking to my commander and he coughed as he was speaking. About 4 inches of a big worm came out of his mouth. I said, "Cough again, Al," and I grabbed the worm and said, "Cough, cough." He coughed and I pulled out a worm a full twelve inches in length. It looked like a big artificial fishing worm, but it was moving. It was about 3/8 inch in thickness and more than ½ inch wide. It looked as if made of rubber, but was an intestinal worm. I had it grasped in my hand and both it's ends were wiggling.

Al started coughing again. "Keep coughing, Al, keep coughing, tickle your throat." He did. Over the next fifteen minutes I pulled a dozen of these things out. I had them held them in my hand. This was right out of a horror movie, except it was real life. I said, "Great Al, that's good!" "Al, we got those suckers out of there. I'm glad they're not inside anymore." That's what I said. Meanwhile, I'm thinking, "Lord, how can we fight this? What can we do about this?"

BUCKET OF WORMS

We had hunger pains because there was so little food. But one morning a POW in my cell named George (name changed) didn't eat. None of us could afford not to eat. We had lost too much weight already. Because of the conditions, some men would stop eating and when they did, they died. So I was very concerned.

I said, "George, you didn't eat any food."
He said, "Yeah, I don't feel like it, but I'll eat some this afternoon."
I said. "Okay."
But he didn't eat in the afternoon.
"George!" I said.
He said, "Guy, I'll eat in the morning, I will eat tomorrow."
The next morning he didn't eat.
"George, what's happening?"

He said, "I just don't feel like eating, I'll eat this afternoon."

"Really?"

He said, "Yeah," because he knew what I was worried about.

He didn't eat in the afternoon. "George!"

He said, "Tomorrow morning." This would be the third day. "I will eat tomorrow for sure."

The next day he didn't eat.

"George, we have to talk."

He said, "Guy, I really don't feel like eating. I can't eat."

"What's wrong?"

"I'm just so full."

I said, "Well, we can handle that, maybe if you tickle your throat it could free everything up."

He tickled his throat over one of the buckets and filled it up about an inch and a half with thousands of these little white, intestinal worms. He was so full of worms that he literally couldn't eat.

COULD NOT WORRY AND LIVE

When we saw these parasites in each other and in ourselves and the results they caused, we had to stop focusing on thoughts of them. We tried to protect our mind from many things, like thoughts of the worms, interrogations, torture and men disappearing from the camps who never came back. We couldn't think of or worry about negative things over which we had no control and still keep our sanity.

HOT, COLD AND BORED

The cells were hot in the summertime. My cellmate and I were in a tin roofed building with no ventilation (no windows and a solid door). We were on the south side of the cellblock under direct sun. We spent the summers lying on the concrete floor, breathing through the crack under the door. This was to get one hundred degree air from the outside because it was so much hotter inside. During the summer we didn't care if we were cold for the rest of our lives, but please, no more heat.

CELL INSPECTION. USED WITH PERMISSION FROM *Prisoner of War*, BY MIKE McGRATH

The winter temperature lows were in the 30's and 40's in North Vietnam. With one blanket and a couple of pair of pajamas, this was cold. We huddled under the blanket as often as we could. We would wear both pair of pajamas all winter long. This was not enough to stop the shivering. We shivered for days and sometimes weeks at a time.

In the summer, we prayed with all our hearts for it to be cold, and assured God that we would never complain about it being cold again, if He would get rid of the heat. In the winter, we prayed for it to be hot, and assured God that we would never complain about it being hot again, if He would get rid of the cold.

So our prayer would switch about every six months. There was never a break from the heat or the cold for weeks at a time. No hot drinks or heater in the winter; no cold drinks, air conditioning or cool breezes in the summer. I have never in my life been as hot or cold before or since.

As typical Americans, both in the United States and during combat, we were constantly involved in activities and completing our mission. There was never an idle moment. It was fulfilling flying close to the ground in heavy anti-aircraft fire and knocking out trucks supplying the enemy army in South Vietnam. I was in an outstanding unit, every man a volunteer. We were full of pride in who we were and what we were doing. But we rarely had time to think or pray.

We went from that environment to being in a cell with absolutely no contact with the world. It was perfectly still and quiet. This inactivity and resultant boredom was tough to handle. There was no entertainment; no books, no television, no radio, no windows, no ability to go outside. Locked in the cell for 24/7 year after year alone or with one other POW at the most, it was an extreme shock to our minds.

WHAT MOON LANDING?
There was no way to know what was going on in the outside world. No news whatsoever for year after year. We didn't find out about the Moon landing until two years after it occurred.

WHAT FAMILY?
It looked like we would live the rest of our lives up there in those conditions, with no knowledge of our families or anything else ever again. For the first two and one half years, we were not allowed to receive any letter or any other communication from our wives or relatives, and not allowed to send any letter with word that we were alive.

TURNED FROM WITHOUT TO WITHIN
We finally learned to be self-sufficient within ourselves by asking God for help and becoming close to Him in prayer. This took more than a year and was a wrenching transition.

But this resulted in great peace and joy even in prison camp. I believe anyone can obtain this peace and joy by simple prayer to God. It took prison camp to rearrange many of my values. So I thank God for having me shot down and having my pride humiliated.

PRIDE DECREASED

Prison camp inexorably beat into my head the truth I was expendable. I was young and strong then like you are now. And also like you, I had always been able to fix any problems I faced. But in prison camp, I was helpless to change the horror. This was a humbling revelation for a 25-year-old. There were many other consistent humiliations in a communist prison camp, for example, daily harsh treatment by the guards, interrogations and tortures, filthy food and hygiene, rats crawling all over us, parasites crawling out of us and a seemingly hopeless, endless existence without chance of escape in a living hell on earth.

GUY IN PRISON CAMP. NORTH VIETNAMESE FILE PHOTO FROM DOD

KICKED AROUND

The guards screaming at us and running us around the camp was also a different experience. They didn't speak English. They would use their feet or hands to give us the direction to go. I then understood what being "kicked around" or "slapped around" meant. A kick meant the guard wanted me to go a certain way. He indicated the direction by kicking me in that direction from behind. It was difficult to restrain a physical reaction. If anyone retaliated, it was the end of him. I wanted a chance to get back and rejoin my wife and children, so I controlled myself.

SURPRISE BLOW TO SOLAR PLEXUS. USED WITH PERMISSION FROM *Prisoner of War*, BY MIKE MCGRATH

KICKS TO KIDNEYS

Many of the POWs were in agony from taking severe kicks to the kidneys. The effects of the damage such as blood in the urine and terrible kidney pain lasted for years. It came and went like malaria. The communists would kick us all over our bodies during day-to-day abuse or during torture. They had no rules of basic humane treatment. For example, they reveled in clubbing and kicking the wounded on their wounds. Can you imagine what a broken bone feels like when it is clubbed and kicked?

USED WITH PERMISSION FROM *Prisoner of War*, BY MIKE MCGRATH

ONLY HOPE WAS GOD

We turned to God, because it was wrong to quit. Trusting in God gave us hope. Otherwise, we had no hope.

DID NOT DARE COMPLAIN

Some POWs stopped eating and died quickly, since we had lost so much weight already. We noticed this hopelessness because we were all tempted to it. Suicide was sometimes triggered by a bad torture or sickness but could also be triggered by somebody complaining. So we never complained.

ISOLATED FOR PROPAGANDA

As I mentioned, when in a little cell with another POW, it was never permitted to see anyone else in the other cells. Each one or two man cell was isolated so they could work on us individually with interrogations. They were always staging interrogations; one, two, three, four, five, six, seven, eight or more times a week for each POW.

INTERROGATIONS WERE OFTEN CONDUCTED WHILE A POW WAS ON HIS KNEES. AFTER SEVERAL HOURS, HIS KNEES BECAME FLATTENED, RED AND SWOLLEN. HERE, I HAVE DEPICTED A POW BEING FORCED TO WRITE AN "APOLOGY" TO THE CAMP COMMANDER FOR HIS "BAD ATTITUDE." IF QUICKER RESULTS WERE DESIRED, A SMALL ROCK WOULD BE PLACED UNDER EACH KNEE.

I ONCE SPENT 30 HOURS IN TWO DAYS ON MY KNEES AS PUNISHMENT BECAUSE A GUARD HAD CAUGHT ME PEEKING OUT OF MY ROOM THROUGH A FLOOR LEVEL VENT. USED WITH PERMISSION FROM *Prisoner of War*, BY MIKE MCGRATH

They tried to find weaknesses, tried to get us to agree with them, tried to get information from us, and tried to do something with us to use for propaganda. More important than military information to the communists was the use of POWs for propaganda, for example, to meet the sympathetic delegations from Europe and the United States. The communists used these people to carry their message back home to the States. They called them "useful idiots." They also had a Russian word for them meaning "crap-eaters," because these sympathizers believed their crap.

MANY MEN WERE FORCED BY TORTURE TO APPEAR BEFORE "PEACE DELEGATIONS" FROM THE UNITED STATES. A POW WOULD BE TORTURED UNTIL THE VIETNAMESE WERE SURE HE WOULD READ A PREPARED STATEMENT. THE STATEMENT MIGHT READ, "I HAVE RECEIVED LENIENT AND HUMANE TREATMENT FROM THE PEACE-LOVING VIETNAMESE."

IN THIS DRAWING, A POW TRIES TO SHOW A MEMBER OF THE DELEGATION THE UGLY ROPE BURNS AND SCARS ON HIS WRISTS. SHE IGNORES HIM BECAUSE SHE IS INTERESTED IN ONLY ONE THING — ANTI-UNITED STATES PROPAGANDA. USED WITH PERMISSION FROM *Prisoner of War*, BY MIKE McGRATH

That required considerable torture because we were just like the people here. I'm sure nobody here wants to be a traitor to the United States on some news network. POWs didn't want to do this in any way. They would take the torture to keep from being forced to proclaim propaganda. Hence the isolation of individual cells. They had to keep us isolated so they could work on us one at a time.

COMMUNICATION UNITES FOR THE FIGHT

A major part of the struggle was to unite all the POWs by communicating so we could resist as a unit. We developed many methods of communication.

This emphasis on communication so broadly implemented by the senior POWs in North Vietnam is a consistent characteristic of fine leadership. You are future leaders. Remember that communication is vital. It must be honest and this includes above all being honest about problems and failures. This means when people point them out, that there are no negative repercussions for them. Instead, thank them. Then you can make corrections to training and procedures both in wartime and/or peacetime.

THE TAP CODE THROUGH WALLS

Communicating was done primarily by the *tap code*. At first we started with Morse Code. Remember, there were 12 to 16 inch thick walls of stone and concrete between cells. With Morse code communication, this would be a dash and this would be a dot (Guy slowly tapped the dash and a dot on the podium to demonstrate). Even performed slowly it is hard to distinguish between them. But it was not done slowly. Communication with Morse code becomes extremely fast with practice and it became harder and harder to differentiate the dashes and the dots through the walls. By the time I arrived in December of 1967, a replacement had been found for Morse code. The new technique had spread rapidly throughout the camps.

One of the US CIA prisoners in North Vietnam had read a book about a prison camp in another war. The communication that had been used was to first make the alphabet a 25 letter alphabet by throwing out the letter K. If we wanted to transmit "K," we used the letter "C." Now the letters could be arranged in five rows and five columns. So the alphabet looked like this:

A B C D E
F G H I J
L M N O P
Q R S T U
V W X Y Z

For each letter, we would first tap the row of the letter, one through five. Then we tapped the column of the letter, one through five. We transmitted or tapped one letter at a time. So we could transmit "A" with tap, pause, tap. We could transmit "C" with tap pause tap, tap, tap. "F" was tap, tap, pause, tap. We could transmit any letter in the alphabet with two series of taps. Using this technique, it doesn't matter if it is a long tap or a short tap, which had been necessary but so difficult with Morse Code. Instead, each letter was simply two sequences of taps. This eliminated the confusion.

The session would begin when one cell would call up the other with a series of taps in the tune known as "shave and a haircut." The response by the adjoining cell was two taps (two bits). This meant he had his ear on the common wall ready to receive. The ear had to be on the wall to hear because the tapping was very lightly done. It had to be done quietly because the guards were always listening for these communications. When caught communicating, the punishment was generally two to three days and nights of torture.

COMMUNICATIONS WERE THE LIFELINES OF OUR COVERT CAMP ORGANIZATION. IT WAS ESSENTIAL FOR EVERYONE TO KNOW WHAT WAS HAPPENING IN CAMP, WHETHER THE NEWS WAS ABOUT A NEW TORTURE OR JUST A FRIENDLY WORD OF ENCOURAGEMENT TO A DISHEARTENED FELLOW POW.

THE PRIMARY MEANS OF COMMUNICATION WAS BY USE OF THE "TAP" CODE. THE CODE WAS A SIMPLE ARRANGEMENT OF THE ALPHABET INTO A 5 X 5 BLOCK.

So the transmitting POW on the wall tapped the first word. After the first word, he paused. The POW listening responded with a quick double tap, indicating he understood. If not, he tapped repeatedly five to ten times. Then the word was retransmitted until understood, that is, until the listener tapped the double tap. Then in the same way, each additional word was transmitted. This method provided for abbreviations and also for shortening of words if the listener understood what was coming because of the context of the sentence. For example, the transmitter came to a sentence with the word "because." He tapped for "B", then for "E" and then for "C" - but the listener would double-tap early meaning that he understood the whole word, so the transmitter could go on to the next word.

It was text-messaging including abbreviations, but only one word at a time. It's the same concept, with immediate feedback word by word. It sounded like a bunch of mad woodpeckers in the walls. We tapped whenever possible. When not tapping, we were clearing for guards. We gave constant warnings signaling the guards' locations and their direction of travel. There were normally five guards making the rounds in the little camp we were in. When they came near our cell, we stopped until clear again.

The guards were constantly opening up the little peephole doors in the big cell doors to catch us communicating. We watched for their approach by lying on the concrete floor and looking through the crack under the cell doors.

COUNTLESS HOURS WERE SPENT IN THIS POSITION AS WE "CLEARED THE HALLWAY" FOR GUARDS. EACH MAN GLADLY TOOK HIS SHARE OF CLEARING, BECAUSE THE CONSEQUENCES OF GETTING CAUGHT WHILE COMMUNICATING COULD RESULT IN TORTURE AND MONTHS OF A MISERABLE EXISTENCE IN IRONS OR "CUFFS."

ALL THE POWs BECAME "PEEKERS" AS WE FOLLOWED THE DAILY ACTIVITIES AROUND CAMP. EVERYTHING WAS NOTED, ESPECIALLY THE MOVEMENT AND INTERROGATION OF PRISONERS. THE NEWS WAS QUICKLY PASSED FROM ROOM TO ROOM IN THE TAP CODE. USED WITH PERMISSION FROM *PRISONER OF WAR*, BY MIKE MCGRATH

NEVER STOPPED COMMUNICATING

Communication was constantly going on under their noses. They knew it from the results of the interrogations. When they tortured us effectively it became obvious what was going on. But they never stopped it the entire time we were there. They would have had to be sitting by every cell watching us through the little doors. And it would have had to have been a 24/7 watch.

WE STANDARDIZED OUR NAMES FOR THE GUARDS AND OFFICERS TO FACILITATE IDENTIFICATION AND COMMUNICATION. NAMES WERE USUALLY PICKED ACCORDING TO SOME EASILY IDENTIFIABLE CHARACTERISTIC SUCH AS THE SPOOKY EYES AND MANNERISMS OF "SPOOK," THE LARGE PROTRUDING EARS OF "RABBIT" (A MASTER AT TORTURE), AND THE LARGE WHITE BIRTHMARK ON THE CHIN OF "SPOT." OTHER COMMON NAMES ABOUT THE CAMPS WERE: "ICABOD," (ALSO KNOWN AS "GOOSE"), "FOX," "BUSHY," ELF," "JAWBONE," "POX," ETC. USED WITH PERMISSION FROM *Prisoner of War*, BY MIKE MCGRATH

GOD BLESSES OBEDIENCE TO AUTHORITY

Communication was extremely important for morale and being able to resist well. We obeyed the *Code of Conduct*. The commander of each cell, of each cell block and of each prison camp was the officer with the earliest date of rank. We obeyed their orders.

"How should we handle this? How should we handle that? What to do here? How to get together on this." Our commanders made the decisions.

We obeyed those decisions. We would sink or swim together. We simply did as we were told, regardless of our opinion, and things worked out well. This reaffirms we should always obey lawful orders from our command structure, because the Lord is behind authority.

RESISTED

As the years passed, especially after the bombing halt for North Vietnam in 1968, it seemed as if nobody (on earth) was going to get us out. It looked like we were going to be there the rest of our lives. That was tough to take but we accepted it. What choice did we have?

I think one of the great moments of America was reflected by the fact that we had three hundred of the old timers (men that had been captured for many years) up there at that time, and the enemy was constantly trying to get us to do things to get special favors or special treatment. Nobody that I knew accepted special favors. Instead the communist propagandists were fought tooth and nail in everything. They wanted us to meet delegations and they wanted us to give them information. And the only time they ever got anything was under serious torture, and what we gave them was garbage. So the Americans in the prison camps, all of us relatively well off and spoiled compared to most of the world, had a loyal spirit under pressure when all seemed hopeless.

FREEDOM COMES FROM GOOD CHRISTIAN SOLDIERS

This supports my opinion that Christians have always made the best soldiers. I emphasize that one reason we should pray to never let the country give up Christianity is because fine fighting men result from it. If you look at history, the Christian armies are the ones who know how to fight to the death, where after the loss of nine out of ten men, the tenth man keeps going. This is a great blessing for the country. It is the reason why we are free. I believe Christianity is the true strength of the country.

Part 2. TORTURE

TORTURE WORKS

The interrogations and tortures were very frightening to us after we realized that torture could alter our behavior. We had believed that we were strong enough to endure any torture. After we had been through it for days at a time, we knew we could be broken. We had been told this in the military's survival school training, but we didn't believe it then.

Our approach was to indicate that torture was not a concern to us. The communists were greatly encouraged if they saw fear. They sensed blood. Meanwhile, we would be in agony while trying to give the impression we could take this level of pain indefinitely. Most of the time, they would eventually get what they wanted, but it would be inaccurate and worthless.

Our leaders told us to resist as best we could, then give them false or misleading information. Then the next time we were to make them go through the whole process again. I believe these procedures were effective and were followed well.

ANTICIPATION KILLS THE SHEEP

The tortures and interrogations caused great mental stress. The anticipation of the torture was worse than the torture itself. This is best illustrated by experiments done with sheep. When hooked up to electrodes and randomly shocked with 50 volts or so, the sheep did fine for months. But upon repeating the experiment with different sheep and ringing a bell two minutes before the electric shock, all the sheep died within a month. The mental stress from anticipating the pain was worse than the pain itself.

Torture is the same way. This is why it was so necessary to control our thoughts and not think about the torture. But whenever we were taken for interrogation, the guard would open the cell door and would make a certain gesture. He would tap a wrist with his other hand. This gesture meant put on our long-sleeved pajamas. The idea was to be as well-dressed as we could be. Formal pajamas for the interrogation!

The gesture for long pajamas was different from the behavior that a guard would have when distributing food. There were two food calls a day. They would simply open the door and wait.

WE WERE THE SHEEP

The interrogation gesture generated the same kind of fear in our stomachs an athlete feels just before going out on the football field or into the boxing ring. I recognized that feeling because I played football and did a lot of boxing. It was fear, and after about six months or a year in the cells, we would be fighting for control over fear every time that the guard made the long pajamas gesture, similar to football or getting into the ring. But the fear was of much greater magnitude and went on constantly, because we were interrogated regularly. Torture came with the interrogations.

We became the sheep dying from the bell.

TORTURE FOR ALL

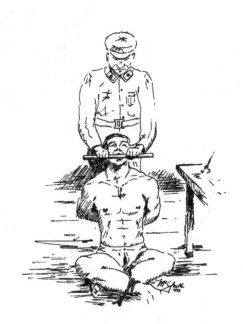

AN INTERROGATION. THE GUARD IS FORCING AN IRON BAR INTO THE PRISONER'S MOUTH TO QUIET HIS SCREAMS. USED WITH PERMISSION FROM PRISONER OF WAR, BY MIKE McGRATH

ROPE TRICKS

They used a number of different tortures. One would begin by tying ropes tightly
around our arms just above our elbows. Then they would pull the ropes to make our
elbows touch behind our back. This took four or five men. This often dislocated one or
both shoulders. Then with the elbows tied behind the back and circulation cut off to
the lower arms, they put us on our knees. We already had leg irons on our ankles.

They tied the ropes from our elbows behind our backs to the ankle irons and pulled tight to put us in a very painful stretched position, with the body arched backwards. A variation was to tie the rope from the elbows over the shoulder to the ankle irons and double up the POW forward. Either position was agony. We were left in this position 24/7 for days or weeks until we agreed to answer their questions.

HERE, I TRIED TO DEPICT THE "VIETNAMESE ROPE TRICK." THE ARMS ARE REPEAT-EDLY CINCHED UP UNTIL THE ELBOWS ARE FORCED TOGETHER BEHIND THE BACK. SOME-TIMES AT THIS POINT THE "HELL CUFFS" ARE APPLIED. THE "HELL CUFFS" ARE HAND CUFFS WHICH ARE PUT ON THE UPPER ARMS AND PINCHED AS TIGHTLY AS POSSIBLE ONTO THE ARMS, CUTTING OFF THE CIRCULATION. THE RESULTING PAIN IS EXTREME. IF THE PRISONER HAS NOT BROKEN DOWN BY THIS TIME, HIS ARMS ARE ROTATED UNTIL THE SHOULDERS DIS-LOCATE. WORDS COULD NEVER ADEQUATELY DESCRIBE THE PAIN, OR THE THOUGHTS THAT DO THROUGH A MAN'S MIND AT A TIME LIKE THIS. USED WITH PERMISSION FROM *PRISONER OF WAR*, BY MIKE MCGRATH

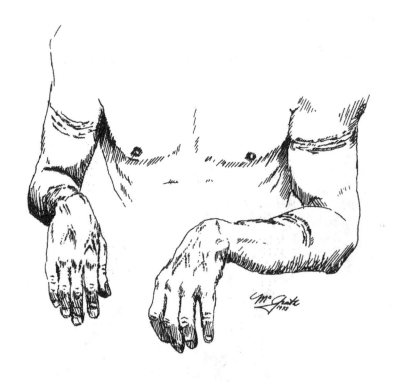

HERE IS A PICTURE OF A MAN WHO HAS BEEN TORTURED THROUGH THE USE OF ROPES OR NYLON PARACHUTE STRAPS. SOMETIMES THE GUARDS WOULD RAP RAGS AROUND A PRISONER'S LIMBS BEFORE BINDING THEM WITH ROPE. THIS WOULD PREVENT THE MARKS OF TORTURE FROM APPEARING. IF THE "V" WERE CARELESS OR OVER-AGGRESSIVE, THE ROPES SLIPPED OFF THE RAGS AND CAUSED ROPE BURNS. THE BURNS BECAME INFECTED AND LEFT UGLY WHITE SCARS.

WHEN THE "V" LEFT A MAN TIGHTLY BOUND FOR AN HOUR OR MORE, THERE WAS A GOOD POSSIBILITY THAT THE MAN WOULD SUFFER NERVE DAMAGE IN HIS ARMS AND WOULD NOT BE ABLE TO LIFT HIS HANDS FOR WEEKS, SOMETIMES MONTHS. USED WITH PERMISSION FROM *Prisoner of War,* BY MIKE MCGRATH

HANGING BY THE ELBOWS

To force us to meet the delegations sympathetic to North Vietnam, additions were made to the standard rope tricks. First the elbows were tied touching behind the back. Then the rope from the elbows went forward over our shoulder, then to our ankles and then tightened to double us up as usual. Then the POW was hung by the elbows from fan hooks on the ceiling. They hung us there for about an hour while they beat us with clubs on our bones. They didn't beat on the bottom or on muscles. They beat us on elbows. They beat us on shoulder blades. They beat us on ankles. They beat us on wrists. They beat us on all our bones and then let us down in about an hour or two.

THE UNBEARABLE PAIN OF TORTURE INVARIABLY BROUGHT SCREAMS FROM THE PRISONERS. TO PREVENT THE SCREAMS, THE VIETNAMESE GUARDS WOULD STUFF DIRTY RAGS INTO YOUR MOUTH WITH A RUSTY IRON BAR THAT WOULD CHIP THE TEETH AND TEAR THE SKIN OFF THE ROOF OF THE MOUTH. IF YOU RESISTED BY GRITTING YOUR TEETH, THE GUARD WOULD CONTINUE TO SHOVE UNTIL YOUR TEETH BROKE OR YOU OPENED YOUR MOUTH.

AS PICTURED HERE, SOME MEN WERE HUNG UPSIDE DOWN FROM THE RAFTERS — THEN BEATEN TO UNCONSCIOUSNESS. USED WITH PERMISSION FROM *PRISONER OF WAR*, BY MIKE MCGRATH

They loosened the ropes for a few minutes and then tightened them up again. They hung us up again. They did this many cycles each day, seven days a week. Part of the effectiveness is that no time is allowed for sleep. This was a favorite torture to force people to meet delegations. The longest time I heard of a man resisting this was thirteen days and nights. It was a very productive torture for their propaganda. It didn't leave any permanent marks. People couldn't tell torture had been done. It could be denied by the communists. They call lies the "sacred lies for the cause." This is why negotiations seem impossible. Their word and their commitments mean nothing.

HOT ROOMS
There were hot rooms. This also left no marks. We were put in the hot room in the sun in the summertime. Heat is an effective torture.

COLD ROOMS
In the wintertime the hot rooms became cold rooms. With temperatures in the 30s and 40s, a POW was stripped and put in irons and ropes on his knees, in the position described above. Then each hour the communists would enter the cold room, beat him on his bones and throw a bucket of cold water on him.

Perpetually shivering and in agony, three days and nights of this as John experienced was one of the tortures used if we were caught communicating with other POWs. But it was used for other reasons as well.

IRONS
Irons were always present. Ankle irons and wrist irons or handcuffs were used on almost everyone. It was painful just being in them for days and weeks at a time. But when tightened, they were much more painful. The pain didn't stop hour after hour and day after day. Many men had permanent scars resulting from irons eating into the flesh.

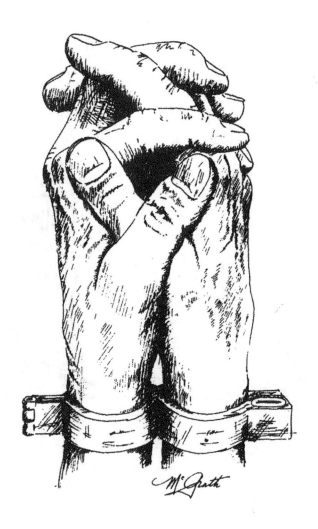

THESE ARE THE MANACLES, DREADED BY EVERYONE. THEY WERE MADE OF TWO FLAT BANDS OF STEEL, WITH THE "W" SHAPES HINGED AT ONE END AND LOCKED AT THE OTHER. THE WRIST OPENINGS WERE SMALL, SO THE FLAT BANDS WOULD CUT INTO YOUR WRISTS, IF YOU RELAXED ENOUGH TO LET YOUR ELBOWS SEPARATE.

IF YOUR WRISTS WERE IN FRONT OF YOU, YOU WERE ALWAYS IN POSITION FOR A QUICK PRAYER. IF THE MANACLES WERE APPLIED WITH YOUR WRISTS BEHIND YOUR BACK, YOU WERE IN FOR A LOT OF PAIN AND DISCOMFORT. THE MANACLES WERE ALSO USED FOR TRANSPORTING MEN BETWEEN CAMPS, BUT WERE MORE OFTEN USED AS A FORM OF PUNISHMENT. THEY WERE SOMETIMES LEFT ON FOR WEEKS AT A TIME. USED WITH PERMISSION FROM *PRISONER OF WAR*, BY MIKE MCGRATH

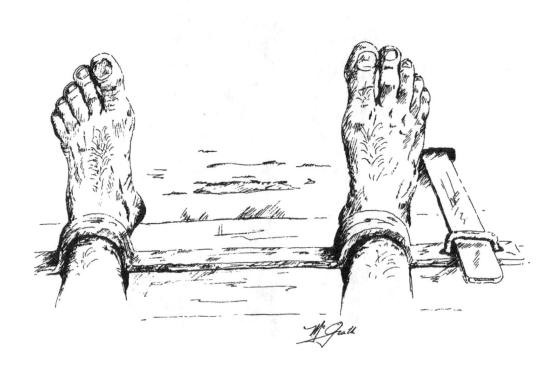

MANY OF THE HANOI PRISON ROOMS HAD STOCKS INSTALLED ACROSS THE FOOT OF THE BEDS. THE BASE WAS MADE OF WOOD. THE TOP BAR WAS OF RUSTY IRON, AND THE SLIGHTEST SCRATCH WOULD CAUSE AN INFECTION. THE LOCKING BAR WAS INSERTED AND LOCKED BY THE GUARD FROM OUTSIDE THE CELL, SO IT WAS IMPOSSIBLE TO PICK THE LOCKS AT NIGHT.

IN SOME CASES, WHEN A MAN'S ANKLES WERE TOO SWOLLEN TO FIT INTO THE STOCKS, THE GUARD WOULD STAND ON THE TOP BAR TO FORCE IT SHUT. THIS WOULD RIP THE SKIN OFF THE ANKLES AND CAUSE EXCRUCIATING PAIN. USED WITH PERMISSION FROM *PRISONER OF WAR*, BY MIKE MCGRATH

DURING THE SUMMER OF 1969, MY ROOMMATE WORE THESE IRONS CONTINUOUSLY FOR 76 DAYS. AT THE TIME, THE VIETNAMESE HAD TAKEN AWAY OUR BED BOARDS AND WE WERE SLEEPING ON THE TILE FLOOR. WHEN JIM WANTED TO TURN BACK FROM HIS BACK TO HIS STOMACH, HE WOULD THROW THE IRONS INTO THE AIR AND FLIP OVER LIKE A PANCAKE. THE IRONS WOULD BANG AND RATTLE ON THE FLOOR. IN THE BEGINNING NEITHER OF US GOT MUCH SLEEP, BUT JIM SOON BECAME ACCUSTOMED TO THE IRONS, AND I TO THE NOISE.

THESE IRON SHACKLES WERE USED LIKE HORSE HOBBLES. VARIOUS IRON BARS WERE USED, SOME WEIGHING AS MUCH AS THIRTY POUNDS. WHEN THE VIETNAMESE WANTED TO MAKE THINGS ROUGHER, THEY WOULD TURN THE LEG LOOPS AROUND SO THE IRON BAR RESTED ON TOP OF YOUR ANKLES. USED WITH PERMISSION FROM *PRISONER OF WAR*, BY MIKE MCGRATH

SOME MEN LIVED IN IRONS FOR MONTHS AT A TIME. THE "V" WOULD NOT TAKE THE IRONS OFF SO YOU COULD WASH YOUR DIRTY UNDERWEAR. WE DISCOVERED THAT IF YOU REALLY WANTED TO CHANGE SHORTS, THEY COULD BE REMOVED BY SLIPPING THEM THROUGH THE IRON LOOPS AND OVER THE TOES, ONE LEG AT A TIME. USED WITH PERMISSION FROM *PRISONER OF WAR*, BY MIKE MCGRATH

24/7 STANDING/KNEELING/SITTING

Another technique was to make us stand up day and night. They would beat us to keep us standing up. After two or three days of standing, our feet would be as big as basketballs. Kneeling was similar. They would have us kneel in irons, elbows tied to ankles. And when they caught me praying, they would put me on my knees on the concrete for many hours. They said, "You want to pray, good, we are going to let you pray."

MANY MEN WERE HANDCUFFED OR TIED TO A STOOL AS A MEANS OF SLOW TORTURE. THE POW SAT IN ONE POSITION, DAY AND NIGHT. EACH TIME HE WOULD FALL OVER, THE GUARDS WOULD SIT HIM UPRIGHT. HE WAS NOT ALLOWED TO SLEEP OR REST.

EXHAUSTION AND PAIN TAKE THEIR TOLL. WHEN THE POW AGREED TO COOPORATE WITH HIS CAPTORS AND ACQUIESCED TO THEIR DEMANDS, HE WOULD BE REMOVED. HERE, I HAVE PICTURED A GUARD NAMED "MOUSE," WHO LIKED TO THROW BUCKETS OF COLD WATER ON A MAN ON COLD WINTER NIGHTS.

SOME MEN, IN HEROIC EFFORTS TO RESIST THE "V," REMAINED SEATED FOR 15 TO 20 DAYS. ONE MAN MADE A SUPER-HUMAN EFFORT TO RESIST. HE LASTED 33 DAYS ON THE

WHIPPINGS

Another standard torture was whipping with hoses or fan belts. These whippings were given in the cases of breaking the camp "regulations." For example, we broke camp regulations by not answering questions, by not meeting delegations, by communicating through the walls with other POW's, or by talking louder than a whisper. A communist prison camp has a rule of silence. We were not allowed to make any noise, ever. We always had to whisper quietly. If the guard ever heard us, it became an excuse for beatings.

DURING THE SUMMER OF 1969 MANY MEN WERE BEING BEATEN WITH RUBBER HOSES AND STRAPS. ONE MAN VERY NEARLY DIED WHEN HE RECEIVED 100 STROKES A DAY FOR NINE DAYS. ANOTHER MAN WAS TORTURED TO COMPLETE INSANITY DURING THIS PERIOD. HE REPORTEDLY DIED (NEVER CAME HOME). THE MAN IN THE CELL NEXT TO ME WAS TORTURED TO DEATH (WHIPPED TO DEATH) AFTER AN UNSUCCESSFUL ESCAPE ATTEMPT. I WAS BEATEN BECAUSE I ASKED AN OFFICER FOR MEDICAL ATTENTION FOR A ROOMMATE'S INFECTED EARS. FROM *PRISONER OF WAR*, BY MIKE MCGRATH

WHIPPINGS TO DEATH

For something more serious, as for example the two men I mentioned earlier who had escaped, it was worse. One of the men was whipped to death over a period of three months. The other man was whipped and his flesh laid open every day for six months, but he didn't die. Part of the beating was putting salt on the open wounds. I wasn't in the camp with the man that died, but I was told that they would often hear his screams, "No, no, not that again," right after they saw the torturers go by with a bag of salt. They would dump salt over his raw back just to increase the effect of the whipping. But the whippings with the fan belts even without salt produced a high level of pain.

It is impossible to list all tortures used because the various torturers all had variations performed at will. But the above were some of the most common.

LANCE BEATEN TO DEATH

Over a period of a month, the communists beat Lt. Lance Sijan, a fellow pilot, to death. At first he was in a cell separated from Bob Craner and me. We were in our own cells about six feet away. The majority of the beatings took place in the cell. It was a horrible way to die. They killed him with brutal beatings on his wounds. I developed a tremendous anger and hatred for these torturers, which in turn almost killed me.

(Please see Chapter 9 for more detail on Lance's struggle)

HATE THE TORTURERS, IF YOU WANT TO COMMIT SUICIDE

After six months of hatred, I started getting suicidal thoughts. I finally realized my hatred was the trouble. I couldn't sleep. All I could think about was how I was going to torture and kill these men in some terrible way. Then I had thoughts in my mind telling me to stop eating and sit in the corner. They became more insistent the more I resisted them.

ASKED GOD FOR HELP

I knew enough to know that suicide was not allowed by God. I believed I was being inspired by the wrong spirits. I tried to stop these thoughts on my own, but failed. Finally, I went down on my knees and prayed, "I'm sorry, God. Obviously, I'm not allowed to hate these men."

FORGIVENESS FINALLY

After three or four months of trying to pray for my captors, I eventually was given the grace to at least form the words of forgiveness in my mind, but I didn't mean them. However, after six months I was praying for them in earnest. I was praying for their repentance and their conversion and I meant it. For the last three or four years of the prison camp I had peace. Everything was a lot easier because I wasn't in constant hatred of the torturers. That was what almost killed me. I think it might have killed a number of people. There was great temptation to hate, and the spiritual writers say it is the greatest sin. I believe it. I had never hated before in my life. I never want to again.

Part 3. LEADERSHIP

LEADER DIED FOR HIS MEN

WHAT ARE LRRPs?

The 173rd Airborne Brigade had Ranger Units with personnel trained to operate as six man patrols behind enemy lines or as long-range scouts (Please see Chapter 13 for more detail of the LRRPs-Long Range Reconnaissance Patrols). Their job was not to make contact with the enemy, but rather to gather intelligence. One of their jobs was to set up listening posts on remote trails in the jungle.

Moving through the jungle is not easy. It requires established trails. In a typical hundred mile section of jungle, the trails are few and far between. So it is only necessary to watch a few trails to determine enemy movement. To try to hack the way through such jungle with machetes, especially when silence is necessary for tactical surprise, would be ridiculous. Everyone uses the trails.

One of the men in the 173rd Airborne Brigade realized this. He developed a methodology and trained units for monitoring the trails. These six man units would stay hidden on the side of the trail with radios to report enemy movements. They were called LRRPs. Then if any enemy unit moved through that trail, the main force unit received warning from the LRRP and they could meet the attack without being surprised. With a few of these special well-trained units on the job the main force was protected from surprise attacks by enemy units sneaking up on them from a rugged area in any direction. The patrol or LRRP would generally be inserted well behind possible enemy lines by chopper and extracted by chopper after a week or weeks, depending on mission requirements.

TOP COVER OVER LONG RANGE RECONNAISSANCE PATROL (LRRP)

The *TONTO* FACs of the 173rd would fly top-cover for LRRPs. This story is about a listening mission by a LRRP along one of the common jungle ridge-line trails that was used by the enemy in the Dak To, Vietnam, area. This was a series of valleys where the enemy would bring in four or five hundred man units from Laos and wipe out little Montagnard villages there. They would surround them and kill all the men and take all the women away. They had wiped out 24 of 25 villages in this way before we were brought in there. There was only one village left.

LRRP HIT

On a late afternoon, in the summer of 1967, one of these LRRP units was watching the main trail the enemy was using to come in from Laos. I was assigned to fly top cover in their approximate area, when the commander of the unit (through the radio man) called me with my call sign, which was "TONTO 5." He said they had to be very quiet because a major unit was moving down the trail, and for me to relay that it looked like an attacking force. Just as he was speaking to me, multiple automatic rifles opened up. The enemy had spotted them, snuck up on them quietly and wounded two of them immediately with the first volley. The six men started retreating down a thousand-foot high mountain that was near the trail. One man on the team was hit in the head and another hit in the leg. The other four were trying to support and carry them as best they could.

Real combat is not like the Rambo movies. When a small unit is in contact with a unit of many hundreds of men, the six men don't win the fight.

The only chance is to either delay the enemy force or to find an alternate way out.

So the Rangers moved down the hill with two wounded. The commander of the unit was Sergeant Thomas (name changed). These men in the LRRPs were carefully picked men, considered by many to be the best infantry soldiers we had. Sgt. Thomas told his men, "Get the wounded down the hill. I will delay them." They went, leaving him behind. I was flying in a small light plane over this action. But there was no longer contact with the unit because the radioman was one of the men hit. That probably is why he was wounded. Many times the radioman is the first hit because they are more visible and vulnerable when on the radio. Also, this particular unit was in such a desperate situation that there was no time to use the radio.

THE SERGEANT DELAYED PURSUIT

I heard a burst from the Sergeant's M16, which had a different sound than the AK47s of the enemy. I heard AK47's answer. I thought, "Well, that's it, he's dead." I had called for troop ships and gun ships for rescue, but we didn't know where the patrol was because of the loss of radio contact. All I knew was which direction they were going. I repeatedly tried to reach them on the radio, but no contact. I flew as low as I could over the jungle, pretending that we had some airpower as support and threat. But nothing on the ground was visible from the air over jungle. The LRRP was on its own.

The Sergeant was shooting, with the enemy answering his fire each time. He would shoot and move immediately. He apparently shot from positions that allowed him to move quickly out of whatever cover he was using. Five times I heard him fire and retreat, fire and retreat. The sixth time they got him. But this slowed up the enemy and gave his men time and distance.

CHOPPER RESCUE

Meanwhile, the rescue choppers arrived and circled for between half an hour and forty five minutes. They finally saw five men break out into a clearing over the next ridge behind me. The five men on the run included the two wounded. The choppers picked them up. It was late in the afternoon just prior to dusk.

BODY RECOVERED

An airborne company was inserted by chopper at first light the next morning. They found Sergeant Thomas. The enemy had emptied many clips into his dead body. He was badly mutilated.

The good leader has the responsibility, the moral duty, to put his life on the line to save one or more men in his unit.

LEADER INSPIRED THE IMPOSSIBLE

LRRP AFTER ENEMY PRISONER

Late one afternoon I was once again flying top cover for a long range reconnaissance patrol, a LRRP going into an enemy regimental area. As I mentioned, part of the LRRPs' job was to look for and monitor trails in the jungle. Another of their missions was to take enemy officers prisoner. They did this very effectively.

Our Rangers were excellent soldiers who moved very quietly. I went out with them on one patrol and was amazed at how silent they were. You would never even know they were there. One of their tricks was to wait by the latrine of an enemy main force unit. They waited until what appeared to be an officer came out. When the man was totally defenseless, they would hit him hard, knock him out and carry him away, then call a chopper and we would have a prisoner.

But it was very dangerous to be anywhere near a main force enemy unit.

Again, it is nothing like the movies, because the enemy doesn't sit by their campfires waiting to be attacked. Main force units have recon patrols going out many miles in every direction. Ambushes are set up on any trails that might approach the unit's position. An infantry unit is never without eyes in the woods or in the jungle. They are constantly covering their flanks and their surroundings in all directions. They have ambushes set up for anybody that might be following them, in case another unit or an enemy scout is trailing them. The way a military unit moves through rugged terrain is a work of art. To get close to a unit like that and capture somebody is tough. Only superb soldiers have a chance.

The LRRP had to be put in by chopper near the enemy main force unit. The insertion was always a vulnerable time because an enemy patrol might detect it. This particular afternoon the ceiling (the "ceiling" is the height of the clouds above the ground) was down on the treetops. A helicopter troopship set down the LRRP with a couple of helicopter gun ships covering it. They were put in at 5:30 PM. I was with them as a Forward Air Controller. My job was to bring in fighters if necessary for fire support and to act as a radio relay back to base if contact was made after the choppers left. The LRRP's radios were only short range. Nightfall would be at 7PM, so they would soon have the cover of darkness in case of enemy attention. With darkness they might be able to break contact and put enough distance between themselves and the enemy to allow them to make it through the night. Then the next day they could again attempt to accomplish their mission.

LRRP COMPROMISED

The insertion was initially uneventful. But contact with the enemy occurred about an hour later. One of the enemy patrols had seen the choppers insert the LRRP team and closed on them. I was flying an O-1 aircraft, which is like a little Cessna, a little front and back seat single engine plane. It was the Air Force version of an artillery observer's plane, which was called the L-19. I was flying on the tree tops with only the ground visible beneath me. The weather was so bad there was no way of bringing fighter strikes in. All the choppers had gone back to base and the weather had become even worse. It was the heavy rain of the monsoon, and flying was only possible skimming the trees to keep them in sight.

LEADER RESPECTED

IMPOSSIBLE FLYING CONDITIONS FOR CHOPPER RESCUE

When the six man patrol was hit, I could see the enemy and pretended I had some firepower. I fired my little smoke rockets at the bad guys and fired my automatic rifle out the side window of the O-1. It seemed to slow them up a bit. They had to worry when we did that. Targets marked with smoke rockets are normally followed by bombs, rockets and cannon fire from attack fighter aircraft. They didn't know enough about flying to know that there was no way that we could bring in fighters in that weather condition. But they were still on our men and they were going to get them. I called up the helicopter unit to request an extraction and they said, "No, we can't, it's impossible to come, we can't fly in these conditions. We just can't do it."

The choppers were always flying VFR (Visual Flight Rules, meaning you had to be able to see where you were going). They were not flying instruments. It was not possible to fly instruments in the jungle in mountainous terrain at low altitude.

I said, "Can I speak to the Captain." I talked to the Captain who was in charge of the choppers that day.

I asked, "Sir, we have six men here who are going to die if we don't get a chopper up. Can you get a volunteer?"

He said, "I can't get a volunteer. I have tried a couple of times."

Lt. Colonel Allison (name changed) was in charge of both the troopships and gun ship helicopters for the more than four thousand man 173rd Airborne Brigade. From the briefings Allison gave each day, it was obvious he was a good man and a great commander. The superior work the choppers did gave evidence of this.

I said, "Well, can you talk to Colonel Allison, maybe he has an idea?"

He said, "Let me let you talk to him." I talked to Colonel Allison and told him the situation.

HE ASKED FOR THE IMPOSSIBLE

Allison asked his unit for a volunteer. He had about forty chopper pilots. One man stepped forward, a troopship pilot. He took the chopper up by himself with no co-pilot, no gunner, no crew, no covering gunship. A gunship is a chopper with heavy firepower that normally supports troopship choppers on insertions and extractions. He came out to the pickup area in about a twenty-minute flight on the treetops through the mountains. He followed a dirt road through the mountains on the deck in a monsoon driving rain. I rendezvoused with him and led him to the LRRP. He set the chopper down, picked the LRRP up and brought them back. The patrol lived.

HE SAVED THE LRRP

The reason that happened was the leader's character. Allison saved those six men just as much as the volunteer pilot did. When he asked for that volunteer, nobody should have gone up. But because it was Allison, someone did. One of his men said to himself, "I don't care about the conditions, I'm going."

A unit with a leader of good character excels in everything it does and it really can do the impossible.

LEADER SUPPORTED HIS MAN

DO WE GO HOME?

It was two days before our release from prison camp in March of 1973. The B-52's and the fighters by order of President Nixon had extensively bombed North Vietnam. This was called the Christmas bombing of 1972. As a result, North Vietnam had agreed to a peace treaty and to withdraw their troops from South Vietnam. The peace treaty was signed in early January of 1973, and part of that peace treaty was the repatriation of all the POWs in four main releases. Our camp was in the third release. We were in our go-home camp. There were about a hundred POWs there.

By this time, after many years of crushing disappointment, it was hard to believe that we were ever going to go home. Something always happened to keep things from working out. Even though it looked different this time, we didn't dare believe it. Because getting our hopes up and having them dashed was just so hard on our mental state. We were all on the edge by that time because of the constant pressure, lack of good food and sunshine, and everything else. We couldn't handle a mental letdown.

RAY RUINS OUR CHANCES

Two days before the release date, they brought Russian reporters and photographers into our camp. They opened the cell doors and set up volleyball nets and said, "Okay, you men can go play volleyball." Our commanding officer, Colonel Flynn, said, "No, don't go out. They obviously want to take pictures. Stay in your cells." So we all stayed in the cells.

However, the Russian photographers needed pictures for their papers. They had big, old press cameras, big rectangular boxes like in the old movies. They came into Ray's cell where there were three POWs. Ray motioned to them and told them, "No pictures." The Russian picked up the camera to take one anyway. Ray, raised on a Kansas farm, grabbed the camera from the Russian photographer and ripped it off his body because it had a strap on it. He lifted it up over his head and smashed it into the concrete floor of the cell.

Everyone in camp thought, "I knew it, that's it, another five years, man, that's it." This action in a communist prison camp was completely beyond the pale.

RAY NOT GOING HOME

They called Ray and Colonel Flynn and the deputy commander in. The deputy commander told me this story.

The communist camp commander said, "He can't go home. We cannot have this. He just insulted us in front of the Russians. We will keep him here."

LEADER TOOK RESPONSIBILITY

Colonel Flynn immediately said in a loud and decisive voice, "Why him? It was my order. I told them not to let anyone take pictures. If you want to keep someone here, keep me. I'm staying. He's going." Just like that. I was stunned, because it was so hard to even think of giving up going back to the States in that environment.

I have never in my life seen anything greater than Colonel Flynn standing up for Ray in that situation. The story had a good ending. Ray came home and Colonel Flynn came home. But without Colonel Flynn, Ray never would have come home.

AND NO ONE WAS BETTER THAN RAY

Ray was one of the finest of men. He held off an entire North Vietnamese battalion for three days and three nights with a 50-caliber machine gun from a bluff overlooking a Montagnard mountain village in Laos. While he did this, the entire Montagnard village with all their women and children made it two miles to safety across an open valley with their possessions. At the end it was only a CIA chopper pilot that saved Ray, bringing his chopper in under heavy fire and picking him up.

To have lost Ray because of that incident would have been terrible.

That story illustrates a commander taking responsibility for his men's actions. Col. Flynn never let anything be his men's fault and in this case, it was so unfair to Flynn. Flynn's directive was understood clearly - the way to avoid getting your picture taken was to turn around and face the wall. That way they can never get a good picture- But Ray is one of those men that gives 100% and he took the order as literally "Don't let them take a picture."

THE BUCK STOPS HERE

What can we learn from Colonel Flynn? Well, if our unit or anyone in it makes a mistake, when we don't achieve the goal, when we don't accomplish the job, when we just mess up as a unit or an individual in our unit messes up, we should treat it solely as our fault to our superior leaders. We will always have a superior, whether in the military or in civilian life. Even if we are the chief of staff of the armed forces, we have a superior leader in the president. If we are the president, we have a superior leader in the American people. If we are a corporate CEO, we are responsible to our customers.

When relating mistakes to our superior, the right answer is that it was our problem, not the unit's problem or the individual's problem. This was explained well by President Truman when he said, "The buck stops here."

Our superior may try to give us a way out, "Well, I guess your men messed up." But our response should be, "No Sir, I didn't explain it properly to them. They were caught unprepared. It is my problem, sir. I have super people here." It should always be the same. Our unit and the personnel in it should be represented as outstanding to senior leadership.

A LEADER ALWAYS SUPPORTS HIS SUPERIORS

It goes the other way too. When there are complaints in the ranks about weird orders coming from top leadership and we have to follow the orders, they are never stupid orders. They are excellent orders, "They know things that we don't know. We will do exactly what they say." No matter what, we should not say, "Oh, I hate to ask you to do this, but they tell us we have to do this. I just have to do what I am told," or words to that effect. None of that! The attitude should always be, "We have very good leadership, and they know what they are doing. Their perspective is better than ours. We do not see everything as clearly as they do. Just execute perfectly with no complaints."

THE BUCK STOPS HERE FROM ABOVE OR BELOW

We will see mistakes coming from both top and bottom of our position. Let the buck stop with us both ways. We should always take the hit. No complaining and no ruining anyone else's reputation.

I can't imagine there could be tougher conditions than those under which Colonel Flynn did it. If he could do it, we can do it.

COLONEL (LATER LT. GENERAL) JOHN PETER FLYNN, USAF

LEADER WITH STRONG FAITH

The leader's faith is obvious to the command. They will know by the morality of his actions whether his faith is sincere. Colonel Robbie Risner was a good Christian and a great fighter pilot. He led the first raid into the Hanoi-Haiphong area. Colonel Risner was the overall commander of all POWs in prison camps in North Vietnam. The first thing Colonel Risner had us communicate to new POWs when they were first captured was telling them about our common church service. This was the initial communication after we taught them the tap code. Every Sunday at noon we would have a church service no matter where we were, in torture or not. We would all say the *Our Father, The 23rd Psalm,* and *The Pledge of Allegiance.* When the communists sounded gongs for their noontime siesta, we would start the service. Even though we were in separate cells or in separate camps, we would all be united every Sunday. We also prayed almost constantly on our own. God was our shepherd in the hopeless situation in North Vietnam. He brought us home. You can count on him too.

COLONEL RISNER ESTABLISHES CHURCH SERVICE IN POW CAMP
Three years later in November of 1970, the very brave men of the Army Special Forces and supporting special ops personnel descended on a little prison camp called Son Tay, where there were about 50 POWs. The intent was to rescue them. They killed all the guards and everything went according to plan. However, the POWs had been moved out the week before. The Son Tay Raiders thought the raid was a failure and were sad and disappointed.

But from the POW's perspective, it was the most successful rescue mission ever undertaken. It forced the communists to take us out of those different camps and concentrate us in the Hanoi Hilton in seven large dungeons. There were 35 to 50 men in each one. It was wonderful being with that many other men compared to being solo or with one other.

When we were placed in the dungeons, Colonel Risner told us we would have a church service on Sunday at the same time as usual, twelve noon. It would be a two hour service. As the first step, men were chosen to act as Chaplains of each dungeon. The service was to start out with eleven hymns of thanksgiving such as the *Star Spangled Banner*, the *Battle Hymn of the Republic* and *Amazing Grace*. Almost everyone knew these. Then the Chaplains assigned different men to preach on various passages of the Bible.

In a communist prison camp with strict regulations to maintain absolute silence, three hundred men belted out the Star Spangled Banner at the top of their lungs on Sunday at twelve noon. They brought in the guards with machine guns. They stood us up against the wall. They took the commanding officers of the dungeons and put them in torture rooms. They left. Based on date of rank, the next commanders stood up and said, "Gentlemen, they interrupted our church service. Let's begin again." We started singing the Star Spangled Banner again. The guards came in and took those commanders to the torture rooms. This was repeated. Each time the new commanders would start the service again.

Finally all torture rooms were filled up. We continued our service and finished it.

The next day I was monitoring an interrogation. We could put our ear on the concrete floor and hear conversations in buildings about 50 yards away. It was my turn to monitor.

TORTURE OR KILL, BUT WE WILL WORSHIP

They called in Ed Mechenbier. The camp commander said, "You know the camp regulations, rule of silence. Any more of those church services and everyone will be tortured and killed if necessary. We will not be embarrassed like that." And Mechenbier said, "You can kill every one of us, but as long as one of us is alive, we are having that service."

This shows how much God had meant to us in those previous three to seven years. Everybody knew the only reason we had made it was God. Nobody wanted to desert him. Our feeling was, "He is the reason we are here. He is the reason we are alive."

We meant it and the North Vietnamese knew it. They let us have that church service from then on.

The sincere hope, faith and trust Colonel Risner had in God was not disappointed in prison camp and in his life since. God makes a leader like Colonel Risner successful.

LEADER BY EXAMPLE

I witnessed a man following the *American Fighting Man's Code of Conduct* perfectly. The *Code* was to govern our conduct if captured. This meant trying to escape as often as we could, obeying the leadership of the people appointed over us, no favors from the enemy, no compromise in any way, making it tough for them to get anything out of us, etc. The provisions of the *Code* are clear.

LT. LANCE SIJAN

Please see the expanded Lance Sijan testimony given at the US Air Force Academy in Chapter 9 in this book.

LANCE DIED FOR US

They would take him out, torture him, and we would hear his screams. Then they would bring him back. This went on many times every day. There was nothing we could do. We were in irons in cells just a few feet away. He was dying slowly, getting weaker and weaker. He died after thirty days. He would never give them anything but name, rank, service number and date of birth. Bob Craner and I would beg him, "Lance, just give them some false answers. Just answer their questions." But he wouldn't answer them. He obeyed the *Code of Conduct* perfectly.

There were slightly over 3500 aircrew members shot down over North Vietnam in the years 1964 to 1973 who were not rescued. In 1973, 591 POWs came home from all services and all countries in Southeast Asia of which 472 came home from North Vietnam. The Russians and North Vietnamese tortured to death or killed in one way or another six out of seven of us in North Vietnam. Lance was one of them.

He was a leader by example to every POW in North Vietnam.

He died for every one of us.

Conclusion:

YOUR TRAINING IS LIKE LANCE'S

Lance graduated from a service program like that you are in. He played on a sports team, the football team. He walked the halls and attended classes. I think every officer should strive to live up to his standards. It takes self-discipline and integrity. It takes fidelity to keep trying as hard as you can all the time. He was only in his twenties when he died. He was a man perfectly obedient. He gave everything he had. Few of us will ever be tested like he was. But we should all be as ready. If we are, we will have great confidence in this life. We will never be worried about anything. We can take prison camp. We can take dying. We can take being crippled. We can take anything in the world if we have that kind of confidence. The training starts here. Our goal should be to uphold the honor that the position carries. There is a great honor in being a military officer. We defend the families of this country.

BE UNSELFISH

It is similar to being a captain of a police force in a city. There is no possible excuse for not fulfilling the responsibilities the nation honors us with. Everything can be done correctly. Being tired or hungry or in pain or any similar discomfort and letting it affect performance is wrong. Life is not about our minor personal problems. Everything should be done with the best possible effort, with patient perseverance through difficulties. We are tested in training and combat. We must react quickly. If we don't react without questioning orders, we won't be able to fight well. A person's responses in war will directly correlate to their responses in training.

LISTEN TO INSTRUCTORS

The officers responsible for training here are trying to train military officers in a way that has been proven over time to result in both the best combat leaders and the best leaders in the service. It is important that you give it your best shot. Follow orders. Do exactly as told. Try to learn well, because the way you train is the way you will fight. Your fighting ability depends on your training right now. It will be instinct. You will do your job well in war because the training here is outstanding. You won't even have to worry about it.

ALWAYS DO THE RIGHT THING

This life is short, but if you follow the example of Lance and so many other good men and always do what's right, you will always sleep well. It is nice to be able to sleep soundly. The Lord will shepherd you carefully through this life, the easy times and the tough times. He does the same for everyone trying to do their best.

Remember, the common trait that everyone must have to be a good leader or a good follower is doing the right thing. Nothing remains hidden. Sooner or later, everything will become known. Live to be happy and content in that moment.

ALWAYS GIVE MAX EFFORT

Everyone should always give maximum effort like Lance and the other soldiers, sailors, airmen and marines did that I witnessed in Vietnam. Then, when tested, it will result in a job well done.

YOU WILL HAVE PEACE

Always striving to do the right thing will be a source of deep peace. Whether or not the world recognizes it, you will know you have done well and will have the peace that results.

I hope and pray that God blesses your service in every way. Thank you for the attention and thank you in advance for your service.

Lord,
Keep our Troops forever in Your care
Give them victory over the enemy...
Grant them a safe and swift return...
Bless those who mourn the lost.

"Soldiers! Let us humble ourselves before the Lord, our God, asking through Christ, the forgiveness of our sins, beseeching the aid of the God of our forefathers in the defense of our homes and our liberties, thanking Him for His past blessings, and imploring their continuance upon our cause and our people."

"Knowing that intercessory prayer is our mightiest weapon and the supreme call for all Christians today, I pleadingly urge our people everywhere to pray. Believing that prayer is the greatest contribution that our people can make in this critical hour, I humbly urge that we take time to pray - to really pray."

"Let there be prayer at sunup, at noonday, at sundown, at midnight - all through the day. Let us pray for our children, our youth, our aged, our pastors, our homes. Let us pray for the churches."

"Let us pray for ourselves, that we may not lose the word 'concern' out of our Christian vocabulary. Let us pray for our nation. Let us pray for those who have never known Jesus Christ and His redeeming love, for moral forces everywhere, for our national leaders. Let prayer be our passion. Let prayer be our practice."

General Robert E Lee, 1863

This page blank.

13

COMBAT, SOUTH VIETNAM, 173RD AIRBORNE

TALK NARRATIVE: On February 19, 2011, I had the honor of speaking to an Air Force Reserve F-16 Fighter Wing at Homestead AFB, Fl, just south of Miami. They requested Forward Air Controller (FAC) combat stories in South and North Vietnam. I was assigned to the US Army for help with air support as a Forward Air Controller. These are some stories of that time in South Vietnam in 1967.

Dak To Special Forces Camp, Aerial View

A Special Forces Camp Attacked

In the summer/fall of 1967, there was a concerted offensive by North Vietnamese regular units to take over the area northwest of Kontum in the Central Highlands of Vietnam. This area was adjacent to the tri-border region where Laos, Cambodia and South Vietnam meet.

The mountains in the Central Highlands are some of the highest mountains in Vietnam. They are four to eight thousand feet high and very rugged, covered in thick, virtually impassable jungle, unless a trail can be found. If there was no trail, then machetes would have to be used to cut a path through the jungle. Can you imagine trying to sneak up on an enemy unit as you cut a trail with machetes? So all soldiers, ours and theirs, generally traveled on the trails.

DAK TO SPECIAL FORCES CAMP FROM THE AIRFIELD

When a Special Forces led company of indigenous soldiers (Montagnards) 150 strong was ambushed and killed to a man by North Vietnamese regular soldiers southwest of the Special Forces Camp of Dak To, the 173rd was asked to help with recovery of the American and Vietnamese bodies. They were also asked to protect the local civilians and to support the Special Forces Camps in the area. These Camps were named Dak To, Dak Seang and Dak Pek in the Kontum Province of South Vietnam.

Our commander, General Dean, moved one battalian of the 173rd Airborne Brigade to the Dak To Special Forces Camp as a base for operations supporting the Special Forces Camps in the area. Captain Buddy Roberts and I accompanied the battalion as FACs for air support. Our infantry recovered the one hundred and fifty bodies of the ambushed unit and brought them back to the base.

The other two Special Forces Camps, Dak Seang and Dak Pek, were closer to the Laotian border. Dak Pek was the closest, located about 5 miles west-northwest of Dak To.

Copyright © 2005 Dana Kelly

DAK SEANG SPECIAL FORCES CAMP FROM THE AIR. USED WITH PERMISSION OF DANA KELLY

Dak Seang was 10 miles north-northwest of our base at Dak To. It was in a mountain valley, with high mountains forming a circle around it. The only break in that circle was the river that entered the valley from the north and exited to the south. This same river flowed by Dak Pek and finally passed by Dak To on the way to Kontum and points south. Dak Seang was built on the valley floor with the Montagnard villages located generally to the north and east. This Special Forces A-Team was protecting 300 or more Montagnard civilians, who were living in the valley with their families. The A-team was composed of eleven well-trained soldiers led by a Captain. Their mission was to protect the Montagnard civilians in this area from the North Vietnamese communist soldiers.

DAK SEANG SPECIAL FORCES CAMP FROM THE AIRFIELD. USED WITH PERMISSION OF DANA KELLY

The Dak Seang Special Forces camp was vulnerable to attack because it was located close to the border with Laos. Our war policy allowed the North Vietnamese safe bases in Laos and Cambodia all along the western border of South Vietnam. We were not allowed to attack these bases. The North Vietnamese would repeatedly raid targets in South Vietnam and then retreat back into their safe areas in Laos or Cambodia.

In the summer of 1967, taking advantage of the monsoon season, the communists sent a regiment across the border to take Dak Seang. After crossing the border, they set up positions on two extensive ridgelines that overlooked the Special Forces Camp. They ambushed any Special Forces patrols attempting to clear the ridgelines and methodically tightened the circle around Dak Seang. As the days progressed, patrols were ambushed closer and closer to the Camp. Finally, any friendly patrol was ambushed as soon as it departed the Camp. After ten days the Special Forces were confined to their Camp. The enemy was able to set up recoilless rifles and heavy machine guns (Russian 12.7mm machine guns, closely equivalent to our .50 calibers and I will refer to them as .50s from now on) with direct fire down into the Camp and the villages around it.

NORTH VIETNAMESE GUN POSITIONS IN THE MOUNTAINS BEHIND THE CAMP YOU SEE IN THE FOREGROUND HERE LED TO DEEP TROUBLE WITH DIRECT FIRE DOWN ON TO THE CAMP. USED WITH PERMISSION OF DANA KELLY.

As this attack began, the Special Forces called for support from the 173rd. However, the terrain was so rough and the rains so heavy that they precluded any attempt at relief by infantry moving over the mountains. The helicopters could not fly in the terrible monsoon rains and so infantry could not be airlifted to reinforce them. The only help we might be able to give was air support, but for the first ten to twelve days, we were unable to fly up the river valley to reach Dak Seang. The clouds were down on the trees with constant heavy rain. This was the summer monsoon.

They called us, "We need help. There is an overwhelming force up here, at least five hundred regulars. We have eleven Americans and some 100 or so civilian irregulars." Our airmen in the command center at Dak To asked, "Can you hold out for a weather change?" They said, "They are tightening the noose, it looks bad." After a few days, they were saying, "We don't have a chance unless you can get to us." Because reinforcing ground forces could not get to them, the help would have to be air power. This required that an O-1 forward air controller aircraft reach them, corresponding with weather good enough for the FAC to bring in fighter aircraft and direct strikes on the enemy. We used WP (white phosphorous rockets) to mark targets for fighters.

O-1 Bird Dog Forward Air Controller Aircraft. This aircraft was the en-abler of strikes by Fighter Aircraft in support of US Infantry Units. Otherwise, such strikes were impossible because of the danger to friendly forces.

I tried to fly up the mountainous river valley each day to Dak Seang. But I would have to turn back after less than a mile or two because the river valley rose in elevation on the way to their camp and the clouds would eventually reduce visibility on the river to zero feet. Then I would climb straight ahead into the clouds to 200 feet above the indicated altitude I had on the river. I would make a 270 degree turn to the right and then a 90 degree turn back to the left, let back down on the river where I could see again, and follow the river back to Dak To.

By this time, the situation in Dak Seang was a true disaster. The enemy had taken away all ability to maneuver (patrols were ambushed as they left the camp) and was obviously preparing for a final assault on the Camp and the neighboring villages. After more than ten days of flying up the river bed and having to turn back, one day I finally had a clear tunnel along the river through the mountains, and I was able to go all the way up the river to Dak Seang.

THE RIVER FROM DAK TO UP TO DAK SEANG THROUGH THE MOUNTAINS; THE CLOUDS WERE DOWN BELOW THE TREETOPS ALONG THE RIVER BANK. I WAS FLYING IN A TUNNEL ON THE WATER UNDER THE CLOUDS UNTIL THE CLEARING APPEARED OVER THE SPECIAL FORCES CAMP OF DAK SEANG. USED WITH PERMISSION OF DANA KELLY

When I arrived in the valley, there was a large clearing ("big hole" to a pilot) in the clouds right over the valley. The high circling mountains around Dak Seang had evidently been responsible for a hole in the monsoon clouds, extending up to 10,000 feet. So I had room to bring in the fighters for strikes. I asked control to give me all the F-100s that were airborne or could be scrambled, and directed them to a mileage marker over the Dak Seang Valley off the Kontum TACAN (a navigation beacon) at 10,000 feet. The fighters scrambled and started north.

To attack, I needed to obtain locations of the enemy positions to mark on large scale 1:50,000 maps I had in my O-1 aircraft. I called the Captain in the Special Forces camp. I had an FM radio, a VHF radio and a UHF radio in this little forward air controller plane, the O-1. The Captain said "The main enemy forces are concentrated on two main ridgelines." He was not sure of the coordinates on the map and I was unable to locate the enemy positions from the air. There were scores of peaks and ridgelines surrounding Dak Seang. I said, "Then I have to come down and get the enemy locations from you, because I can't see them." He said, "You can't land, they have direct fire on us." I said, "I have to land. I have no choice." So I landed on a 600-foot strip in the valley. A sergeant met my plane with a jeep and we drove to the command bunker, turning constantly to avoid incoming fire. In the bunker on his large map, the Captain showed me where the enemy positions were on the ridgelines, and I marked them on my map.

Meanwhile the enemy was firing artillery and recoilless rifles down on the camp, trying to hit my little plane. There was no other aircraft on the strip, of course. So I said, "Okay, I know where they are. I have to get to my plane." The captain just looked at me. The sergeant said, "I will take you, sir." So we jumped in the jeep and were again dodging fire as we went to the plane. I jumped out of the jeep while it was still moving and into my plane. I taxied, turned around, took off and just barely reached flying speed at the end of the runway as it fell away off a cliff. Then I had to circle in the valley to gain altitude.

But now I had the coordinates of the two primary ridgelines from the Captain. I flew over them and finally could make out the foxholes under the trees. There were hundreds of them. They had cleared lanes of fire down onto the camp. They also had .50 caliber machine guns and recoilless rifle artillery firing from positions on additional perpendicular ridgelines extending downhill from the two primary ridgelines. Those ridgelines also had numerous dug-in soldiers.

DAK SEANG SPECIAL FORCES CAMP AERIAL VIEW, CENTRAL HIGHLANDS OF SOUTH

VIETNAM. USED WITH PERMISSION OF DANA KELLY

They could fire either directly down into the camp or at aircraft. The .50 calibers had me under heavy fire. The F-100 fighters arrived on station. I told the pilots I had them in sight overhead and had a good target for them.

I used my smoke rockets to mark two of the guns on the ridge line and the F-100's dive bombed them. After three bombs were dropped, a 500-pound bomb hit between two .50-caliber gun emplacements, which were about 30 yards apart. So I thought we had wiped those two positions out, and prepared to switch to the others. But on the next dive in, those two fifty caliber gun positions opened up on the diving aircraft. I was amazed. It convinced me that bombs were not going to take these men out. Bombs are typically not effective on infantry in foxholes unless there is a direct hit or unless the crater includes the foxholes. These were 500-pound bombs with zero time delay fuse on impact. There was no crater, because the bombs were exploding immediately as they hit the ground. Two of the F-100s were badly hit by the .50 calibers and had to return to base during the initial attacks.

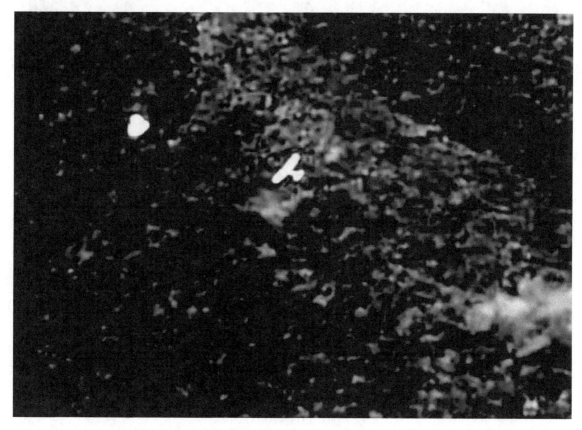

O-1 MARKING THE ENEMY TRENCHES WITH WP (WHITE PHOSPHOROUS) ROCKETS

So I told the next fighters coming in that I needed 20mm strafe (cannon fire) and it had to be high-angle strafe, with the fighters firing from a steep dive, because these men were in foxholes. Low-angle strafe (a shallow dive) would not get them. I felt that with the high-angle strafe we might have a chance. Now the F100's came in diving but using strafe (20 mm cannons) instead of bombs. They had four 20 millimeter cannons, 1500 rounds per minute rate of fire each, so they had equivalent rate of fire of a Gatling gun, which is 6000 rounds a minute, or 100 rounds a second. But the fire system of the F-100 was superior to a gatling gun, because they covered a wider area due to the natural dispersal of the shells from four separate, independent cannons. They started applying high-angle strafe on the foxholes, as well as rockets and bombs.

F-100 ON THE ATTACK

Meanwhile, I again asked the command center at Dak To to request and send to me all the fighters they had in theater. I had an outstanding target. Numerous four-ship flights of F-100's came in. They all applied high-angle strafe, and we raked the ridges with the foxholes back and forth, back and forth. I called my commander and asked him to come up the river. He replaced me. Then another man replaced him. We spent six hours guiding in F-100 strikes that day, as long as the weather held. We guided at least 25 to 30 flights of four F-100s each on this attack. That is more than 100 fighter aircraft. The F-100's fired more than 80,000 rounds of 20 millimeter high-angle strafe on all the enemy positions on all the ridgelines, along with numerous rockets and bombs. The enemy called off the attack and ran back to Laos.

Two or three days later, the Special Forces Team sent patrols out of their perimeter, which they had not been able to do for some time. Their patrols didn't run into anyone. They kept going further and further. Finally they went about a mile up the mountain to where the enemy positions had been. There was no one there. There were body parts all over the trees. There were many mass graves with 20, 30 or 40 men in them. Intelligence gave us a radio intercept they had received by the enemy unit returning across the border. The intercept was to the effect that "Such and such regiment is returning to North Vietnam. We have lost all our officers and most of our men. We are no longer an effective fighting unit. We cannot stay."

These F-100 fighters had stopped the enemy attack with primarily strafe (20mm cannon). Of course, they also had dropped bombs and fired rockets, but the bombs did not seem to be as effective. The high-angle strafe took out the soldiers in the foxholes. I would hate to be in an infantry unit fixed in foxholes or any other position if the enemy had air superiority. I hope we never lose it.

F-100 TWO-SHIP, OFF-TARGET, EMPTY, MISSION COMPLETE, HEADED HOME. USED WITH PERMISSION OF ROGER "WILLY" WILLIAMSON.

A Village Attacked

We had been sent to Dak To because the villages in their area of responsibility were getting crushed by the North Vietnamese regular army. They had lost 24 villages out of 25 in extended action over time that had been taking place in a huge valley between the Dak To Special Forces Camp and the Dak Pek Special Forces Camp. Further north, the Dak Seang Special Forces Camp discussed above still had their villages because the Special Forces Camp was right next to them. But the villages that Dak Pek and Dak To were trying to protect were all isolated. They had been independently surrounded and attacked. The communists would kill all the men. The women and children were left to the whims of the attacking soldiers. That happened to 24 villages before we got there.

Our continuing mission was to provide support and cover for the infantry in this valley, which was north of Dak To. Two days after we arrived, a patrol that consisted of the village chief of the remaining village and eleven of his men was watching a trail. The "friendlies" observed an enemy main force unit moving down the trail. The enemy detected the friendly patrol. The patrol managed to get off a radio signal to the Air Force liaison officer for the South Vietnamese at the District Capital, and then they were killed. But the village was warned.

The enemy unit was obviously coming down the trail to wipe out the remaining village. So the friendly forces in that village called us and asked for help. It was just a little after dark. The clouds were down low. We had about a thousand-foot ceiling in the valley. And because we had just arrived in the area a few days earlier, we didn't yet know the terrain. The Air Force liaison officer gave me the coordinates of the village.

As we came down the pitch-black valley to the village, it was lit by all kinds of fire. The enemy was raking the village's fort with different types of weapons; mortars, heavy machine guns, light machine guns and grenades. I could see the enemy sappers running up with their TNT charges to the walls of the fort defending the village. It was their job to blow up the fort's defenses and breach the wall with explosive charges. I was at low altitude, varying between 400 to 800 feet. I could clearly see what the enemy soldiers were doing. They were running up and destroying the barbed wire emplacements around the fort. There were 38 civilian militiamen in the fort. They were the remainder of the 50 able bodied men originally in the village.

After I had received the first warning of the enemy coming down the trail, I had called up Pleiku and said, "I need a scramble of your alert A1's (The A1 is a World War II propeller fighter aircraft called the Skyraider that could come in low and slow with 20mm cannons and other firepower in weather conditions that jet fighters could not fly in. This was the case during this action. The ceiling was 1000 feet in the mountains and no jet could have flown in those conditions in the Dak To area). I need them to come up the river valley, straight up from Pleiku , past Kontum, and I will pick them up as they are following the river to this location." They asked, "Are troops in contact?" I said, "No, but they will be in contact soon." They said, "Sorry, we can't scramble unless the troops are in contact." I said, "You have to scramble them. We have a serious problem here. We are going to lose a village if you don't scramble."

They scrambled the A1's. I said. "Also give me your gun ship, your AC47 gun ship that has the side firing Gatling guns." So they sent that modified C47 aircraft up. I also asked that they, "Give me some more A1's, scramble as many as you can."

Just as the enemy started firing on the village fort, the first two A1's came up the river south of the fort. The fort was just south of the village on the river, with a cleared field between. The main enemy force was attacking the fort from the north side, with the village to its rear. They were blowing up the defenses protecting the fort from that side preparing for the final assault.

As the A1's were coming up the river, I said, "Continue going straight ahead. You see the heavy fire on that little triangular fort. Go straight ahead. The enemy is attacking from the north side and they are right up to the walls, so you're cleared in hot, take them out." The A1's have four 20mm M-3 cannon on their wings. They started strafing these men off the barbed wire and off the walls of the fort on their very first strafing run. They made tight turns and came back in. Back and forth, run after run. The .50 caliber machine guns of the enemy units were turned on the A1's, but when the guns were not on them, they turned on me. I was in a continuous turn at 80 knots to avoid their fire, and the .50 caliber tracers were coming right under my fuselage. Because I was turning hard, at max power of the aircraft, the turn made the .50 caliber tracers go under my fuselage.

Because I was so low in altitude and relatively slow (The O-1 was equivalent to a light Cessna aircraft), the gunners were right on. They didn't have to lead me with their aim. But my constant turning at a 60 degree or greater bank made them miss me just barely under the belly of the aircraft. This fight went on for two hours. Two of the A-1s were hit badly and had to crash land, one at Dak To. After the A1's had concentrated their fire on the north side, the enemy moved over the west side. Meanwhile eight more A1's came in. We started strafing with 20mm cannon fire all over the field to the west side, and after two hours the enemy broke off the attack and went back to Laos, taking ten hostages with them.

After a few miles, they let the hostages go. The hostages told us the enemy was carrying about 100 of their dead with them, another 50 or so wounded, and they left 38 bodies on the battlefield.

The lifting of the seige of the Special Forces Camp at Dak Seang and the defense of this little village were two actions where air power clearly played a major role.

LRRPs (Long Range Reconnaissance Patrols – The best of the best)

A few weeks later, we were establishing a LRRP (Long-Range Reconnaissance Patrol) in the hills and mountains south-southwest of Pleiku.

The long-range reconnaissance patrols were six-man patrols inserted by helicopter behind enemy lines to gather intelligence on enemy operations. The LRRPs were composed of carefully selected soldiers. This included requiring approval of any new additional soldier by every soldier currently assigned to the unit. On their missions, one bad soldier could get all of them killed. We had just arrived in the Pleiku area, supporting the Fourth Infantry Division.

The following was adopted by the 173rd Airborne Brigade LRRPs;
From Shakespeare's *Henry V*, 1598:

KING HENRY V:

This story shall the good man teach his son;
And Crispin Crispian shall ne'er go by,
From this day to the ending of the world,

But we in it shall be remember'd;
We few, we happy few, we band of brothers;
For he to-day that sheds his blood with me
Shall be my brother; be he ne'er so vile

This day shall gentle his condition:
And gentlemen in England now a-bed
Shall think themselves accursed they were not here,
And hold their manhoods cheap whiles any speaks
That fought with us upon Saint Crispin's day.

One of the capabilities that the 173rd Airborne Brigade had was excellent long-range reconnaissance patrols (LRRPs). The 173rd had developed the concept in the jungles of Okinawa before the Vietnam War even started. Every other unit acknowledged we had the best LRRPs. So the Fourth Infantry Division asked us to get some information on one of the mainline North Vietnamese Regiments in the area. The mission was to put in a LRRP close to the enemy headquarters. Its job would be to capture an officer of the North Vietnamese Army and bring him back for interrogation.

It was my responsibility to provide air cover for the insertion of this particular long-range reconnaissance patrol. We always had a FAC (Forward Air Controller) flying over them initially, because the most dangerous time was when they were first inserted. When the enemy would see a chopper come into the area, even if they weren't sure that the chopper had landed, they would be on guard. The LRRP mission was very dangerous because sometimes the enemy would be sure that the chopper had landed. It was hard to disguise a drop off when you had a chopper fly down and land in a little clearing in the jungle, although they used many tactics that tried to do just that. For example, they would have many choppers fly low over the jungle in the area of insertion with constant activity and noise.

If the LRRP was noticed and attacked immediately by the main force unit, the six men did not have much of a chance.

The only radio contact the LRRP had after being dropped off was with the FAC overhead because of the rugged terrain and their short range radios. Again, this particular evening I was monitoring them. We put this patrol in at about 1730 hours

(5:30PM in the afternoon). A couple of troopship choppers with a couple of gunship choppers providing fire support dropped them off in a clearing. It was monsoon season and there was a bad rainstorm going on. The ceiling (the ceiling is the height of the clouds above ground level) was coming down and the rain was getting heavier and heavier. It was such a driving rain that I couldn't see out of the front windshield of my O-1 aircraft. I could only see out of the open side windows. I stayed until 1830 (6:30PM). I always tried to give the LRRPs an hour close by overhead, just in case of contact.

Initially, there were no problems. But I always stayed until darkness fell, because I hoped that when it was dark, they would be relatively safe. But the patrol was hit about 15 minutes later by a strong enemy force. Our men were trying to distance themselves from the enemy force and called me on the radio. I quickly came directly overhead and since there was still a bit of light, I could see them running. It was a two hundred-foot ceiling. So I dove on the enemy forces that were chasing them about a hundred yards behind, and fired my smoke rockets. I also turned and fired my CAR15 out of the side window (the CAR15 is a jungle carbine version of the AR15, which was the standard infantry rifle in Vietnam). (Laughter from the audience.) I knew you guys would laugh about that, but believe it or not it slowed the enemy down. They had to worry about fighters following the smoke mark with bombs and cannon fire. They did not know that fighters could not be put in during weather like that.

And our guys started to put a little bit of distance between themselves and the enemy. I called the 173rd Airborne control center and told them the LRRP needed a scramble of a couple of gun ships and a couple of troop ships to extract them.

They replied, "We can't, the weather is too bad. We can't make it out, the ceiling has really dropped." So I asked them to let me talk to their flight commander or to the captain or to whoever was in charge. I talked to the captain and he said. " I'm sorry, I can't force anyone to go out in this. This is volunteer weather and I can't get anybody to volunteer." I said, "Let me talk to the colonel." I knew the colonel was a good man and well-respected by all the chopper pilots. I said to the colonel, "These guys will all die, without a doubt, if you can't get a chopper to pick them up. Please ask for a volunteer."

He had one volunteer, a troop ship pilot. He took off with no crewmen and no gunship in support. The troop ship came down the dirt road to our area, and I showed him the friendly location. The pilot landed and took the LRRP soldiers on-board, and the troop ship went back to base. The 173rd forward operating base was fairly close by, so everything worked out well.

But now I had to return to my base at Pleiku, which was north through the mountains. I was flying a VFR (visual flight rules) aircraft. I didn't have good instruments. The O-1 was the Air Force designation for the Army's L-19 artillery observer aircraft. I had to follow a dirt road back to Pleiku through mountainous terrain. But as you followed this road back to Pleiku, it led directly to a sudden cliff on the side of a mountain in line with the road. This mountain was the remains of an old volcano, and it was covered with trees on both the outside and the inside of the crater. I knew it rose steeply to my front in the direction I was flying. On the side of that mountain were about ten crashed aircraft that were plastered to it from following the road in weather, just like I would have to. But my only chance was to follow it. I had an advantage, because I knew what happened if you made a mistake.

The trouble was, as I mentioned, I couldn't see out of the front windshield of the aircraft. It was dark now in a driving rain. All I could do was turn back and forth over the road right on the treetops with quick reversing turns. As I would cross over the road, I could again see where it was because its color was slightly different from the jungle, then immediately turn back the other way. This let me follow the road north.

As the road approached the steep mountain, it went to the left with a sharp 90-degree turn to avoid the cliff-face straight ahead. Then it circled around the mountain to the west side and resumed its course north to Pleiku after making a semi-circle around the mountain. What I was hoping for was that when I turned to the left and did not see the road, I could continue the turn, pick that road up and follow it around the mountain on the west side and back to Pleiku.

But what happened was that instead I was in a right turn when the road disappeared. There was nothing to the right except jungle, and I knew that the cliff was under the belly of the aircraft and very close by. So I pulled into a hard four-G turn, which is about the max you can do without pulling the wings off in that type of aircraft. Of course, I was right on the treetops. So I put it into a hard four-G turn and I had bad vertigo for the first time in my life.

I had been all through pilot training with extensive unusual attitude recovery training, but the instructors had never been able to induce vertigo in me. So I didn't even worry about vertigo. I had thought that the training about vertigo was boring.

But after I went into a hard right turn, I experienced it. My body and brain told me I was rolling into the ground, but the instruments said I was holding altitude in the turn. One of the hardest things I ever had to do was trust the instruments as I had been told to do by the instructors, hold the plane on altitude, roll out on a southerly heading and blindly climb to 5000 feet through mountains in monsoon clouds on a pitch-black night. There was nothing else I could have done. If I hit a mountain, I hit it. I had never been scared like that. I had never been in stark terror like that is what I should say.

I had helped a number of Special Forces soldiers out of terrifying situations when they were out on patrols. For example, their patrol might have just been attacked or ambushed by an NVA unit, and all the Montagnards disappeared into the jungle. Then the American soldier would be all-alone with a radio surrounded by the enemy. When you first talked to him, every other word said was unintelligible. So the first thing I would do is to calm the man down so he would be able to pop a smoke grenade and I could locate him in the jungle. Then I would bring in fighter strikes and literally clear a path through the jungle back to the Special Forces Camp with bombs and strafing runs.

I had done that at least twice. But I always wondered, "How can a man be so afraid?" As I was climbing through those mountains, I no longer wondered how they could have been so afraid. Because I was now in the same situation and I wasn't even surrounded by the enemy. I said to myself, "This is ridiculous. Either you are going to hit a mountain and die or you're not. So why are you so afraid?" But these thoughts didn't help any. I think the vertigo destroyed my confidence.

At 5000 feet, I finally broke out into a layer of clear air between the cloud layers. Then I could see where the mountain tops were. So I made a 180 degree turn back to Pleiku. Now I was proceeding on an ADF (ADF is an old navigation aid) heading to

Pleiku, which we were not supposed to do, because the ADF was unreliable, especially in storms. But I took up the ADF heading and followed the needle, even though I knew I should call Pleiku and request a radar vector. The reason I didn't dare call Pleiku was because I knew if I called for that vector, I would be talking irrationally. I didn't trust my voice. My pride wouldn't allow it. I would rather have died.

When the ADF needle flipped, showing station passage over Pleiku, I still didn't call. I turned right to a heading of east, because there was a plain to the east of Pleiku, and I started letting down in altitude. I was going to let down until I got to a level of 20 feet above the ground. I broke out of the clouds at 50 feet. I turned to a westerly heading and saw the lights of the Pleiku airport in the distance. I didn't call the control tower. Pleiku was a very busy airport. They had A1's stationed there. There were many planes and choppers going in and out of Pleiku all the time. It was the major airport in the central highlands. There were planes constantly coming in on approaches, especially in weather like that. I didn't call the tower. No one knew I was landing. There was no excuse for this. Only by God's grace was a collision avoided. I landed on the very end of the runway, and turned off on the first taxiway. Usually I taxied my O-1 fast, but that day I just inched along the side taxiway, amazed at being alive. I didn't get out and kiss the ground, but I wanted to. After that mission, I would never again knock anyone who was scared.

(The rest of the talk to the F-16 Wing was on the mission of the *MISTY* Forward Air Controllers flying F-100s over North Vietnam and a description of the first time I was shot down. There was also interest in Lance Sijan, the *Medal of Honor* winner, and I related what had happened to him. For detail on these topics please see Chapter 1, "My General Talk" and Chapter 9, "Lance Sijan").

GUY IN THE COCKPIT OF AN F-16 AT HOMESTEAD AFB, FLORIDA

What is a Fighter Pilot?

A fighter pilot is noted for intelligence, independence, integrity, courage, and patriotism. "Fighter Pilot" is a state of mind, not a job title. Therefore, not all people who fly fighters are fighter pilots, nor do all fighter pilots fly fighters, some of them drive trucks.

From *Red River Valley Fighter Pilot's Association* Website

- The F-100 Fighter Aircraft, as mentioned in my story of the Special Forces Camp of Dak Seang, flew more than 24,000 combat missions (Wikipedia) in support of US Infantry in South Vietnam.

One Fighter Pilot's thoughts;

"This is about my first fighter, the F-100 Super Sabre (The Hun). I checked out in it at the age of 21 and flew it for 10 years, compiling 2,000 hours in it, one combat tour and 11 of my 13 ocean crossings in it. I stood many hours of nuke (nuclear) and non-nuke alert with it, far from home, civilization and my family for months at a time, cumulatively totaling many years." Norm Turner

Ode to the Hun

I have been joyous in it,
  triumphant in it,
    lost in it
      and terrified in it.
I crashed the first one I soloed but accomplished many victories in it as well.
    It took me to nine different countries
      and brought me home in impossible weather.
It was the most difficult to fly
    and least forgiving of all jet fighters,
      and, from time to time
        it scared all of us who flew it.
It was the backbone of the Air Force's fighter corps for many years,
    and even after it was technically obsolete,
      it was the favorite jet of those troops in Vietnam who needed help
        when things got tough.
There are a lot of aging vets - former soldiers and marines - walking around
    alive and well today because I and a lot of guys like me were very
      good in it and could visit deadly destruction on the enemy with it
        when called upon.
It is gone now,
    but still alive in my heart
      and in the memory of those who flew it.

From *The Intake*, Journal of the *Super Sabre Society*, Spring 2013, Issue 21, p13

ABOUT THE AUTHOR

A U.S. Air Force Captain, Guy Gruters, of Sidney, Ohio, flew more than 400 combat missions during the Vietnam War. Captain Gruters was awarded more than 30 combat awards, including two Silver Stars, two Distinguished Flying Crosses, two Bronze Stars for Valor, two Purple Hearts, the P.O.W. Medal, and more than twenty Air Medals. But it was his faith that carried Guy to victory in the biggest battle of his life. Shot down twice during the Vietnam war, Guy was captured the second time and spent a grueling five years and three months in communist prison camps. Captain Gruters has spoken around the country sharing his unique message, a joyful, positive one full of faith and hope. He and his wife, Sandy, have been married for almost fifty years, raised seven children and have adopted an eighth.

"I was in my early twenties when I volunteered to go to Vietnam. I was very healthy and strong, both physically and emotionally. I had been through four years of school at the Air Force Academy. It included significant physical training and mental discipline. I was on Judo and Boxing teams there, and took parachute training with the US Army. I also attended Purdue University where I earned a Masters Degree in Astronautical Engineering, then completed pilot training and fighter gunnery school.

"It was a different world back then. Our country was fearful of communism and rightfully so. We were engaged in a war in Vietnam to stop communism from spreading and taking over the whole world. Communism had already grown like a horrible cancer to include Russia, China, all of the Eastern European nations, North Korea, and North Vietnam. Now South Vietnam was being invaded.

"It had to be stopped. This is what the leaders of our country thought. I agreed and as a soldier was happy to be able to contribute to this struggle.

"I volunteered for Vietnam. I served there a total of six years and 15 days. The first seven months were as a forward air controller with the 173rd Airborne Brigade, an excellent U.S. army unit. This Brigade fought in many parts of Vietnam. During the last months of my service assigned to this unit in 1967, it was stationed at the Dak To Special Forces Camp in the Central Highlands. Combat action was continuous because we were the "Fire Brigade," and it was our job to finish up the tough battles. Then I volunteered for the *MISTYs*, a top-secret all-volunteer fighter unit flying Forward Air Controller missions over North Vietnam. I was surrounded by heroes."